SO YOU WANT TO SING THE BLUES

So You Want to Sing

Guides for Performers and Professionals

A Project of the National Association of Teachers of Singing

So You Want to Sing: Guides for Performers and Professionals is a series of works devoted to providing a complete survey of what it means to sing within a particular genre. Each contribution functions as a touchstone work not only for professional singers but also for students and teachers of singing. Titles in the series offer a common set of topics so readers can navigate easily the various genres addressed in each volume. This series is produced under the direction of the National Association of Teachers of Singing, the leading professional organization devoted to the science and art of singing.

So You Want to Sing Music Theater: A Guide for Professionals, by Karen S. Hall, 2013
So You Want to Sing Rock 'n' Roll: A Guide for Professionals, by Matthew Edwards, 2014
So You Want to Sing Jazz: A Guide for Professionals, by Jan Shapiro, 2015
So You Want to Sing Country: A Guide for Performers, by Kelly K. Garner, 2016
So You Want to Sing Gospel: A Guide for Performers, by Trineice Robinson-Martin, 2016
So You Want to Sing Sacred Music: A Guide for Performers, edited by Matthew Hoch, 2017
So You Want to Sing Folk Music: A Guide for Performers, by Valerie Mindel, 2017
So You Want to Sing Barbershop: A Guide for Performers, by Diane M. Clarke & Billy J. Biffle, 2017
So You Want to Sing A Cappella: A Guide for Performers, by Deke Sharon, 2017
So You Want to Sing Light Opera: A Guide for Performers, by Linda Lister, 2018
So You Want to Sing CCM (Contemporary Commercial Music): A Guide for Performers, edited by Matthew Hoch, 2018
So You Want to Sing for a Lifetime: A Guide for Performers, by Brenda Smith, 2018
So You Want to Sing the Blues: A Guide for Performers, by Eli Yamin, 2018

SO YOU WANT TO SING THE BLUES

A Guide for Performers

Eli Yamin

Allen Henderson
Executive Editor, NATS

Matthew Hoch
Series Editor

A Project of the National Association of Teachers of Singing

ROWMAN & LITTLEFIELD
Lanham • Boulder • New York • London

Published by Rowman & Littlefield
An imprint of The Rowman & Littlefield Publishing Group, Inc.
4501 Forbes Boulevard, Suite 200, Lanham, Maryland 20706
www.rowman.com

Unit A, Whitacre Mews, 26-34 Stannary Street, London SE11 4AB

British Library Cataloguing in Publication Information Available

Library of Congress Cataloging-in-Publication Data

Names: Yamin, Eli, author.
Title: So you want to sing the blues : a guide for performers / Eli Yamin.
Description: Lanham : Rowman & Littlefield, 2018. | Series: So you want to sing | Includes bibliographical references and index.
Identifiers: LCCN 2018013704 (print) | LCCN 2018014130 (ebook) | ISBN 9781442267046 (electronic) | ISBN 9781442267039 (pbk. : alk. paper)
Subjects: LCSH: Singing—Instruction and study. | Blues (Music)—Instruction and study.
Classification: LCC MT820 (ebook) | LCC MT820 .Y36 2018 (print) | DDC 783/.0643143—dc23
LC record available at https://lccn.loc.gov/2018013704

∞™ The paper used in this publication meets the minimum requirements of American National Standard for Information Sciences—Permanence of Paper for Printed Library Materials, ANSI/NISO Z39.48-1992.

Printed in the United States of America

CONTENTS

LIST OF FIGURES AND TABLE

SERIES EDITOR'S FOREWORD

S*o You Want to Sing the Blues: A Guide for Performers* is the thirteenth book in the NATS/Rowman & Littlefield So You Want to Sing series and the tenth book to fall under my editorship. For this title, we have engaged blues singer and pedagogue Eli Yamin, who travels internationally performing and presenting workshops to both experienced blues musicians as well as newcomers to the style. He brings decades of experience singing and teaching the blues to these chapters, and his wisdom is evident throughout this volume.

While some topics in the So You Want to Sing series present us with dozens of prospective authors from which we must pick, the blues is a genre that seems to exist somewhat separately from the traditional voice-teaching community. In conversation with NATS colleagues, I initially had difficulty identifying who would be the "right" author for this book. Then one day, my friend and colleague Jeannette LoVetri gave me the answer: Eli Yamin. Jeanie could not have been more correct, and these pages you are about to read resoundingly affirm that Eli Yamin is the perfect author for this topic.

During the first year of our correspondence, Eli and I communicated with each other only via phone and e-mail. Then, at the NATS national conference in Chicago in 2016, I had the opportunity to meet Eli in person for the first time. Experiencing him "live" was a transforming experience: Eli doesn't just sing the blues and write about the blues—he *lives* the blues. The genre completely inhabits him. While reading these pages and exploring Eli's online resources, I truly feel as if he is in the room talking to me. His excitement is contagious.

Like other books in the series, there are several "common chapters" that are included across multiple titles. These chapters include a chapter on voice science by Scott McCoy, one on vocal health by Wendy LeBorgne, and one on using audio enhancement technology by Matthew Edwards. These chapters help to bind the series together, ensuring consistency of fact when it comes to the most essential matters of voice production.

The collected volumes of the So You Want to Sing series offer a valuable opportunity for performers and teachers of singing to explore new styles and important pedagogies. I am confident that voice specialists, both amateur and professional, will benefit from Eli Yamin's important resource on singing the blues. It has been a privilege to work with him on this project. This book is an invaluable resource for performers who are interested in adding the blues to their stylistic vocabulary.

Matthew Hoch

ACKNOWLEDGMENTS

Thank you to Walter Perkins, Joe the bartender, Gwen Cleveland, Bross Townsend, C. I. Williams, John Dooley, and everyone else at the Skylark Lounge for your welcome and helping me become a professional bluesman.

Thank you to Amiri Baraka, author of the seminal work *Blues People*, and Amina Baraka for taking me under your wings when I first came to Newark, New Jersey, as a teenager. I am so grateful for the lessons I received at the Barakas' house listening to music and performing and receiving their encouragement in their basement club, "Kimako's Blues People."

Thank you to my friends and mentors at WBGO/Jazz 88 and the Institute of Jazz Studies at Rutgers Newark and the worlds you opened up to me: Dorthaan Kirk, Wylie Rollins, Rhonda Hamilton, James Browne, Michael Anderson, Michael Bourne, Chico Mendoza, Becca Pulliam, Richard Skelly, Duke Markos, Alfredo Cruz, Felix Hernandez, Dan Morgenstern, Ed Berger, Vincent Pelote, Loren Schoenberg, Gary Walker, and Bob Porter, with whom I had the distinct honor and good fortune to produce "Portraits in Blue," a weekly look at great American artists of black music.

Thank you to the members of my blues band for the miles we have traveled and the hearts we have touched: Bob Stewart, Kate McGarry, LaFrae Sci, Howard Johnson, Charenee Wade, Ben Stapp, Chanell Crichlow, Antoinette Montague, and Dwayne "Cook" Broadnax.

Thank you to the U.S. Department of State and all the diplomats who truly believe in the power of the blues and its ability to open hearts and build friendships around the world and across cultures, especially Bob Keefe, Ambassador Todd Robinson, Dawn Suni, Sarah Saperstein, and Cultural Affairs Assistants Maria Taff, Basilia Lopez, Ruxandra Todiras, Matilda Vangjeli, Markella Karagiorga, Slavica Rosica, and Edvaldo Amorim.

Thank you, Maja Popovic, the amazing producer of Jazz Art Montenegro (JAM), for your great support and encouragement bringing blues and jazz to the people of Montenegro.

Thank you to support team from Jazz at Lincoln Center's Rhythm Road American Music Abroad team—Susan Johns, Monak Chunn, Alexis Ortis, Shana Bromberg, and Jasna Radonjic—and two and a half generations of the education team at Jazz at Lincoln Center: Phil Schaap, Erika Floreska, Samantha Samuels, Michelle Schroeder, Beatrice Anderson, Asata Viteri, Joanna Massey, Todd Stoll, Seton Hawkins, Justin Poindexter, Jake Blasini, Matt Buttermann, Maegan McHugh, Alison Magistreli, Antoinette Henry, Cedric Easton, and Executive Directors Adrian Ellis and Greg Scholl and Managing and Artistic Director Wynton Marsalis.

Thank you fellow musicians, scholars, and teachers who share this passion for teaching the power of the blues. Your guidance and collaboration are dear to me:

For breaking ground on how to teach African American singing to everyone: Dr. Bernice Johnson Reagon, Dr. Horace Boyer, and Dr. Trineice Robinson-Martin.

On how to teach jazz and blues language and creative practice: Barry Harris; James McBride; Kenny Barron; Catherine Russell; Marion Cowings; Shemekia Copeland; Tammy McCann; Evan Christopher; Alvin Atkinson Jr.; Uma Karkala; Adam Bernstein; Ravi Best; Ari Roland; Stefan Schatz; Mickey Davidson; Zaid Nasser; Camille Thurman; Darrell Smith; Chris Byars; Dr. Josh Renick; Dr. William Rodriguez, founder of Celia Cruz Bronx High School of Music; Todd Williams of Indiana Wesleyan University; Ronald Carter of Northern Illinois University; Rodney Whitaker of Michigan State University; Marcie Hutchinson of Arizona State University; Dr. Dara Byrne of John Jay College, City University of

New York; Dr. John Hollwitz of the Fordham Graduate School of Business; Dr. Chris Washburne of Columbia University; and Tom Dempsey of LaGuardia Community College.

Thank you to Judi Holifield of the Mississippi Arts Commission, Scott Barretta of the Mississippi Blues Trail and Oxford University (Ole Miss), Howlin' Mad Perry of the Delta Blues Museum, and Bill Perry Jr. in Mississippi for guiding me into the riches of Mississippi culture, history, and music.

Thank you to Clifford Carlson of the Louis Armstrong Middle School in Queens, New York, for our fruitful collaborations on jazz musicals and aesthetic education practice.

Thank you to Dr. Maxine Green, Cathyrn Williams, Scott Noppe-Brandon, Holly Fairbank, Dacia Washington, Sonya Robinson, Barbara Ellman, Jerry James, Jean Taylor, David Wallace, Patrick McKearn, Jessica Meyer, April Armstrong, Dan Levy, David Wallace, and the Lincoln Center Institute for the Arts in Education for providing a nurturing space for me and other educators and artists to collaborate and make a living through the imagination.

Thank you to the board of directors, staff, and supporters of the Jazz Power Initiative for supporting our mission of transforming lives through jazz arts education: Shireen Dickson, Roberto Benitez, Phil Bertelsen, Rondi Charleston, Ron Claiborne, Tom Dempsey, Kirk Imamura, Patricia Pastor, Becca Pulliam Wendy Rothman, Aasha Collins, Janny Gonzalez, Lana Neudorfer, Brian Fender-Shirley, and Jonathan Hernandez-Jimenez.

Thank you to Jeanie LoVetri for your groundbreaking work in voice pedagogy and your vigorous encouragement to go deep into it in support of blues and jazz artists of all ages.

Thank you to Darrell Lauer for helping me heal my voice and find new pathways to learn how to help others as well as cowriting chapter 2 of *Blues Voice Pedagogy*.

Thank you to my students far and wide who take chances with me, find yourself in the blues, and share it.

Thank you for my grandfather, Samuel Yamin, who as a lawyer for Decca Records from 1948 to 1968 was the first member of my immediate family to encourage me to become a professional jazz and blues musician.

I did not realize at that time how much black music was recorded and distributed through Decca. Now I see how my family directly benefited from the commercial success of this music and have made it my life's work to give back as much as possible.

Thanks to my parents Rebecca and Peter Yamin for playing great music during my childhood and giving me professional encouragement once you saw there was no turning back. Thanks to my sister Ariana for helping me understand what "cool" means.

Thank you to my wife Lorraine Yamin and daughter Mani Yamin. You are the love supreme of my life.

INTRODUCTION

Whether you are a performer, a teacher, or a student, this book is for you. It is one of the first books that looks at blues singing from the standpoint of style, history, and technique. It is a resource for understanding the blues inside of you regardless of your cultural background. This book identifies the source of authenticity in the blues and its rich African American origins. By offering concrete explanations and exercises of key elements of the blues, you will find pathways to go deeper with your ability to express yourself in this infinite art form. If you have already been singing the blues for some time, this book offers pathways for you to increase the freedom in your singing by helping you strengthen your technique, providing you with more stamina and flexibility.

In my work as an American musician, I find the blues everywhere. It is the foundation of popular music, rock and roll, jazz, hip-hop, and rhythm and blues. Even country and bluegrass come from the blues. As an educator, I often find the blues missing from school curricula at all levels in all regions of the United States. It seems that despite its seminal influence on American culture, the blues is seldom thought of as a legitimate subject to teach students. Even college jazz programs tend to give the blues short shrift.

At the Lake Placid (New York) Public Library, I found myself surrounded by a collection of a recent edition of the *New Grove Dictionary of Music* in twenty volumes. Naturally, I went straight to the "B" volume and immediately found "Beethoven." The entry surprised me in its length: nearly sixty pages! I braced myself for the blues entry. I could feel a knot form in the pit of my stomach as I shifted through the pages toward the letters "B-L-U." There it was, a mere six pages! How is it that, in 2018, with all of our supposed progress on racial justice, Beethoven, a great composer no doubt but nonetheless a single man, gets sixty pages in *Grove* and a whole genre of music that gave birth to multiple other genres gets just six? (This edition of *Grove* was published in 2001, but the point stands.)

Thankfully, the National Association of Teachers of Singers (NATS)—in partnership with Rowman & Littlefield—has taken on this project to even the scales by publishing this volume, *So You Want to Sing the Blues*, and others in the series focusing on American singing styles. It is our hope that these books will be used by professionals and educators far and wide so that the world may know more clearly the complexity and beauty of the blues and the genres it spawned.

This is a perfect time to turn a page in the book of racial justice and give credit where credit is due by increasing our knowledge of the importance of the contributions of African Americans to American culture. Whereas these contributions run far and wide beyond the scope simply of music, the musical contributions are a phenomenon recognized around the globe. I have seen it with my own eyes and ears as I have traveled with my blues and jazz bands to give performances and workshops in Albania, Austria, Brazil, Chile, China, Colombia, the Czech Republic, Denmark, Ecuador, France, Germany, Greece, Guatemala, Holland, India, Japan, Mali, Montenegro, Norway, Panama, Romania, Russia, Switzerland, and the United Kingdom.

I toured many of these places on behalf of the U.S. Department of State. As a blues and jazz ambassador, I have seen the blues buoy a Romanian audience devastated by the world financial crash of 2008 and a Chilean audience by an earthquake. In Montenegro, I have seen the blues be the cause to celebrate the personal strength and the power of hard physical labor. In India, I have seen the blues bring ecstatic communal joy, and in China, I have witnessed the blues as a welcome opportunity for emotional release. In Mali, I got to sit down and play with master musicians of the Bamako Orchestra and witness how closely the elder musicians resembled the African American masters who raised me.

I grew up in suburban New Jersey and first discovered the blues from listening to recordings of Jimi Hendrix, B.B. King, Elizabeth Cotten, Taj Mahal, the Rolling Stones, the Beatles, and Elvis Presley. The music grabbed me and would not let go. It was a joy and a mystery. Beyond the recordings, I found further clues at the Crossroads Theatre, one of the premiere black theater companies of the United States. There, I became enamored of the *blues aesthetic* as rendered by classic musicals such as *Bubblin' Brown Sugar* and *Ain't Misbehavin'* but also by plays with music such as *Robeson* and *Slow Dance on the Killing Ground*. The latter showed me, more than any other play, how the blues moves, communicates, challenges, and contains powerful emotions, questions, and deep human concerns.

I sought out guides. Fortunately, I found my way to African American master writers and musicians who grew up in the communities in which the blues was created. On my eighteenth birthday, I started working at WBGO/Jazz 88 in Newark, New Jersey, and soon found myself hosting radio shows and producing programs with top jazz historians and legendary blues producers. I met writers Amiri and Amina Baraka, and they welcomed me into their home and basement club, "Kimako's Blues People," where the blues as music, spoken word, dance, and sculpture fused seamlessly. The more I heard and played the blues, the more curious I became to know its source.

On graduating college in 1990 from Rutgers University, drummer Walter Perkins hired me to play in his band at the Skylark Lounge in Jamaica, Queens. Walter was originally from Chicago and came up in the 1950s playing with blues creators Muddy Waters, Howlin' Wolf, and Memphis Slim. My college repertoire was of little use in this club where a mostly middle-class African American community gathered to relax after the workweek. Every third tune we played was a blues. Walter would give a title, such as "Hogmalls and Chitlins," and give a count off, I would call a key, and we were off. I would improvise the melody based on Walter's rhythms and the energy of the room. Later, it would be a different tempo, key, and title, such as "Macaroni and Meatball," and once again we would create. Those were magical times, and I learned a ton.

I learned about the purpose of the blues, that is, as Walter always used to say, "Make people feel *gooooood*, Baby Sweets. That is our job."

I learned about the powerful rhythm of the blues. Walter's shuffle was second to none. I learned about the moan and cry of the blues and how that feeling can be transfigured into ecstatic reverie, release, and joy. I learned how the blues always must *mean something* individually and collectively. Herein lies a paradox. The blues requires you to tune into the people around you—*community*—while at the same time being passionately self-expressive—*individual*. In the Skylark, the tables were so close that the audience was literally on top of us. Their vocal responses and gestures let us know when we were in tune and doing our job to provide communal release. We could feel them breathe. And while our attunement to the audience was of critical importance, I learned that it is also true that to be effective as a blues performer, you have to be truly yourself. No airs, hiding, or holding back.

The bartender at the Skylark was named Joe. I used to order white Russians from him, and he once asked me, "Eli, why you always order *white* Russians? How come you never order *black* Russians?" I said, "Because I *am* a *white* Russian, that's why." We shared a good laugh. Later, Joe honored me by inviting me to play and sing at his family's reunion. I set up my keyboard in the middle of the room surrounded by children and adults—Joe's family members—and did what I knew best: played and sang the blues. There was good feeling all around. When you get the feeling right, the blues always delivers.

Sure, I play and sing other kinds of music—jazz in particular—but I always come back to the blues. The blues is the foundation. The blues is the source. The blues is strength. It connects you with a lineage that goes back hundreds, possibly thousands, of years. The blues is life force and creativity. The blues is personal and collective. The blues makes people move, and the blues is real. When you immerse yourself and share what you have in the blues and your body, mind and soul and those around you are uplifted.

Whereas the blues can do all this, it is not easy. So often, the blues gets defined in small ways. But the blues is not small. The blues is *huge*. Sure, anybody who knows three chords in twelve bars can technically play a blues. But that *ain't it*. To be truly effective, the blues requires a unique level of honesty and emotional range from the performer.

As a singer, the blues presents many challenges. You have to be able to whisper and shout, scream and serenade. You have to let yourself go in the energy of the music and have a voice the next day for the next gig. This requires preparation. The idea of blues training itself may seem paradoxical; however, professional singers who meet the demands of performing night after night and touring have found some way to care for their voice by hook or by crook. Consciously training your voice to sing the blues in the true spirit of the genre can be highly effective in sustaining your career as an artist and/or teacher. B.B. King always kept his dressing room hot because he was looking out for his throat. He spoke freely about his preference for using the full voice from the top to the bottom. Catherine Russell trained as an actor and classical singer before embarking on a career as a vocalist with Steely Dan and David Bowie and now as a Grammy Award–winning blues performer headlining her own band.

Voice training and blues singing have not historically gone together. There are many reasons for this. From the standpoint of the singer already singing the blues, you might be concerned that voice training could take the soul out of your sound. As with any technique, you have to be careful to not throw away everything you already know once you have some new tools in your toolbox. New technique can help you make needed adjustments for using your instrument more efficiently, but you have to use good judgment so as not to get rid of the good stuff and know the difference. If you want to holler, good voice technique can help. The same is true with scooping, sliding, and even growling.

For me, voice training has been a lifesaver. When I started singing the blues, I knew nothing about how the voice works and would generally squeeze my throat to sing high notes and make something sound bluesy. This worked okay for a while but often left me with little or no voice at the end of the gig. Eventually, it was unsustainable. I trained first with Jeanie LoVetri, the founder of Somatic Voicework™, The LoVetri Method, who showed me how you can treat your voice as an instrument and develop its capacity in conscious ways to make the sounds you want to make singing easier and freer. Jeanie taught me to identify the different registers of my voice, head, and chest and mix and develop a daily routine to keep them balanced.

With characteristic exuberance and no small amount of stubbornness, oversinging, screaming, and talking brought me further vocal challenges and a polyp on my vocal chords. To confront this, Jeanie sent me to voice therapist Darrell Lauer, who first helped me learn a new way to talk that put much less strain on my voice. He taught me to speak more on the breath at a higher pitch—more in the middle of my range instead of on the bottom—and smooth out my glottal attacks. It worked, and thankfully I was able to heal the polyp without surgery. I have continued voice training with Darrell, who, a longtime member of NATS, graciously volunteered to cowrite chapter 4 in this book. With no prior publication on this particular subject, his contributions are essential in providing you with time-tested tools in functional voice technique that can help you be more equipped to meet the demands of ongoing performance at a high level.

Before we get into vocal mechanics, chapter 1 deals with the prehistory of the blues. Often, the history of blues is told by beginning with slavery. This is essential to understanding where the blues comes from; however, there is an inherent flaw in starting the story here. It promotes the myth that the Africans who were brought to America in chains were somehow a tabula rasa, a blank slate, shaped only by the trauma inflicted on them. When we start the story of the blues with slavery, we miss the opportunity to delve into the rich cultures from which Africans in the New World were taken and the complex individuals and communities they became in their new world as African Americans.

Since the 1950s, Western music scholars have studied African music and identified antecedents of African American music. We present some keys points of their research in chapter 1 with a particular focus on elements of blues singing that we can learn to embody. As a singer, knowing about these elements and listening to some of the examples cited can deepen your blues-ness. It can also give you tools to teach the fundamentals of the singing style.

Chapter 2, by series author Scott McCoy, gives you an introduction to blues and how it relates to voice science, whereas chapter 3 is an overview of vocal health by Wendy LeBorgne. Chapter 4 is where we look at how to apply knowledge of voice function to the particular demands of blues singing.

Chapter 5 looks at the vocal style of early blues women and chapter 6 at that of early blues men. This is followed by chapters on Chicago blues singers and the modern blues sound and a chapter on making a soulful sound and writing your own blues. Finally, series author Matt Edwards contributes a chapter on audio enhancement technology.

Personally, writing this book has been a tremendous gift. I hope the results of our work will help you go farther on your path as a blues artist and/or educator. Let us use the blues well to offer support and strength to our communities worldwide. And let us always remember to give credit where credit is due.

ONLINE SUPPLEMENT NOTE

So You Want to Sing the Blues features an online supplement courtesy of the National Association of Teachers of Singing. Visit the link below to discover additional exercises and examples as well as links to recordings of the songs referenced in this book.

http://www.nats.org/So_You_Want_To_Sing_Book_Series.html

A musical note symbol ♪ in this book will mark every instance of corresponding online supplemental material.

1

ORIGINS OF THE BLUES

Wise I

If you ever find yourself
Somewhere lost and surrounded
By enemies
Who won't let you speak
In your own language
Who destroy your statues and instruments
And ban your om boom ba boom
Then you are in trouble
Deep trouble
They ban your own boom ba boom
You are in deep, deep trouble

Humph!

Probably take several hundred years
To get out—

—Amiri Baraka

WHAT IS THE BLUES?

Blues is an astounding art form invented by African Americans that transforms sadness into resilience, strength, and, sometimes, good humor. It is defined by personal story, rhythm, and the sound of the voice—whether a human voice or an instrument, authenticity arrives in the presence of a particular combination of African American–derived vocal vocabulary.

Blues singers ranging from Bessie Smith to B.B. King make every song they sing sound like the blues. These artists embody a system of immediate emotional communication with ancient roots that remains perpetually current. Common blues forms in 8, 12, and 16 bars are widespread but secondary in defining the sound of the blues. Samuel Charters, author of the groundbreaking 1959 work *The Country Blues*, writes,

> The blues is a personal song, with intensely personal emotional characteristics. The blues became the emotional outlet for Negro singers in every part of the South, and as the rich confusion of music from the fields began to fall into loose patterns, the blues became a part of the fabric of Negro life itself.[1]

The emotional range of the blues is one its most distinct features. Although having the blues is sad, playing the blues need not be so. In fact, noted historian Paul Oliver once said that we "play the blues to get rid of the blues."

The blues is sung solo with instrumental accompaniment ranging from solo guitar to a full band with piano, bass, drums, guitars, and a horn section. The singer is often telling a story that has a moderately to a severely tragic edge. Sharing the story with others helps relieve some of the singer's burden and in turn the audience's. To facilitate this, blues music requires constant interaction between the singer, other musicians, and audience, creating a life force of community that helps us face life's challenges through fellowship. The blues singer calls, and she is answered by a horn, a guitar riff, or someone in the audience saying, "Alright now." The blues is social music.

Albert Murray in *Stompin' the Blues* highlights some of the magical properties of the blues and the mechanics that make it work when he says that the blues is a "magical combination of idiomatic incantation and percussion that creates the dance-oriented good time music."[2]

In this definition, the importance of steady rhythm is identified—*percussion*—as well as an *incantation*. An incantation is a magical form of vocalizing, such as in a spell or a spiritual chant. This vocalizing and what goes into it is the main focus of this book. However, the rhythm is of equal importance and must be valued as such by every blues performer in order to create the desired effect.

Murray defines the "blues musician [as] being an agent of affirmation and continuity in the face of adversity."[3] Once again, we *play the blues to get rid of the blues*. This act, a radical one to be sure, makes the blues an existential gift to the world.

WHEN DID THE BLUES FIRST EMERGE?

Composer, trumpeter, and bandleader William Christopher (W.C.) Handy heard the blues in Tutwiler, Mississippi, in 1903. Sometime after that, in Cleveland, Mississippi, he saw a "ragtag" trio playing blues and getting showered with coins. This inspired him to take up the music. Widely considered the father of the blues, Handy began publishing his blues compositions in 1912 with "Memphis Blues." Singer Ma Rainey, considered the mother of the blues, started integrating blues into her stage show in 1902. Rainey's early contact with a young Bessie Smith had a significant impact on Smith's development. Smith went on to become the most famous and influential of the early blues singers and is known as "Empress of the Blues." Trumpeter Bunk Johnson of New Orleans said in the 1880s that they played "nothing but the blues."[4] Safe to say, the blues emerged sometime after the Civil War. We don't know exactly when because at the time of the genesis of the blues, there were no recordings, and no one was publishing blues compositions. There are many signs, however, and they lead back to Africa.

WHAT ARE THE ROOTS OF BLUES MELODY AND FORM?

African elements or retentions are essential to understanding how the blues came to be. These African elements are present in the music traditions of enslaved African Americans, such as field hollers, work songs, ring shouts, and spirituals. In fact, according to Africanist Gerhard Kubik, the blues was "a logical development that resulted from specific processes of cultural interaction among eighteenth- to nineteenth-century African descendants in the United States, under certain economic and social conditions."[5]

It is generally understood that African American music is the combination of African and European influences. However, this explanation is too simplistic and negates the complexity of both Europe and Africa. There is no singular European or African culture. Instead, there are interactions, different combinations, and assimilations. Where and when these occur is important to understanding blues. Africans in America had many tools of their culture stripped away during the genocide of American slavery. Drums were banned, and speaking native languages was forbidden. Through the sound of their voice, Africans in America retained a sense of their inheritance, a complex web of many rich cultural traditions from an ancient continent where humanity was born. The sound of the *voice* most clearly defines the blues, and we can trace the blues vocal tradition back to the western Sudanic region of Africa from Senegal and Gambia and across Mali, northern Ghana, and Burkina Faso to northern Nigeria.

However, these countries were not the only ones to have people enslaved and taken to North America. Whereas most Africans enslaved in the United States came from the often Muslim Guinea Coast region and those brought to South America came from the Congo region, there were some who came to Louisiana under French/Spanish rule who also came from Congo. Safe to say, enslaved Africans in America came from many different countries in Africa with a wide variety of musical traditions.

Why did particular traditions prevail in the development of the blues? Western scholars have been writing about African antecedents of the blues since the 1950s. By the 1990s, particular African traditions had been identified as being significant in providing the basis for the rise of particular African American musical traditions. Gerhard Kubik writes in *Africa and the Blues*,

> In situations of population transplant anywhere in the world, we often get a picture of interaction that applies also to the United States in the nineteenth century: one stylistic cluster from a certain region survives in one or two particular genres (e.g., the blues), while another survives in a dif-

> ferent one (e.g. the spirituals). The spirituals were a more or less tolerated outlet for community-based musical manifestations. Therefore, it is not surprising that Western multipart hymn singing was quickly reinterpreted by concepts of homophonic [multi] part-singing long established on the Guinea Coast and in west-central Africa. Parallelism in fourths or fifths, forbidden in nineteenth-century European harmonic theory, crept into "Negro" singing, while the blues remained unaffected by these concepts for a long time.[6]

Kubik makes a strong case for two major sources combining to form the basis Mississippi Delta blues:

1. A declamatory, Arabic-Islamic song style characterized by melisma, wavy intonation, and pitch instabilities within a pentatonic framework—resembling the Muslim call to prayer heard in mosques throughout the world today.
2. An ancient west-central Sudanic tradition of pentatonic song composition related to steady work rhythms with syncopated features dating back thousands of years.

It is important to point out that in Africa, these two song traditions were distinct. The blues tradition *combined them*.[7]

Decades before Kubik completed his research, singer Paul Robeson made similar conclusions when studying in England. Robeson was raised in an African American household and received Western classical music training. He was a genius scholar, musician, athlete, and actor who spoke seven languages fluently, graduated at the top of his class at Rutgers University, was a star on the football team, and went on to become a star of stage and screen. It is fascinating to contemplate Robeson's own insights on African influences on African American music. By studying African languages, he identified similar African influences on the connections between African music and the blues. Robeson wrote in 1934,

> As a first step, I went to the London School of Oriental Languages and, quite haphazardly, began by studying the East Coast languages, Swahili, and the Bantu group which forms a kind of Lingua Franca of the East Coast of Africa. I found in these languages a pure Negro foundation,

> dating from an ancient culture, but intermingled with many Arabic and Hamitic impurities. From them, I passed on to the West Coast Negro languages and immediately found a kinship of rhythm and intonation with the Negro-English dialect which I had heard spoken around me as a child. It was to me like a home-coming, and I felt that I had penetrated to the core of African culture when I began to study the legendary traditions, folksong and folklore of the West African Negro.[8]

Robeson's observation of a "kinship of rhythm and intonation with the Negro-English dialect" and his identification of Arabic and Egyptian (Hamitic) influences by ear in the 1930s is striking. My mother often played Robeson's recordings for me as a child, and they served as a magnificent entry point into the heart and soul of spirituals and African American singing tradition.

"There Is a Balm in Gilead" sung by Paul Robeson ♪

In *Africa and the Blues*, Kubik identifies 11 of blues' style characteristics. We focus on six directly related to singing here. Of course, as with everything in the blues, nothing is absolute. Instead, we are looking for characteristics that contribute to authenticity—a theme that runs throughout *So You Want to Sing the Blues*. I have provided listening examples to illustrate each characteristic listed here. When there is a question about the blues, always source the classic recordings. They have all the answers.

Kubik's blues singing style characteristics from *Africa and the Blues*:

1. Predominantly solo singing tradition with lyrics in the first person.

   "Saint Louis Blues" sung by Bessie Smith ♪

2. Wavy intonation with plenty of melisma, slurs, gliss tones, and timbre-melodic sequences.

   "Devil Got My Woman" sung by Skip James ♪
   "Black Snake Moan" sung by Blind Lemon Jefferson ♪

3. Slow triple or swing tempos.

   "Shipwrecked Blues" sung by Clara Smith ♪

4. Voice/instrument relationship:

   A. Voice guided by simple background drone/ostinato on the instrument with occasional melodic answer on instrument.

      "Nothin' but the Blues" sung by Lightnin' Hopkins ♪

   B. Guitar creates contrasting melodies simultaneously with vocal melody.

      "Crossroad Blues" sung by Robert Johnson ♪

5. Pentatonic melodic line with broad variation margin that does not necessarily directly correspond with Western-style diatonic chord sequences, suggesting tonic, subdominant, and dominant seventh chords.

   "Come On in My Kitchen" sung by Robert Johnson ♪

6. Form: Three-line strophic form with the first line repeated and the third introducing a new textual motif (conclusion). Other forms, such as two-line, four-line, and couplet plus refrain, as well as forms "based on short cycles affiliated to cycles in African music.[9]

The three-line strophic form is the most common blues form in use today, and a good example is Memphis Minnie's "If You See My Rooster." ♪

Minnie sings,

> If you see my rooster, please run him on back home (guitar response) ×2
> I haven't found no eggs in my basket (woo-hee) since my rooster been gone

Notice the call-and-response built into the form. Not only is the first line repeated, then answered by the third line, but there is instrumental commentary from the guitar after each line. This idea of commentary, or "co-signing," is essential in African American music. In blues vocal tunes, the voice is often "answered" by an instrument played by the person singing or by someone else. Another option is for the singer to answer herself as Memphis Minnie does in the second verse of "If You See My Rooster":

I heard my rooster crowing
This morning just about the break of day (rrr rrr rrrrr)
I heard my rooster crowing
This morning just about the break of day (guitar)

Couplet plus refrain is well represented by Tampa Red's "Blues for My Baby." ♪

Red sings,

I wake every morning talking out of head
and thinking about my baby and everything she said
I got the blues for my baby, I'm just a worried man
going back to my baby down in dear old Dixieland

FURTHER AFRICAN RETENTIONS

Once you accept that Africanisms from the western Sudanic belt form the musical origins of blues singing, you can develop a healthy skepticism toward an overemphasis on European-derived frameworks for assessing the blues.

Unfortunately, even though Western researchers first published about complex African sources of the blues in the 1950s, Eurocentric frameworks continue to dominate blues and jazz education materials well into the twenty-first century. It is no wonder that the idea of *blues education* remains an anomaly. Essential guideposts from Africa and African American culture are too often left out or just dismissed altogether.

It is problematic to use Greek-derived terms, such as "rhythm," "melody," and "harmony," when describing African and African American music because they have no exact equivalents in African languages. Furthermore, Western notation emphasizes pitch sequences over aural information prioritized in the blues, such as timbre-melodic and melodic-rhythmic patterns.

The acute awareness of timbre modification and timbre sequences is essential for sounding authentic when singing the blues. Western notation is not designed to capture these kinds of nuances. This is why it is of supreme importance to take cues about the blues from people who possess a deep understanding of the culture it came from. Amiri Baraka, formerly Leroi Jones, was the first African American scholar to publish a book on the origins of jazz and blues. His classic 1963 work *Blues People: The Negro Experience in White America and the Music That Developed from It*, remains in print more than fifty years after its first publication. It is widely read and studied today because it so well integrates emerging research on African origins of the blues with Baraka's own keen observations growing up as an African American in an African American family and community. Baraka writes,

> Melodic diversity in African music came not only in the actual arrangements of notes (in terms of Western transcription) but in the singer's vocal interpretation. The "tense, slightly hoarse-sounding vocal techniques" of the work songs and the blues stem directly from West African musical tradition. In African languages the meaning of a word can be changed simply by altering the pitch of the word, or changing its stress—basically, the way one can change the word "yeh" from simple response to stern challenge simply by moving the tongue slightly.[10]

These nuances in pitch and timbre represent a standard of beauty and excellence that is different than the dominant European one. Baraka continues,

> While the whole European tradition strives for regularity—of pitch, of time, of timbre and of vibrato—the African tradition strives precisely for the negation of these elements. . . . In music, the same tendency towards obliquity and ellipsis is noticeable: no note is attacked straight; the voice or instrument always approaches it from above or below, plays around the implied pitch without ever remaining any length of time, and departs from it without ever having committed itself to a single meaning. The timbre is veiled and paraphrased by constantly changing vibrato, tremolo and overtone effects. The timing accentuation, finally, are not stated, but implied or suggested. The denying or withholding of all signposts.[11]

If we can't have signposts, let's look carefully at the bends in the road.

BLUE NOTES?

In an attempt to distill the essential ingredients of the blues into teachable elements that fit a Western structure, educators often make two significant errors. One is a description of "blue" notes, such as the minor third, flat fifth, and minor seventh, as fixed entities. This flies in the face of what we discussed before in terms of pitch variation. Deep South blues singers from the dawn of the blues don't talk about "blue notes" this way. This characterization appears to be an invention of early jazz literature and has been reinforced for generations in blues education materials. Master blues artists bring much more subtlety in terms of pitch variation, and we offer here a more nuanced perspective in pursuit of a more authentic approach to blues singing. On Western fixed-pitch instruments like the piano, you have to use flat thirds and sevenths because the notes don't bend, but when singing or playing guitar, fiddle, or harmonica, you face no such limitations because you can easily "bend" the notes. When you listen closely to master blues singers, you can hear much more subtle pitch variance around the thirds and sevenths. This is the vocal approach we strive to imbibe.

Another error found widely in blues instructional materials assumes that the tonic, subdominant, and dominant chords commonly used to accompany blues singing are functioning in a Western way. They are not.[12]

Master blues singers combine pitch variation with a wide range of timbre, timing, and inflectional variations to create the tremendous range of expression of the blues. Muddy Waters, one of the finest and most influential blues singers, was originally from the Mississippi Delta. Renowned popular music critic Robert Palmer wrote that "when Muddy sings, he screws up the side of his face and then relaxes it, opens and contracts his throat, shakes his jowls, constantly readjusts the shape (and thus the resonating capacity) of his mouth cavity, all in order to get different, precisely calibrated vocal sounds, from the purest falsetto to deep, quivering moans to a grainy, vibrato-heavy rasp."[13]

"I don't sing on the beat. I sing behind it, and people have to delay to play with me. They got to hang around, wait, see what's going to happen next," said Waters. The ways in which Waters mastered the subtle art of rhythmic and pitch variation are key illustrations of his virtuosity as a singer. Palmer writes,

> Those infinitesimally flattened thirds, majestic falling fifths, and glancing slides between tones all mean something, just as the slightest shift in the pitch level of a person's speech means something when someone who hears as acutely as Muddy does is listening. Exactly how flat he sings a

> note will depend on where in the melody line that note falls (a purely musical values) and on the emotional weight of the feelings the line is meant to convey. As in the singing of the Akan of Ghana, the flatter the pitch, the more intense the feeling. One recognizes in this artful pitch play an unmistakable reflection of the African preoccupation with music as language and, more specifically, of the pitch-tone languages so many Africans spoke when they first arrived in the Americas.[14]

So you can't just say when singing blues to flat the third and seventh of the major scale. Authentic blues singers just don't think like that. Instead, blues musicians maintain an awareness of certain flexible or neutral pitch areas found around the third and seventh degrees of the scale.

Learning the blues as a living oral tradition involves absorbing its sonic language from master blues artists whose execution of the language is second nature. If you are coming from a Western music background mind-set, it is important to let go of needing to associate everything to what you know from traditional Western music training so that you can be open to understanding the full complexity of blues singing. This is why Baraka is emphatic about the New World African tradition of negating the regularity of European musical standards. "While the whole European tradition strives for regularity—of pitch, of time, of timbre and of vibrato—the African tradition strives precisely for the negation of these elements."

And as great as Muddy Waters was in bringing this practice to its highest level, he did not come to it purely from his own imagination. We can see traces of these standards of microtonal pitch modification in the African music of his ancestors.

ELASTIC SCALES

Kubik documented the concept of flexible pitch areas in African musical cultures and coined the term "elastic scales" to describe it.[15] In other words, you can certainly hold the third and seventh in your awareness as a flexible pitch area, but it is most helpful to think of the scale as elastic in a more general sense. The more you absorb blues tonal language from master blues men and women, the more you will find yourself messing around with the thirds, sevenths, fifths, and even sixths. The important thing is to absorb the working melodic vocabulary of the genre to sound authentic and then be freely expressive telling your story and the story of your songs within this framework.

The first blues record by an African American singer, "Crazy Blues," by Mamie Smith (composed by Perry Bradford) was released in 1920, and it was gobbled up by working-class African Americans who paid a dollar a record—a substantial sum for a working-class person in 1920! Why was the record worth so much to the working-class black people who bought it? Many people have noted that hearing someone who *sounded like the listener* on a record was tremendously meaningful to African Americans, who had had their humanity denied for generations during slavery. What made the sound familiar? No doubt, the dialect was an important factor, and we get into this in chapter 5. But also the style of the voice was familiar, and *elastic scales* with *flexible pitch areas* were a big part of that.

WHAT ABOUT THE CHORDS?

Of course, it's true that the blues today uses three fundamental chords: I7, IV7, and V7. However, when you listen to the most authentic blues people, you find that many songs don't use standard 12-bar blues form yet still sound bluesy. Why is that?

A big reason for this is the melodic approach of the singers described above and the accompaniment, but researchers have also uncovered African antecedents for non-Western usage of Western chords in the blues that are worth noting here.

When we say standard 12-bar blues form, we are talking about this:

I/I/I/I7/IV7/IV7/I/I/V7/IV7/I/I

Notice that the dominant V7 chord is the least used. It appears in one bar only—bar 9. This is no accident. As Kubik explains, "Musicians tend to circumvent, avoid, or quit the dominant chord quickly, as if it lacked oxygen." The blues is based on a central tonality or tonic. The fifth degree up is important melodically and can function like a dominant chord leading the listener back to the tonic, but the dominant chord itself can be seen as a bit of a compromise where the blues singer is concerned.[16]

As mentioned before, you can find examples of blues songs based around a single tonic such as the following:

"Smokestack Lightnin'" sung by Howlin' Wolf ♪
"Shake Your Hips" sung by Slim Harpo ♪
"Preachin' Blues" sung by Robert Johnson ♪

You can also find blues songs that basically have two pitch centers: one based on the tonic and the other based either a whole step down from the tonic or on the subdominant IV.

A strong case can be made for a return to the exploration of these non–chord progression expressions of the blues. It is certainly a great tool to use in training blues musicians. Personally, I find that playing the blues on one chord or just two, the tonic I and the subdominant IV, with a possible quick transition on the V, makes a lot of sense. It allows you to focus on the voice in a different kind of way than when you are negotiating a lot of dominant–tonic relationships. There is certainly a time and place for the latter, and this becomes very important in 1920s blues songs. However, when I first got into the blues, I recall vividly how a more pared-down chordal concept drew me toward the heart of it. Blues on one or two chords can be artistically effective as well as extremely helpful in teaching students to feel the soul of the music. Let the more elaborate chord progressions come later.

It is interesting to note that Kubik's research involved separating the vocal and instrumental tracks of some of the early blues singers' recordings. By doing this, you can see very clearly that the melody doesn't always correspond with the chords. Researchers have explored this idea with regard to early New Orleans music having two different tonalities operating simultaneously: a melodic and harmonic. In fact, it is safe to say that in addition to polyrhythm, jazz and blues has a polytonal concept dating back to its beginnings in the nineteenth century.

RHYTHM

The most direct way I have always found to help people connect with the rhythm of the blues is simply to have everyone put their hands on their hearts:

What is the sound the heartbeat makes?
Du-duum, du-duuum, du-duuum, or something like that, right?
What do you notice?
It's a steady rhythm that is uneven, broken but not broke. In music, we call it the *shuffle*. It is the essential pulse of the blues. Therefore, I offer you this blues pledge of allegiance. With your hand on your heart you may say:
The heartbeat is the shuffle,
And the shuffle is the heartbeat of the blues.

A great example is "Built for Comfort" sung by Taj Mahal, a modern-era recording with acoustic instruments. ♪

During slavery in North America, it is well known the drum was taken away because it was seen as a threat to white control of the enslaved. African Americans based a whole new music on a rhythm that could never be taken away because *the heartbeat resides in every living person!*

Let's look at the history of its development.

AFRICANS IN THE NEW WORLD

W. E. B. Du Bois once said, "Many have suffered as much as Black people . . . but none of them was real estate." The horror of American slavery cannot be overstated, and it is unique in human history. The first Africans brought to North America thought of themselves as captives and expected to return to their homelands when their period of captivity had ended. In addition to forced labor, enslaved Africans were separated from family members and forbidden to speak their native languages and had their drums taken away. The drum had been identified by slave masters as an effective form of communication and therefore had been removed from most communities of enslaved Africans. White slave masters routinely raped black women and beat men on their plantations, inflicting cruel, severe, and repeated trauma. By the mid-nineteenth century, it was clear there was no returning to Africa. Such was the beginning of black people's unique struggle in America. Conditions for enslaved Africans remained extremely cruel and severe for many generations. Baraka points out,

> There was no communication between master and slave on any strictly human level, but only the relation one might have to a piece of property . . . it was this essential conditional of non humanity that characterized the African slave's lot in this country of his captivity, a country which was later and ironically to become his land also. . . . The African cultures, the retention of some parts of these cultures in America, and the weight of the step culture produced the American Negro. A new race.[17]

And this is where the blues comes in. Emerging after emancipation, it is part of a continuum—a new realization of freedom through music and a positive expression of African American identity. "In fact, the African, because of the violent differences between what was native and what he was forced to in slavery, developed some of the most complex and complicated ideas about the world imaginable."[18]

MUSIC TO SURVIVE SLAVERY

Africans brought to the New World music traditions from many nations and cultural frameworks. Renowned African American music scholar Eileen Southern demonstrates in her seminal work *The Music of Black Americans* how these cultures had enough in common to establish an identifiable heritage for Africans in the New World. For one, music making engaged the community and often involved interaction between soloists or leaders with the group as the chorus. Music supported sacred rituals, provided recreational outlets, but also offered a means of communication and a way of sharing in collective experiences, whether of the past or of the present. In addition, music was often combined with dance and/or dramatic elements for storytelling.[19]

Improvisation, both vocally and instrumentally on the fiddle and African banjo, has always been an important part of African American music. African American musicians were often called on to play for dances in both the North and the South. Southern writes,

> The function of music as a communal activity . . . led to the development of slave-song repertories that provided some measure of release from the physical and spiritual brutality of slavery. Despite the interaction of African and European cultural patterns in black communities, with the

> resultant emergence of new, African-American patterns, there persisted among black folk musicians a predilection for certain performance practice, certain habits, certain musical instruments, and certain ways of shaping music to meet their needs in the new environment that had roots in the African experience.[20]

Although music making by enslaved Africans was limited on plantations, especially in terms of drumming, there were gatherings known as "slave festivals" in the North, such as "Pinkster dances" in New York and "jubilees" in Philadelphia and Congo Square in New Orleans, where some African musical tools survived and were passed on through dance and music.[21]

Congo Square in New Orleans was unique in its scope and longevity. Every Sunday for about 150 years (1730s–1880s), hundreds, possibly thousands, of enslaved Africans gathered to share their traditional music, dances, and ceremonies. According to eyewitness accounts, these people represented six different African tribes: Kraels, Minahs, Congos and Mandringas, Gangas, Hiboas, and Fulas.[22] Whereas in most places in North America the drum and traditional languages were banned, here they were allowed with the hope that enslaved Americans would be better slaves if they had an opportunity to express their traditions on Sundays. It was a unique opportunity for African Americans and clearly an important one for keeping connections with African culture strong. Eyewitness William Wells Brown writes,

> The music consisted of two drums and a stringed instrument . . . , [one of which was] a cylindrical drum, about a foot in diameter. . . . The drum was an open staved thing held between the knees. . . . They made an incredible noise. The most curious instrument, however, was a stringed instrument, which no doubt was imported from Africa. On the top of the finger board was the rude figure of a man in a sitting posture, and two pegs behind him to which the strings were fastened. The body was a calabash. It was played upon by a very little old man, apparently eighty or ninety year.[23]

Congo Square was one of the few places African Americans were allowed to use drums. In addition to the presence of the drums, it is important to note the use of a stringed instrument. Blues researchers are quick to point out that the African traditions most retained in the blues are vocal traditions accompanied by strings. These traditions were not suppressed as much as ones involving percussion because they were apparently not perceived as much of a threat.

Pinkster dances in New York and jubilees in Philadelphia also featured African-derived music, dance, and instruments. The performance practices and instruments used resembled those described by travelers to Africa during the eighteenth and nineteenth centuries.[24]

Let us continue to uncover African retentions in African American music while surveying further developments in the music that gave rise to the blues singer.

THE UNDERGROUND RAILROAD

The Underground Railroad, developed in secret in the early nineteenth century, was not an actual railroad but rather a loosely knit organization existing for the sole purpose of helping fugitive slaves escape. The Underground Railroad collectivized the task of freeing enslaved people from slavery and sourced people of good conscience in the North and South. It included "underground roads," "stations," and "conductors." The most famous of these conductors was Harriet Tubman (1820?–1913), called the "black Moses of her race." After escaping slavery herself, she made numerous trips down South to help others escape. There was a special song she always used to indicate her presence:

Dark and thorny is de pathway
Where de pilgrim makes his ways;
But beyond dis vale of sorrow
Lie de fields of endless days.[25]

When enslaved African Americans heard this song, whether or not they could see the singer, they knew that their "Moses" had come after them, and they would get ready to leave.[26] Songs were often used during the process of escapes to convey coded information and keep spirits up.

Songs during this period included the spirituals "Steal Away to Jesus," "Swing Low Sweet Chariot," and "Wade in the Water." These songs were used both for worship and to convey coded messages. Some revealed a "map" on the Underground Railroad—the most famous of these was "Follow the Drinking Gourd."[27]

These songs are basic texts for the blues singer. Modern-day blues singer Catherine Russell recalls her musical upbringing and the importance of singing these songs. For those coming to the blues from a classical background, Catherine specifically recommends "Swing Low Sweet Chariot" as a song to bridge the classical and blues worlds. *Lift Every Voice and Sing*, the African American hymnal edited by Horace Boyer, is an excellent and easily available resource for many of these songs.

"Follow the Drinking Gourd" (figure 1.1) is often used in educational contexts when teaching about slavery. You can see how the melody is built on the D minor pentatonic scale. Minor pentatonic is a good starting point for blues tonality, but, as we just discussed, don't get too fixed on the pitches. Spirituals, like blues, call for similar kinds of pitch variation, and you can experiment with this on this historically important song.

Figure 1.1. "Follow the Drinking Gourd" ***Slave Songs of the United States***

SPIRITUALS AND GOSPEL

I will never forget my first experience playing gospel music when Lance Williams, a high school classmate, asked me to accompany him for a talent show on "Over the Rainbow." I laid down the first chord on piano, and his first phrase, with its magnificent bluesy melisma, told me that we were in a completely different stratosphere of sound. I was mesmerized. Soon after, I experienced a transformation as a member of the audience for the iconic vocal group Sweet Honey in the Rock's live performance at Carnegie Hall. The feeling that these women communicated, led by their founder, Bernice Johnson Reagon, moved me to tears and opened up a world of spirit in music that has shaped the trajectory and purpose of my life.

Sweet Honey in the Rock and the African American spiritual and freedom song tradition they embody showed me how deeply expressive this music can be while simultaneously producing a balm for overcoming despair and meeting it with a call to collective action. Over the years, I have experienced how this feeling is closely connected with the blues. I often include spirituals and freedom songs in blues concerts in a wide variety of contexts and have seen diverse audiences transported from the struggles of daily life through the power of these linked traditions. In many ways, the spirituals are the most direct way to access the spirit from which the blues flows.

Bernice Johnson Reagon (the founder of Sweet Honey in the Rock) writes,

> More than memories, we move with sounds, ways of being, hungers and itches that need to be scratched just so. Even without a drum there are the rhythms, without a song there is a singing stowed up needing to find the air, and there is knowing ordered by generations that plowed this land and their lives with sorrow and glory. And wherever we go, we can carry this load with us and have it as material to form our new present if we make it so.[28]

African American congregation song tradition has provided tremendous opportunities for African American singing traditions to be passed down from one generation to the next. Many blues singers and musicians started in the church playing and singing spirituals and gospel music, including Dinah Washington, Etta James, B.B. King, Sister Rosetta Tharpe, Son House, and Thomas Dorsey.

Thomas A. Dorsey is widely considered the founder of modern black gospel music. He composed "Take My Hand, Precious Lord," made famous by Mahalia Jackson, whom he mentored. The song was a favorite of civil rights icon Martin Luther King Jr.

Dorsey's blues and spiritual roots are intertwined. Born in Georgia, Dorsey's father was a minister and his mother a piano teacher. After studying in Chicago, he got hired by Paramount Records to organize a band to record with Ma Rainey. Later, under the name "Georgia Tom," he teamed up with guitarist-singer Tampa Red, and in 1928, their song "It's Tight Like That" became a blockbuster hit, selling 7 million copies.[29] ♪ After the tragic sudden death of his wife and child in childbirth, Dorsey turned to church music full-time. This is when he wrote "Take My Hand, Precious Lord."

"Take My Hand, Precious Lord" (Thomas Dorsey explaining how he made this composition and then performs it with Marion Williams ♪)

Dorsey bridged the gap between secular and sacred topics furthered by the African American community's view of the street as the place for devils and the church as the place for the saved. As Bernice Johnson Reagon said, "What torture it must have been to have the music of both the church and street resonating from within one's soul! Dorsey was not alone in the struggle; there were others who found it hard to split themselves between church and juke joint."[30]

Dorsey's struggle left an unsurpassed musical legacy in both the blues and the gospel genres. He composed more than five hundred gospel songs and many more blues and jazz compositions.[31] His work had an influence on all gospel musicians who came after, many of whom straddled the musical worlds of black sacred and secular music as he did.

Where do spirituals and the blues meet? How do the sacred songs sung by African Americans during the eighteenth and nineteenth centuries contribute to the development of the blues in the late nineteenth and early twentieth?

In the 1970s, another renowned black sacred music scholar, Dr. Horace Boyer, cofounded with Dr. Fred Tillis a jazz program rooted in spirituals at the University of Massachusetts, Amherst. Boyer's approach to training jazz singers was unique and had a deeply positive impact on contemporary jazz singers, such as the award-winning Kate McGarry, who studied with Boyer every day for four years while a student at the university. Through McGarry, I had the good fortune to meet Dr. Boyer and speak with him about the intersection of spirituals and the blues. Although he passed away in 2009, his legacy remains a great inspiration. Dr. Boyer appears in the documentary film *Too Close to Heaven: The History of Gospel Music*, where he explains that spirituals were as much about social significance as they were about religion: "They were commentary like a Greek chorus in Aeschylus. They commented on their lives and society. They commented on the big man boss in terms which the overseer could not interpret."[32]

In this film, Boyer goes on to beautifully demonstrate one of the saddest songs he knows as "Swing Low Sweet Chariot." He explains that "Jordan" meant death for enslaved Africans and that, as beautiful as this song is, it is essentially a call to death for release from suffering:

Swing Low, Sweet Chariot
Coming for to carry me home
Swing low, sweet chariot,
Coming for to carry me home.

I looked over Jordan, and what did I see
Coming for to carry me home.
A band of angels coming after me,
Coming for to carry me home.[33]

The "spiritual" was in common usage by the 1860s and a great container for emotion and story expressed through singing. In independent black churches, segregated camp and bush meetings, and "invisible" churches on plantations, African Americans seized the opportunity to develop a wide variety of religious songs away from the "surveillance of whites."[34]

Some of these songs are collected in *Slave Songs of the United States: The Classic 1867 Anthology*. A great modern-day resource for spirituals is the widely available volume edited by Boyer called *Lift Every Voice and Sing II*[35] with an introduction by Boyer, with whom Bernice Johnson Reagon collaborated. Reagon's lectures on spirituals are exemplary in that they combine historical information with the practice of engaging her audience to experience the transformational spirit of the music.

"WADE IN THE WATER"

"Wade in the Water" is a spiritual from times of slavery that contains rich multimeaning and infinite soulful *bluesiness*. In my teaching, I often use this song to help students enter the deep treasure well of African American spirituals and invite them to make a soulful sound. Like many spirituals, "Wade in the Water" is based on a minor pentatonic scale. These songs were often passed down orally in African American churches and "raised" rather than read from a book. Here's how I raise the song:

1. Invite everyone to stand in a circle.
2. Give some historical context of slavery in the United States, the families separated, the language and drums stripped away, the brutal conditions, the strenuous nature of the work, the heat, and so on.
3. Close eyes and lead a simple but focused call-and-response on "hum" using the first few notes of a minor pentatonic scale with scale degrees 1, ♭3, 4, and 5. Be sure to share this with characteristic slides up and down. Repeat this as long as it takes until people align with the sound and spirit.
4. Once the group is aligned, begin humming the melody of "Wade in the Water" phrase by phrase in call-and-response fashion. Take your time and imbibe the melody with as much feeling and soul as possible. This is achieved by dramatically leaning into certain notes over others and sliding appropriately into the pitches.
5. When the melody is truly felt by the group, you can begin to add the words phrase by phrase:

   Wade in the water
   Wade in the water children
   Wade in the water
   God's gonna trouble the water.

Once that is established out of time or in a moderate tempo, you can begin to establish the beat by using the stomp/clap.

THE STOMP/CLAP

The stomp/clap is the steady beat created in a congregation by each person stomping a foot and then clapping hands in steady time. This tradition emerged in the New World, not in Africa, and I suspect that it was developed by a combination of African American and Native American traditions. It is the foundational beat of most American music in that it establishes a steady pulse in duple time marking all quarter notes but emphasizing the two and four, often referred to as the "backbeat." I introduce it like this:

> The stomp/clap is an ancient tool from African American culture that has been used to get through very hard times as well as times of celebration. For some of you, it will be like you have been doing it for hundreds of years. For others, it will be quite new. However, rest assured because you too, with practice, can become a master of the stomp/clap.

Make sure the stomp is always first and the beat steady and easeful before combining with vocals. Use of stomping and hand clapping became prevalent in the United States among African Americans because the use of the drum was prohibited. Against the fixed rhythms of the pulse, the melodies moved freely, producing cross rhythms that constantly clashed with the pulse patterns.[36] The best way of understanding these clashes is *polyrhythm*, usually expressed through the constant simultaneous presence of triple and duple meter. We explore this later in the book.

For now, we can say that singing "Wade in the Water" is an ideal pathway to understanding the source of blues music on many levels. The melody is built on a minor pentatonic scale as many spirituals and blues songs are. In addition, the song originates during slavery and holds a double meaning. Outwardly, it is a worship song and related to the Bible story about Jesus coming to the pool of Bathzatha in Jerusalem in John 5:2–9.[37] It also carried a coded message to enslaved people; one strategy to give slave catchers the slip is to *wade through the water*. In this way, dogs that may be used to follow your scent will lose you.

Bernice Johnson Reagon takes this one step further when she investigates the meaning of the *troubled* water that, "once charged by the power of Spirit, has the power to transform and heal. The song said to us, then and now, go ahead, get in the water."[38] Reagon explains,

> As a child, I pondered this song because it had an upbeat, soft swing to it. It felt as if it was saying to go ahead into something that was trouble. My parents, my teacher, all adults around me who loved and cared about me told me over and over again to stay away from trouble. So, what was this song that I had learned from these same people that said that trouble was okay to go into, that it was all right to risk your life and put yourself in trouble? It took my own living to answer the question. It was not until I found myself in a situation where I could choose between an immediate safety and an action that would endanger me that I understood that often, if you want to be changed or healed or to be different, you cannot always steer around trouble. Sometimes you have to go through trouble.[39]

Reagon went on to march for civil rights in Albany, Georgia. She recalls sitting in at police stations during demonstrations and how, when demonstrators raised a spiritual, even the tense atmosphere in a police station during a sit-in could be completely transformed. Singing in the face of "troubled waters" to achieve personal transformation is one thing that spirituals and the blues have in common. Lifting up others in the community around you through the process is another.

"Wade in the Water" sung by Sweet Honey in the Rock ♪

RING SHOUTS

There were many different kinds of spirituals. Some were for worship service, some for "jes' sittin' around," and some for accompanying the shout.[40] After the regular service was over, a special one, more innately African, was held.

William Francis Allen, coeditor of *Slave Songs of the United States* published in 1857, writes,

> The true "shout" takes place on Sundays or on "praise" nights through the week, and either in the praise-house or in some cabin in which a regular

> religious meeting has been held. Very likely more than half the population of the plantation is gathered together. . . . The benches are pushed back to the wall when the formal meeting is over, and old and young, men and women . . . all stand up in the middle of the floor, and when the "sperichil" [spiritual] is struck up, begin first walking and by-and-by shuffling round, one after the other, in a ring. The foot is hardly taken from the floor, and the progression is mainly due to a jerking, hitching motion, which agitates the entire shouter, and soon brings out streams of perspiration.[41]

There are usually at least two groups of shouters, and the melodies of the spiritual are sung in various configurations of call-and-response, unison, improvised variations, use of riffs, body percussion, and *movement*. The ring shouts were known to go on for as long as four or five successive hours. The energy of the movement and repetitive riffs of the music created a communal ecstatic reverie resembling Sufi and Gnawan (Morocco) chant and movement rituals. The shout belonged to no one denomination or to any one region. It simply represented the survival of an African tradition in the New World and showed two essential ingredients:

1. Shouters used dance as a means of communication with God in the same way that song and prayer are used.
2. Shouters reached the highest level of worship when the Holy Spirit entered their bodies and took possession of their souls.[42]

Riff-based music that moves people to dance remains at the center of American music of the twenty-first century. It was important to the development of the blues, swing, rhythm and blues, rock, funk, disco, and popular music of today.

FIELD HOLLER

Contemporary blues artist Shemekia Copeland (featured on the cover of this book) quotes her father, blues man Johnny Copeland, as saying that "blues singing is nothing but hollering like they used to do in the fields."[43]

Author Paul Oliver, in his book *Savannah Syncopators—African Retentions in the Blues* (1970), points to a declamatory singing style in northern Ghana, widespread in the savanna culture area, as a source of the singing style known in the United States as the field holler. Blues researcher David Evans confirms this view:

> It is plain to see how a cattle herding song tradition from Africa could be adapted to another type of largely solitary rural activity since the U.S. South was mostly devoted to crop agriculture, although there was some dairy and beef cattle activity and much more in Louisiana/Texas where there were many black cowboys.[44]

Many blues singers cite the holler as having an important influence on blues singing. Sometimes the songs were merely cries in the field—"cornfield hollers," "cotton field hollers," "whoops," or "water calls." A slave's call or cry could mean any one of a number of things: a call for water, food, or help; a call to let others know where he or she was working; or simply a cry of loneliness, sorrow, or happiness. One cry might be answered by another from a place far distant. Music was a primary form of communication.[45]

In 1853, a traveler in the South described such a sound:

> Suddenly one [a slave] raised such a sound as I had never heard before, a long, loud musical shout, rising and falling, and breaking into falsetto, his voice ringing through the woods in the clear frosty night air, like a bugle call. As he finished, the melody was caught up by another, and then, another, and then, by several in chorus.[46]

One such field holler is "I Know Moonlight" found in the appendix on page 202.

SHOUTING INTO VERSE AND SURVIVING

Sometimes this shoutlike singing was adapted into verses. Many travelers commented on the "wild hymns of sweet and mournful melody" sung by men and women of the slave coffles on the long journey from "Virginny" into the lower South. Gathered together into groups that sometimes numbered in the hundreds, slaves were handcuffed, two by two, and attached to a long chain that ran down the center of the double file. Men on horseback accompanied the coffles, wielding long whips to "goad the reluctant and weary," and fiddlers among the slaves were forced to play on their instruments. Thus, the grim procession took on the bizarre aspect of a nightmarish parade. And the slaves sang about this too.[47] William Wells Brown, a prominent African American abolitionist and writer, recalled the words of one of the songs they sang:

> See these poor souls from Africa
> Transported to America:
> We are stolen and sold to Georgia, will you go along with me?
> We are stolen and sold to Georgia, go sound the jubilee.
>
> See wives and husbands sold apart,
> The children's screams!—it breaks my heart;
> There's a better day a-coming, will you go along with me?
> There's a better day a-coming, go sound the jubilee.
>
> O gracious Lord! When shall it be
> That we poor souls shall all be free?
> Lord, break them Slavery powers—will you go along with me?
> Lord, break them Slavery powers, go sound the jubilee.
>
> Dear Lord! Dear Lord! When Slavery'll cease,
> Then we poor souls can have our peace;
> There's a better day a-coming, will you go along with me?
> There's a better day a-coming, go sound the jubilee.[48]

It was common practice to force slaves to sing and dance under the most tragic of circumstances. This included during transport on slave ships and just before being put up for sale on the auction block. There was usually a slave fiddler made available to play for such dancing, often one of the slaves who, himself, was up for sale.[49]

Frequently, a song summed up all the things the slaves most hated from relatively minor annoyances to dreaded "laying on" of a hundred lashes when a slave failed to meet his or her work quota.[50] Blues man B.B. King writes in his autobiography,

> My great-grandmother who'd also been a slave, talked about the old days. She'd talk about the beginnings of the blues. She said that, sure, singing helped the day go by. Singing about your sadness unburdens your soul.

> But the blues hollerers shouted about more than being sad. They were also delivering messages in musical code. If the master was coming, you might sing a hidden warning to the other field hands. Maybe you'd want to get out of his way or hide. That was important for the women because the master could have anything he wanted. If he liked a woman, he could take her sexually. And the woman had only two choices: Do what the master demands or kill herself. There was no in-between. The blues could warn you what was coming. I could see the blues was about survival.[51]

Through the feeling conjured through context and the shape of these melodies, songs from this period offer a strong base for singing blues.

"Dere's No Rain" and "No More Auction Block for Me" can be found in the appendix on page 202.

WORK SONGS

Work songs are the fabric from which the blues is woven, and you can see why—the steady rhythm required of the work involved, whether it consisted of picking cotton, threshing rice, stripping tobacco, or harvesting sugarcane. Music served the function of easing the monotony of the work and spurring workers on.[52] This practice, as noted before, is connected to an ancient west-central Sudanic African tradition of pentatonic song composition that goes back thousands of years. Work songs, in fact, were common throughout Africa. Frederick Douglass writes,

> Slaves are generally expected to sing as well as to work. A silent slave is not liked by masters or overseers. "Make a noise" and "bear a hand," are the words usually addressed to the slaves when there is silence amongst them. This may account for the almost constant singing heard in the southern states.[53]

The work song always has a *steady beat*, and this helps workers keep in time with one another, whether working in the fields or hammering or some other motion involving physical coordination.

These songs are connected with songs sung on boats to coordinate oarsmen, though those songs tend to be slower in tempo. The English actress and singer Fanny Kemble spent the winter of 1838–1839 on a plantation on the coast of Georgia. Her journal was published in 1863 and contains her observations of the music of enslaved African Americans. As a professional singer who recognized the injustice of slavery, her observations give us something close to an objective observation of African American singing in the 1830s. Her initial impressions include comments about unique singing qualities of African Americans. Kemble writes, "Their voices seem oftener tenor than any other quality, and the tune and time they keep something quite wonderful; such truth of intonation and accent would make almost any music agreeable." However, she expects the sources of the tunes to be from white men: "their overseers or masters whistling Scotch or Irish airs, of which they have reproduced these *rifacciamenti* [adaptations]." On further listening, Kemble recognizes that this is not the case; in fact, the singing and the tunes of African Americans are truly unique, even extraordinary. She continues,

> My daily voyages up and down the river have introduced me to a great variety of new, musical performances of our boatmen, who invariably, when the rowing is not too hard, moving up or down with the tide, accompany the stroke of their oars with the sound of their voices. I told you formerly that I thought I could trace distinctly some popular national melody with which I was familiar in almost all of their songs; but I have been quite at a loss to discover any such foundation for many that I have heard lately, and which appeared to me extraordinarily wild and unaccountable. The way in which the chorus strikes in with the burden, between each phrase of the melody chanted by a single voice, is very curious and effective, especially with the rhythm of the rowlocks for accompaniment.[54]

The first collection of *Slave Songs of the United States* was published in 1867. The editors noted, as Kemble initially did, the Euro-derivative nature of many of the songs. However, like Kemble, they realized that the closer they came to the working slave, the closer they came to the "extraordinarily wild and unaccountable" music that Kemble had heard. One song completely beyond their abilities to transcribe because of its complexity sounded like a minor-keyed wailing song of the West African tribes.[55]

Even when slavery was supposed to end in 1865, it didn't. Southerners quickly forced northern troops to allow them to reimpose restrictions on the rights of new "freedmen." The tipping point was the presidential election of 1876 when narrowly elected Republican Rutherford B. Hayes made a compromise with southern Democrats by agreeing to remove federal troops from the South altogether. This paved the way for white southerners to force blacks into a servitude little better than slavery and gave rise to the infamous Ku Klux Klan. The new order of sharecropping and the widespread imprisonment of black men for invisible offenses kept many black people in, to quote the title of Douglas Blackmon's book on the subject, *slavery by another name*.[56]

Work songs continued to be sung by prison gangs doing hard labor splitting rocks and/or driving spikes for the construction of the railroad. The opening scene of the year 2000 Coen Brothers movie *O Brother, Where Art Thou?* shows such a work chain gang singing. The song was taken from a field recording by Alan Lomax, who asked prisoners to reenact chain gang work.

"Po' Lazarus" sung by James Carter and the Prisoners ♪

EARLY EARLY BLUES

By the late nineteenth century, work songs became what would sound to us now like blues, such as this levee shout heard on the Mississippi River in the 1890s:

> Oh, rock me, Julie, rock me.
> Rock me slow and easy.
> Rock me like a baby.[57]

In 1904, a man in Auburn, Alabama, recalled the following "work song," which referred to the time late at night just before daybreak—"before day blues":

> Some folks say be fo' day blues ain't bad,
> But be fo' day blues am de wust I eber had.[58]

This song was found other places with other variations:

> Be four day blues ain't nuffin'
> But a woman wants a man.
>
> When a woman takes de blues
> She tucks her head and cries.

But when a man catches the blues,
He catches er freight and rides.

If de blues was whiskey
I'd stay drunk all de time.

De blues ain't nothin'
But a poor man's heart disease.

And there was one of the most simple and intense of the early blues verses:

I got de blues,
But I'm too damn mean to cry.[59]

You can hear and feel the legacy of the older work songs in early blues recordings and later ones as well. One of the first widely influential blues men was Blind Lemon Jefferson from Texas. Singing in a high crying voice, many of his recordings were direct reworkings of old field cries and work songs.[60]

"Prison Cell Blues" sung by Blind Lemon Jefferson ♪

SOLO

Whereas working in groups and singing work songs were encouraged, gathering in groups during leisure time was not. It could be that the suppression of community-oriented forms of expression among the slaves on the plantations helped create the need the blues would fill. The blues is known as a solo singing tradition. Once again, African American blues unites two relatively different African performance traditions: sung narratives to the accompaniment of an instrument by a soloist and stories incorporating songs, told to small audiences of adults and children, especially in the evenings, with the audience participating as a responding chorus. All of these incorporated complex literary symbolism, and were sung in the first person.[61]

If it's true that a blues performer plays the blues to rid himself of the blues, then it reasons to follow that "blues texts, with their complaints and intense imagery, occasionally read like quotations from the diary of a patient experiencing or recovering from clinical depression."[62] Of course, the texts are much more poetic than that. As Samuel Charters quotes blues man Baby Tate in *Poetry of the Blues*,

> I'll tell you what gives me the blues. When my wife makes me mad. Make me angry otherwise. A dog go mad. But if she makes me angry. I didn't do all I can do or something like that, and she want me to do something else. She get me angry. Well the first thing I do I'll grab my guitar and walk out of the house to keep from having a fight.[63]

Blues man J. D. Short agreed that singing the blues helped him get through periods of emotional stress:

> Yes, it actual do. It's a lot of times we can get very worried and dissatisfied, and we can get to singing the blues and if we can play music and play the blues we may play the blues for a while until we get kind of pacified. That cuts off a lot of worry.[64]

It seems simple, yet if you think about it, playing the blues to get rid of the blues is one of the most powerful things a human being can do. Studying the origins of the blues has been immensely helpful for me to be able to share the rich emotional content of the music with audiences around the world in performances and workshops. Of course, you don't have to personally experience the cruelty of slavery or its stinging legacy of racism to sing the genre. But if it is not in your experience, knowing about it helps tremendously. Finding a personal connection to the meaning behind the songs is essential for authentic presentation of the blues. Blues music is a platform for resilience, resistance, identity, healing, creativity, and community. Let us continue to give credit to the African American women and men who created this music and honor them and the extraordinary culture they came from by representing this treasure as authentically as we can.

NOTES

1. Samuel Charters, *The Country Blues* (New York: Da Capo, 1975).
2. Albert Murray, *Stompin' the Blues* (New York: Da Capo, 1976), 16–17.
3. Murray, *Stompin' the Blues*, 38.
4. Nat Shapiro and Nat Hentoff, *Hear Me Talkin' to Ya* (New York: Da Capo, 1955), 7.

5. Gerhard Kubik, *Africa and the Blues* (Jackson: University Press of Mississippi, 1999).

6. Kubik, *Africa and the Blues*, 102.

7. Kubik, *Africa and the Blues*, 94

8. Paul Robeson, "The Culture of the Negro," *The Spectator* (London) (1934), 86–87.

9. Kubik, *Africa and the Blues*, 85–92.

10. Amiri Baraka, *Blues People* (New York: Harper Perennial, 1963), 26.

11. Baraka, *Blues People*, 31.

12. Kubik, *Africa and the Blues*, 123.

13. Robert Palmer, *Deep Blues* (London: Penguin, 1981), 102.

14. Palmer, *Deep Blues*, 103.

15. Kubik, *Africa and the Blues*, 125.

16. Kubik, *Africa and the Blues*, 127.

17. Kubik, *Africa and the Blues*, 3–8.

18. Kubik, *Africa and the Blues*, 7.

19. Eileen Southern, *The Music of Black Americans: A History* (New York: Norton, 1997), 19–20.

20. Southern, *The Music of Black Americans*, 21–22.

21. Southern, *The Music of Black Americans*, 53.

22. William Wells Brown, *My Southern Home* (Boston: A. G. Brown, 1880), 121–22.

23. Brown, *My Southern Home*, 121–22.

24. Southern, *The Music of Black Americans*, 138.

25. Southern, *The Music of Black Americans*, 142–44.

26. Sarah Bradford, *Harriet, the Moses of Her People* (New York, 1886), 37.

27. Southern, *The Music of Black Americans*, 144.

28. Bernice Johnson Reagon, *If You Don't Go, Don't Hinder Me: The African American Sacred Song Tradition* (Lincoln: University of Nebraska Press, 2001), 42.

29. Laurence Staig, "Obituary: Thomas Dorsey," *Independent*, January 26, 1993.

30. Reagon, *If You Don't Go, Don't Hinder Me*, 22.

31. Horace Boyer, "Take My Hand, Precious Lord, Lead Me On," in *We'll Understand It Better By and By: Pioneering African American Gospel Composers*, ed. Bernice Johnson Reagon (Washington, DC: Smithsonian Institution Scholarly Press, 1992), 142.

32. From the film *Too Close to Heaven: The History of Gospel Music*.

33. Words traditional, "Swing Low Sweet Chariot."

34. Southern, *The Music of Black Americans*, 181.

35. This volume is "II" because the earlier edition is out of print.

36. Southern, *The Music of Black Americans*, 195.
37. Reagon, *If You Don't Go, Don't Hinder Me*, 129.
38. Reagon, *If You Don't Go, Don't Hinder Me*, 130.
39. Reagon, *If You Don't Go, Don't Hinder Me*, 130.
40. Southern, *The Music of Black Americans*, 181.
41. William Francis Allen, *Slave Songs* (New York: Simpson & Co., 1995), xiii–xv.
42. Southern, *The Music of Black Americans*, 183.
43. Shemekia Copeland, interview with LaFrae Sci (2017).
44. David Evans, quoted in Kubik, *Africa and the Blues*, 65–66.
45. Southern, *The Music of Black Americans*, 157.
46. Frederick Law Olmsted, *Journey in the Seaboard Slave States: With Remarks on Their Economy*, vol. 2 (New York: Dix and Edwards; London: Sampson Low, Son & Co., 1856), 19.
47. Southern, *The Music of Black Americans*, 158.
48. William Wells Brown, *The Anti-Slavery Harp: A Collection of Songs for Anti-Slavery Meetings* (Boston: Bela Marsh, 1848), 29.
49. Southern, *The Music of Black Americans*, 159.
50. Southern, *The Music of Black Americans*, 160.
51. B.B. King, with David Ritz, *Blues All Around Me: The Autobiography of B.B. King* (New York: HarperCollins, 1996), 8.
52. Southern, *The Music of Black Americans*, 161.
53. Frederick Douglass, *My Bondage and My Freedom* (New York: Penguin, 1855).
54. Frances Anne Kemble, *Journal of a Residence on a Georgia Plantation in 1838–1839* (New York, 1864).
55. Charters, *The Country Blues*, 23.
56. Douglas A. Blackmon, *Slavery by Another Name: The Re-Enslavement of Black Americans from the Civil War to World War II* (New York: Doubleday, 2008).
57. Blackmon, *Slavery by Another Name*, 29.
58. Newman I. White, *American Negro Folk Songs* (Cambridge, MA: Harvard University Press, 1928).
59. Charters, *The Country Blues*, 30.
60. Charters, *The Country Blues*, 57–72.
61. Charters, *The Country Blues*, 27.
62. Charters, *The Country Blues*, 29.
63. Baby Tate, quoted in Samuel Charters, *The Poetry of the Blues* (New York: Oak Publications, 1963), 13.
64. J. D. Short, quoted in in Charters, *The Poetry of the Blues*, 13.

2

SINGING AND VOICE SCIENCE

Scott McCoy

This chapter presents a concise overview of how the voice functions as a biomechanical, acoustic instrument. We will be dealing with elements of anatomy, physiology, acoustics, and resonance. But don't panic: the things you need to know are easily accessible, even if it has been many years since you last set foot in a science or math class!

All musical instruments, including the human voice, have at least four things in common, consisting of a power source, sound source (vibrator), resonator, and a system for articulation. In most cases, the person who plays the instrument provides power by pressing a key, plucking a string, or blowing into a horn. This power is used to set the sound source in motion, which creates vibrations in the air that we perceive as sound. Musical vibrators come in many forms, including strings, reeds, and human lips. The sound produced by the vibrator, however, needs a lot of help before it becomes beautiful music—we might think of it as raw material, like a lump of clay that a potter turns into a vase. Musical instruments use resonance to enhance and strengthen the sound of the vibrator, transforming it into sounds we identify as a piano, trumpet, or guitar. Finally, instruments must have a means of articulation to create the nuanced sounds of music. Let's see how these four elements are used to create the sounds of singing.

PULMONARY SYSTEM: THE POWER SOURCE OF YOUR VOICE

The human voice has a lot in common with a trumpet: both use flaps of tissue as a sound source, both use hollow tubes as resonators, and both rely on the respiratory (pulmonary) system for power. If you stop to think about it, you quickly realize why breathing is so important for singing. First and foremost, it keeps us alive through the exchange of blood gases—oxygen in, carbon dioxide out. But it also serves as the storage depot for the air we use to produce sound. Most singers rarely encounter situations in which these two functions are in conflict, but if you are required to sustain an extremely long phrase, you could find yourself in need of fresh oxygen before your lungs are totally empty.

Misconceptions about breathing for singing are rampant. Fortunately, most are easily dispelled. We must start with a brief foray into the world of physics in the guise of Boyle's Law. Some of you no doubt remember this principle: the pressure of a gas within a container changes inversely with changes of volume. If the quantity of a gas is constant and its container is made smaller, pressure rises. But if we make the container get bigger, pressure goes down. Boyle's law explains everything that happens when we breathe, especially when we combine it with another physical law: nature abhors a vacuum. If one location has reduced pressure, air flows from an area of higher pressure to equalize the two, and vice versa. So if we can create a zone of reduced air pressure by expanding our lungs, air automatically flows in to restore balance. When air pressure in the lungs is increased, it has no choice but to flow outward.

As we all know, the air we breathe goes in and out of our lungs. Each lung contains millions and millions of tiny air sacs called alveoli, where gases are exchanged. The alveoli also function like ultra-miniature versions of the bladder for a bag pipe, storing the air that will be used to set the vocal folds into vibration. To get the air in and out of them, all we need to do is make the lungs larger for inhalation and smaller for exhalation. Always remember this relationship between cause and effect during breathing: we inhale because we make ourselves large; we exhale because we make ourselves smaller. Unfortunately, the lungs are organs, not muscles, and have no ability on their own to accomplish this feat. For this reason, your bodies came from the factory with special muscles designed to enlarge and compress your entire thorax (rib cage), while simultaneously moving your lungs. We can classify these muscles in two main categories: any muscle that has the ability to increase the volume capacity of the thorax serves an inspiratory function; any muscle that has the ability to decrease the volume capacity of the thorax serves an expiratory function.

Your largest muscle of inspiration is called the diaphragm (figure 2.1). This dome-shaped muscle originates from the bottom of your sternum (breastbone) and completely fills the area from that point around your ribs to your spine. It's the second-largest muscle in your body, but you probably have no conscious awareness of it or ability to directly control it. When we take a deep breath, the diaphragm contracts and the central portion flattens out and drops downward a couple inches into your

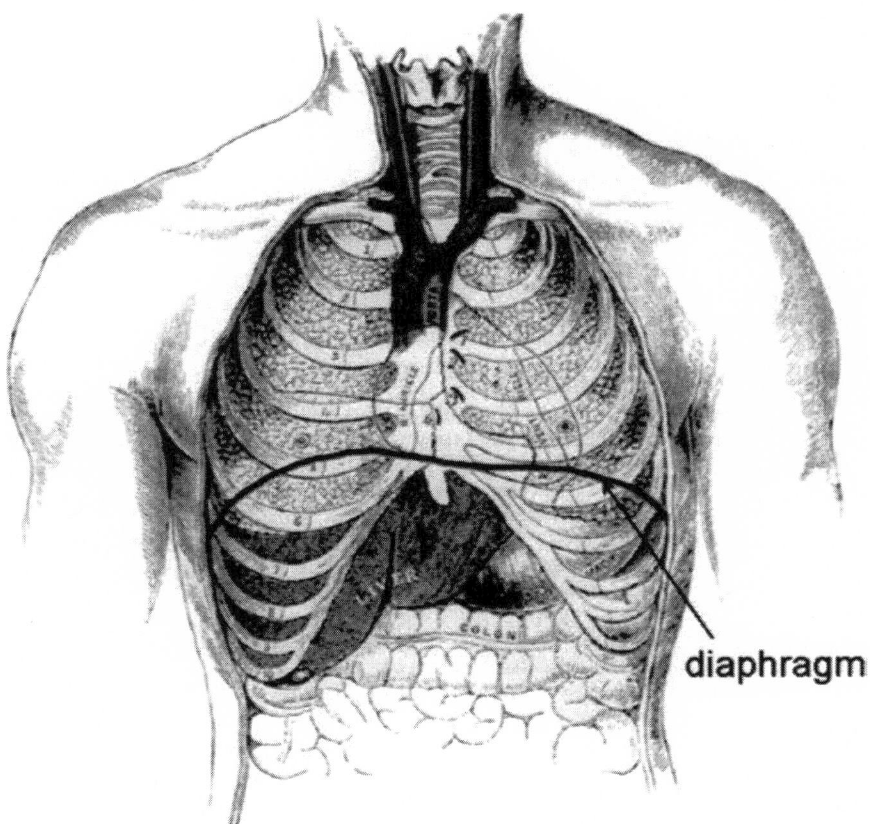

Figure 2.1. Location of Diaphragm. ***Dr. Scott McCoy***

abdomen, pressing against all of your internal organs. If you release tension from your abdominal muscles as you inhale, you will feel a gentle bulge in your upper or lower belly, or perhaps in your back, resulting from the displacement of your innards by the diaphragm. This is a good thing and can be used to let you know you have taken a good inhalation.

The diaphragm is important, but we must remember that it cannot function in isolation. After you inhale, it relaxes and gently returns to its resting position through an action called elastic recoil. This movement, however, is entirely passive and makes no significant contribution to generating the pressure required to sustain phonation. Therefore, it makes no sense at all to try to "sing from your diaphragm"—unless you intend to sing while you inhale, not exhale!

Eleven pairs of muscles assist the diaphragm in its inhalatory efforts, which are called the external intercostal muscles (figure 2.2). These muscles start from ribs one through eleven and connect at a slight angle downward to ribs two through twelve. When they contract, the entire thorax moves up and out, somewhat like moving a bucket handle. With the diaphragm and intercostals working together, you are able to increase the capacity of your lungs by about three to six liters, depending on your gender and overall physical stature; thus, we have quite a lot of air available to power our voices.

Eleven additional pairs of muscles are located directly under the external intercostals, which, not surprisingly, are called the internal intercostals (figure 2.2). These muscles start from ribs two through twelve and connect upward to ribs one through eleven. When they contract, they induce the opposite action of their external partners: the thorax is made smaller, inducing exhalation. Four additional pairs of expiratory muscles are located in the abdomen, beginning with the rectus (figure 2.2). The two rectus abdominis muscles run from your pubic bone to your sternum and are divided into four separate portions, called bellies of the muscle (lots of muscles have multiple bellies; it is coincidental that the bellies of the rectus are found in the location we colloquially refer to as our belly). Definition of these bellies results in the so-called ripped abdomen or six-pack of body builders and others who are especially fit.

The largest muscles of the abdomen are called the external obliques (figure 2.3), which run at a downward angle from the sides of the rec-

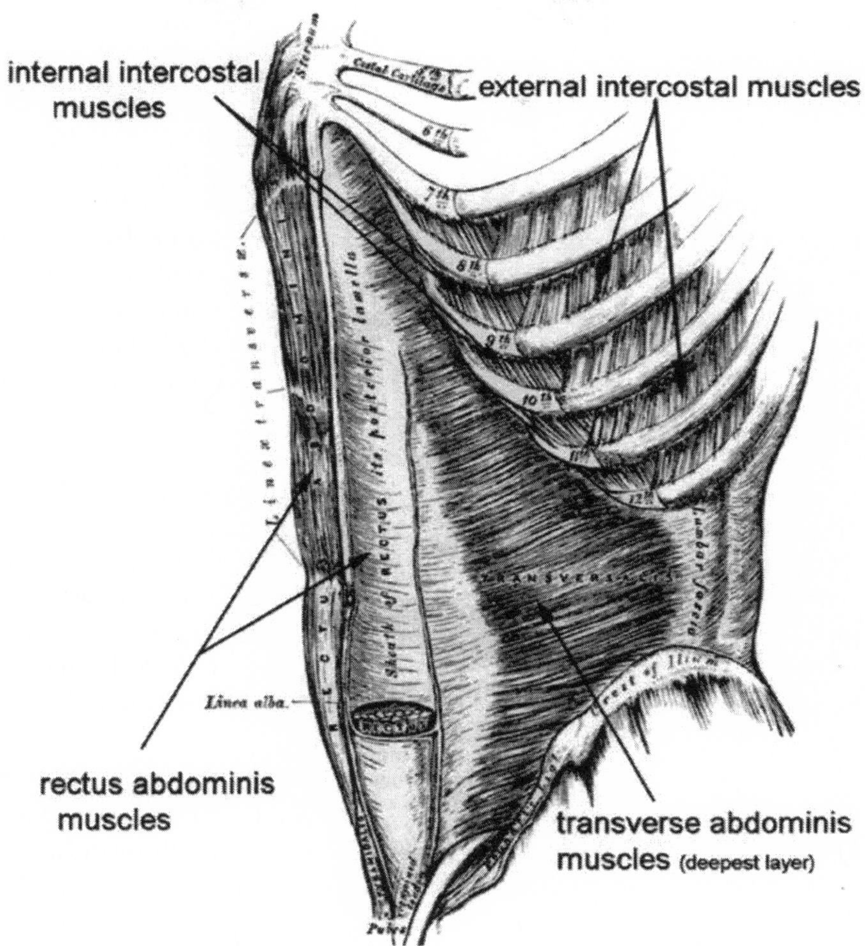

Figure 2.2. Intercostal and abdominal muscles. ***Dr. Scott McCoy***

tus, covering the lower portion of the thorax, and extend all the way to the spine. The internal obliques lie immediately below, oriented at an angle that crisscrosses the external muscles. They are slightly smaller, beginning at the bottom of the thorax, rather than extending over it. The deepest muscle layer is the transverse abdominis (figure 2.3), which is oriented with fibers that run horizontally. These four muscle pairs completely encase the abdominal region, holding your organs and digestive system in place while simultaneously helping you breathe.

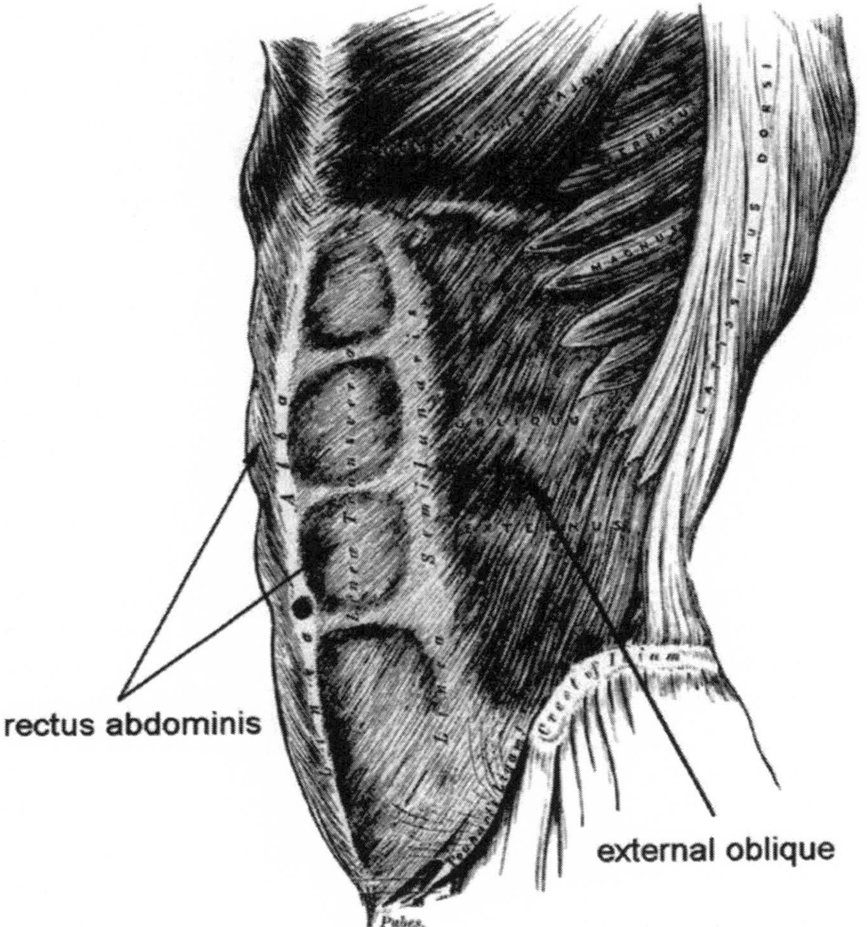

Figure 2.3. External oblique and rectus abdominus muscles. ***Dr. Scott McCoy***

Your expiratory muscles are quite large and can produce a great deal of pulmonary or air pressure. In fact, they easily can overpower the larynx. Healthy adults generally can generate more than twice the pressure that is required to produce even the loudest sounds; therefore, singers must develop a system for moderating and controlling airflow and breath pressure. This practice goes by many names, including breath support, breath control, and breath management, all of which rely on the principle of muscular antagonism. Muscles are said to have an antagonistic relationship when they work in opposing directions, usually pulling on a common point of attachment, for the sake of increasing stability or motor control. You can see a clear example of muscular antagonism in the relationship between your biceps (flexors) and triceps (extensors) when you hold out your arm. In breathing for singing, we activate inspiratory muscles (e.g., diaphragm and external intercostals) during exhalation to help control respiratory pressure and the rate at which air is expelled from the lungs.

One of the things you will notice when watching a variety of singers is that they tend to breathe in many different ways. You might think that voice teachers and scientists, who have been teaching and studying singing for hundreds, if not thousands of years, would have come to agreement on the best possible breathing technique. But for many reasons, this is not the case. For one, different musical and vocal styles place varying demands on breathing. For another, humans have a huge variety of body types, sizes, and morphologies. A breathing strategy that is successful for a tall, slender woman might be completely ineffective in a short, robust man. Our bodies actually contain a large number of muscles beyond those we've already discussed that are capable of assisting with respiration. For an example, consider your latissimi dorsi muscles. These large muscles of the arm enable us to do pull-ups (or pull-downs, depending on which exercise you perform) at the fitness center. But because they wrap around a large portion of the thorax, they also exert an expiratory force. We have at least two dozen such muscles that have secondary respiratory functions, some for exhalation and some for inhalation. When we consider all these possibilities, it is no surprise at all that there are many ways to breathe that can produce beautiful singing. Just remember to practice some muscular antagonism—maintaining a degree of inhalation posture during exhalation—and you should do well.

LARYNX: THE VIBRATOR OF YOUR VOICE

The larynx, sometimes known as the voice box or Adam's apple, is a complex physiologic structure made of cartilage, muscle, and tissue. Biologically, it serves as a sphincter valve, closing off the airway to prevent foreign objects from entering the lungs. When firmly closed, it also is used to increase abdominal pressure to assist with lifting heavy objects, childbirth, and defecation. But if we gently close this valve while we exhale, tissue in the larynx begins to vibrate and produce the sounds that become speech and singing.

The human larynx is a remarkably small instrument, typically ranging from the size of a pecan to a walnut for women and men, respectively. Sound is produced at a location called the glottis, which is formed by two flaps of tissue called the vocal folds (aka vocal cords). In women, the glottis is about the size of a dime; in men, it can approach the diameter of a quarter. The two folds are always attached together at their front point but open in the shape of the letter V during normal breathing, an action called abduction. To phonate, we must close the V while we exhale, an action called adduction (just like the machines you use at the fitness center to exercise your thigh and chest muscles).

Phonation only is possible because of the unique multilayer structure of the vocal folds (figure 2.4). The core of each fold is formed by muscle, which is surrounded by a layer of gelatinous material called the lamina propria. The vocal ligament also runs through the lamina propria, which helps to prevent injury by limiting how far the folds can be stretched for high pitches. A thin, hairless epithelial layer that is constantly kept moist with mucus secreted by the throat, larynx, and

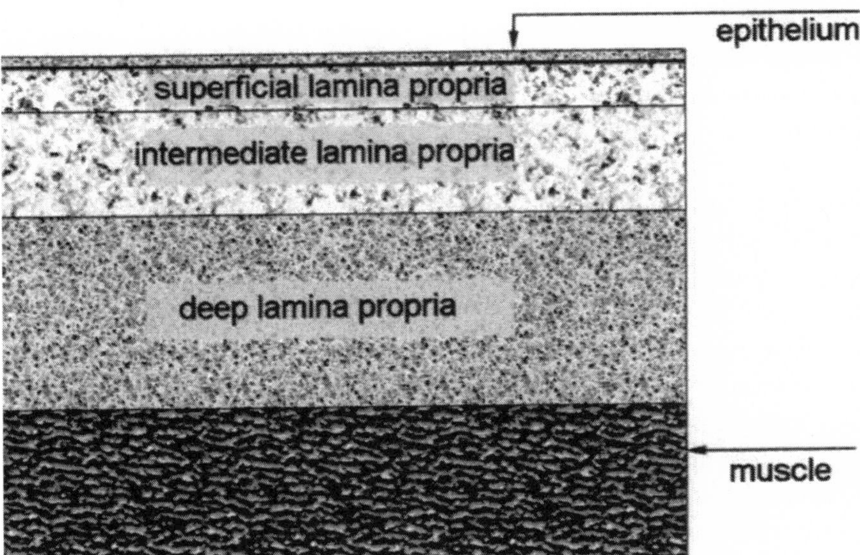

Figure 2.4. Layered structure of the vocal fold. ***Dr. Scott McCoy***

trachea surrounds all of this. During phonation, the outer layer of the fold glides independently over the inner layer in a wavelike motion, without which phonation is impossible.

We can use a simple demonstration to better understand the independence of the inner and outer portions of the folds. Explore the palm of your hand with your other index finger. Note that the skin is attached quite firmly to the flesh beneath it. If you poke at your palm, that flesh acts as padding, protecting the underlying bone. Now explore the back of your hand. You will observe that the skin is attached quite loosely—you easily can move it around with your finger. And if you poke at the back of your hand, it is likely to hurt; there is very little padding between the skin and your bones. Your vocal folds combine the best attributes of both sides of your hand. They provide sufficient padding to help reduce impact stress, while permitting the outer layer to slip like the skin on the back of your hand, enabling phonation to occur. When you are sick with laryngitis and lose your voice (a condition called aphonia), inflammation in the vocal folds couples the layers of the folds tightly together. The outer layer no longer can move independently over the inner, and phonation becomes difficult or impossible.

The vocal folds are located within the five cartilaginous structures of the larynx (figure 2.5). The largest is called the thyroid cartilage, which is shaped like a small shield. The thyroid connects to the cricoid cartilage below it, which is shaped like a signet ring—broad in the back and narrow in the front. Two cartilages that are shaped like squashed pyramids sit atop the cricoid, called the arytenoids. Each vocal fold runs from the thyroid cartilage in front to one of the arytenoids at the back. Finally, the epiglottis is located at the top of the larynx, flipping backward each time we swallow to prevent food and liquid from entering our lungs. Muscles connect between the various cartilages to open and close the glottis and to lengthen and shorten the vocal folds for ascending and descending pitch, respectively. Because they sometimes are used to identify vocal function, it is a good idea to know the names of the muscles that control the length of the folds. We've already mentioned that a muscle forms the core of each fold. Because it runs between the thyroid cartilage and an arytenoid, it is named the thyroarytenoid muscle (formerly known as the vocalis muscle). When the thyroarytenoid, or TA muscle, contracts, the fold is shortened and pitch goes down. The folds

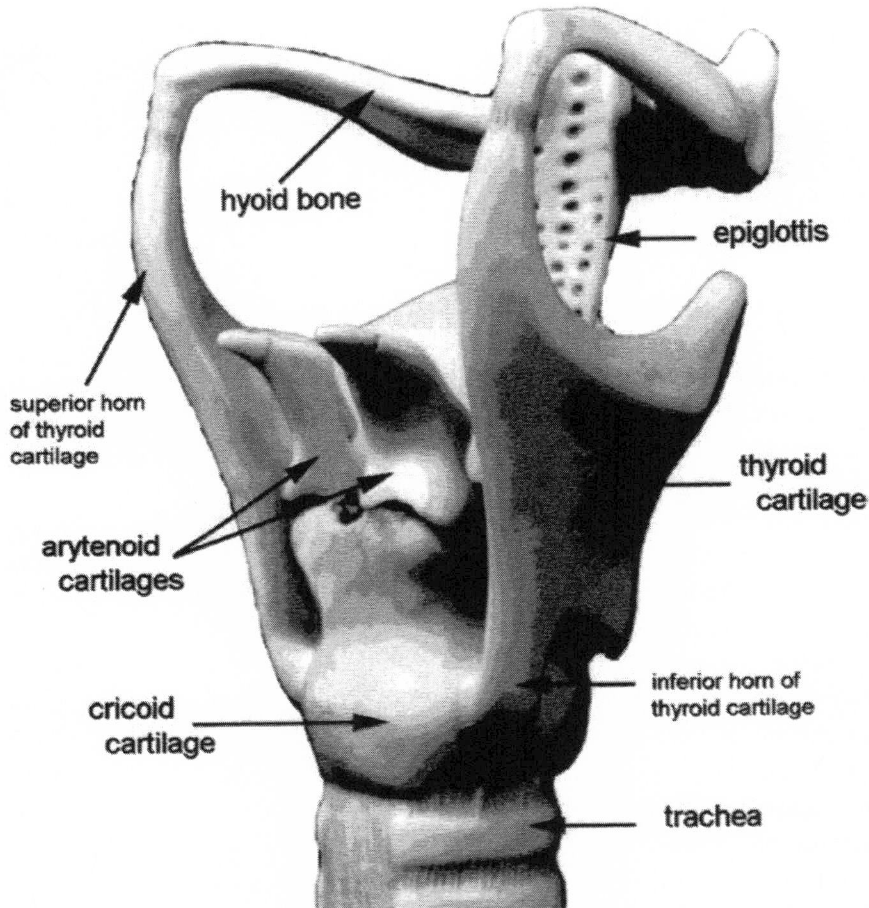

Figure 2.5. Cartilages of the larynx, viewed at an angle from the back. ***Dr. Scott McCoy***

are elongated through the action of the cricothyroid, or CT muscles, which run from the thyroid to cricoid cartilage.

Vocal color (timbre) is created by the combined effects of the sound produced by the vocal folds and the resonance provided by the vocal tract. While these elements can never be completely separated, it is useful to consider the two primary modes of vocal fold vibration and their resulting sound qualities. The main differences are related to the relative thickness of the folds and their cross-sectional shape (figure 2.6). The

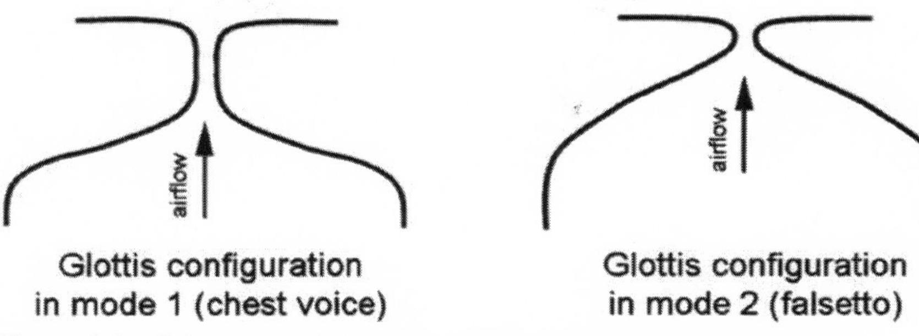

Figure 2.6. Primary modes of vocal fold vibration. ***Dr. Scott McCoy***

first option depends on short, thick folds that come together with nearly square-shaped edges. Vibration in this configuration is given a variety of names, including mode 1, thyroarytenoid (TA) dominant, chest mode, or modal voice. The alternate configuration uses longer, thinner folds that only make contact at their upper margins. Common names include mode 2, cricothyroid (CT) dominant, falsetto mode, or loft voice. Singers vary the vibrational mode of the folds according to the quality of sound they wish to produce.

Before we move on to a discussion of resonance, we must consider the quality of the sound that is produced by the larynx. At the level of the glottis, we create a sound not unlike the annoying buzz of a duck call. That buzz, however, contains all the raw material we need to create speech and singing. Vocal or glottal sound is considered to be complex, meaning it consists of many simultaneously sounding frequencies (pitches). The lowest frequency within any tone is called the fundamental, which corresponds to its named pitch in the musical scale. Orchestras tune to a pitch called A-440, which means it has a frequency of 440 vibrations per second, or 440 Hertz (abbreviated Hz). Additional frequencies are included above the fundamental, which are called overtones. Overtones in the glottal sound are quieter than the fundamental. In voices, the overtones usually are whole number multiples of the fundamental, creating a pattern called the harmonic series (e.g., 100 Hz, 200 Hz, 300 Hz, 400 Hz, 500 Hz, etc. or G2, G3, D4, G4, B4—note that pitches are named by the international system in which the lowest C of the piano keyboard is C1; middle-C therefore becomes C4, the fourth C of the keyboard) (figure 2.7).

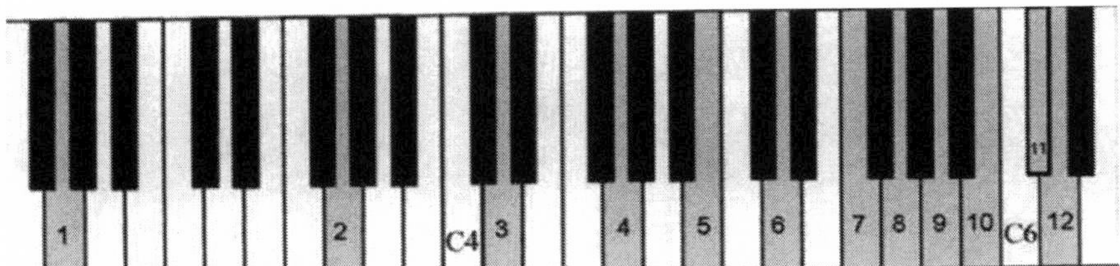

Figure 2.7. Natural harmonic series, beginning at G2. ***Dr. Scott McCoy***

Singers who choose to make coarse or rough sounds as might be appropriate for rock or blues often add overtones that are inharmonic, or not part of the standard numerical sequence. Inharmonic overtones also are common in singers with damaged or pathological voices.

Under most circumstances, we are completely unaware of the presence of overtones—they simply contribute to the overall timbre of a voice. In some vocal styles, however, harmonics become a dominant feature. This is especially true in throat singing or overtone singing, as is found in places like Tuva. Throat singers tune their vocal tracts so precisely that single harmonics are highlighted within the harmonic spectrum as a separate, whistle-like tone. These singers sustain a low-pitched drone and then create a melody by moving from tone to tone within the natural harmonic series. You can learn to do this too. Sustain a comfortable pitch in your range and slowly morph between the vowels [i] and [u]. If you listen carefully, you will hear individual harmonics pop out of your sound.

The mode of vocal fold vibration has a strong impact on the overtones that are produced. In mode 1, high-frequency harmonics are relatively strong; in mode 2, they are much weaker. As a result, mode 1 tends to yield a much brighter, brassier sound.

VOCAL TRACT: YOUR SOURCE OF RESONANCE

Resonance typically is defined as the amplification and enhancement (or enrichment) of musical sound through supplemental vibration. What does this really mean? In layman's terms, we could say that resonance makes instruments louder and more beautiful by reinforcing the original vibrations of the sound source. This enhancement occurs in two primary ways, which are known as forced and free resonance (there is nothing pejorative in these terms: free resonance is not superior to forced resonance). Any object that is physically connected to a vibrator can serve as a forced resonator. For a piano, the resonator is the soundboard (on the underside of a grand or on the back of an upright); the vibrations of the strings are transmitted directly to the soundboard through a structure known as the bridge, which also is found on violins and guitars. Forced resonance also plays a role in voice production. Place your hand on your chest and say [a] at a low pitch. You almost certainly felt the vibrations of forced resonance. In singing, this might best be considered your private resonance; you can feel it and it might impact your self-perception of sound, but nobody else can hear it. To understand why this is true, imagine what a violin would sound like if it were encased in a thick layer of foam rubber. The vibrations of the string would be damped out, muting the instrument. Your skin, muscles, and other tissues do the same thing to the vibrations of your vocal folds.

By contrast, free resonance occurs when sound travels through a hollow space, such as the inside of a trumpet, an organ pipe, or your vocal tract, which consists of the pharynx (throat), oral cavity (mouth), and nasal cavity (nose). As sound travels through these regions, a complex pattern of echoes is created; every time sound encounters a change in the shape of the vocal tract, some of its energy is reflected backward, much like an echo in a canyon. If these echoes arrive back at the glottis at the precise moment a new pulse of sound is created, the two elements synchronize, resulting in a significant increase in intensity. All of this happens very quickly—remember that sound is traveling through your vocal tract at more than seven hundred miles per hour.

Whenever this synchronization of the vocal tract and sound source occurs, we say that the system is in resonance. The phenomenon occurs at specific frequencies (pitches), which can be varied by changing the position of the tongue, lips, jaw, palate, and larynx. These resonant frequencies, or areas in which strong amplification occurs, are called formants. Formants provide the specific amplification that changes the raw, buzzing sound produced by your vocal folds into speech and singing. The vocal tract is capable of producing many formants, which are labeled sequentially by ascending pitch. The first two, F1 and F2, are used to create vowels; higher formants contribute to the overall timbre and individual characteristics of a voice. In some singers, especially those who train to sing in opera, formants three through five are clustered together to form a super formant, eponymously called the singer's formant, which creates a ringing sound and enables a voice to be heard in a large theater without electronic amplification.

Formants are vitally important in singing, but they can be a bit intimidating to understand. An analogy that works really well for me is to think of formants like the wind. You cannot see the wind, but you know it is present when you see leaves rustling in a tree or feel a breeze on your face. Formants work in the same manner. They are completely invisible and directly inaudible. But just as we see the rustling leaf, we can hear, and perhaps even feel, the action of formants through how they change our sound. Try a little experiment. Sing an ascending scale beginning at B♭3, sustaining the vowel [i]. As you approach the D♮ or E♭ of the scale, you likely will feel (and hear) that your sound becomes a bit stronger and easier to produce. This occurs because the scale tone and formant are on the same pitch, providing additional amplification. If you change to a [u] vowel, you will feel the same thing at about the same place in the scale. If you sing to an [o] or [e] and continue up the scale, you'll feel a bloom in the sound somewhere around C5 (an octave above middle C); [a] is likely to come into its best focus at about G5.

To remember the approximate pitches of the first formants for the main vowels, [i]-[e]-[a]-[o]-[u], just think of a C-major triad in first inversion, open position, starting at E4: [i] = E4, [e] = C5, [a] = G5, [o] = C5, and [u] = E4 (figure 2.8). If your music theory isn't strong, you could use the mnemonic "every child gets candy eagerly." These pitches

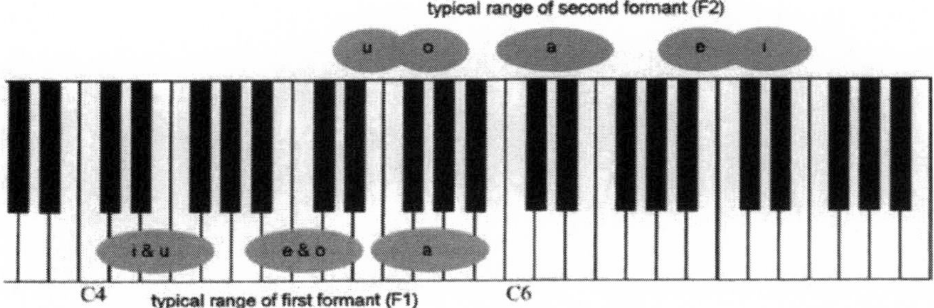

Figure 2.8. Typical range of first and second formants for primary vowels. ***Dr. Scott McCoy***

might vary by as much as a minor third higher and lower but no farther: once a formant changes by more than that interval, the vowel that is produced must change.

Formants have absolutely no preference for what they amplify—they are indiscriminate lovers, just as happy to bond with the first harmonic as the fifth. When men or women sing low pitches, there almost always will be at least one harmonic that comes close enough to a formant to produce a clear vowel sound. The same is not true for women with high voices, especially sopranos, who routinely must sing pitches that have a fundamental frequency higher than the first formant of many vowels. Imagine what happens if she must sing the phrase "and I'll leave you forever," with the word "leave" set on a very high, climactic note. The audience won't be able to tell if she is singing leave or love; the two will sound identical. This happens because the formant that is required to identify the vowel [i] is too far below the pitch being sung. Even if she tries to sing leave, the sound that comes out of her mouth will be heard as some variation of [a].

Fortunately, this kind of mismatch between formants and musical pitches rarely causes problems for anyone but opera singers, choir sopranos, and perhaps ingénues in classic music theater shows. Almost everyone else generally sings low enough in their respective voice ranges to produce easily identifiable vowels.

Second formants also can be important, but more so for opera singers than everyone else. They are much higher in pitch, tracking the pattern [u] = E5, [o] = G5, [a] = D6, [e] = B6, [i] = D7 (you can use the mnemonic "every good dad buys diapers" to remember these pitches) (figure 2.8). Because they can extend so high, into the top octave of the piano keyboard for [i], they interact primarily with higher tones in the natural harmonic series. Unless you are striving to produce the loudest unamplified sound possible, you probably never need to worry about the second formant; it will steadfastly do its job of helping to produce vowel sounds without any conscious thought or manipulation on your part.

If you are interested in discovering more about resonance and how it impacts your voice, you might want to install a spectrum analyzer on your computer. Free (or inexpensive) programs are readily available for download over the Internet that will work with either a PC or Mac computer. You don't need any specialized hardware—if you can use Skype or FaceTime, you already have everything you need. Once you've installed something, simply start playing with it. Experiment with your voice to see exactly how the analysis signal changes when you change the way your voice sounds. You'll be able to see how harmonics change in intensity as they interact with your formants. If you sing with vibrato, you'll see how consistently you produce your variations in pitch and amplitude. You'll even be able to see if your tone is excessively nasal for the kind of singing you want to do. Other programs are available that will help you improve your intonation (how well you sing in tune) or enhance your basic musicianship skills. Technology truly has advanced sufficiently to help us sing more beautifully.

MOUTH, LIPS, AND TONGUE: YOUR ARTICULATORS

The articulatory life of a singer is not easy, especially when compared to the demands placed on other musicians. Like a pianist or brass player, we must be able to produce the entire spectrum of musical articulation, including dynamic levels from hushed pianissimos to thunderous fortes, short notes, long notes, accents, crescendos, diminuendos, and so on. We produce most of these articulations the same way instrumentalists do, which is by varying our power supply. But singers have another layer of articulation that makes everything much more complicated; we must produce these musical gestures while simultaneously singing words.

As we learned in our brief examination of formants, altering the resonance characteristics of the vocal tract creates the vowel sounds of language. We do this by changing the position of our tongue, jaw, lips, and sometimes palate. Slowly say the vowel pattern [i]-[e]-[a]-[o]-[u]. Can you feel how your tongue moves in your mouth? For [i], it is high in the front and low in the back, but it takes the opposite position for [u]. Now slowly say the word Tuesday, noting all the places your tongue comes into contact with your teeth and palate and how it changes shape as you produce the vowels and diphthongs. There is a lot going on in there—no wonder it takes so long for babies to learn to speak!

Our articulatory anatomy is extraordinarily complex, in large part because our bodies use the same passageway for food, water, air, and sound. As a result, our tongue, larynx, throat, jaw, and palate are all interconnected with common physical and neurologic points of attachment. Our anatomical Union Station in this regard is a small structure called the hyoid bone. The hyoid is one of only three bones in your entire body that do not connect to other bones via a joint (the other two are your patellae, or kneecaps). This little bone is suspended below your jaw, freely floating up and down every time your swallow. It is a busy place, serving as the upper suspension point for the larynx, the connection for the root of the tongue, and the primary location of the muscles that open your mouth by dropping your jaw.

Good singing—in any genre—requires a high degree of independence in all these articulatory structures. Unfortunately, nature conspires against us to make this difficult to accomplish. From the time we were born, our bodies have relied on a reflex reaction to elevate the palate and raise the larynx each time we swallow. This action becomes habitual: palate goes up, larynx also lifts. But depending on the style of music we are singing, we might need to keep the larynx down while the palate goes up (opera and classical) or palate down with the larynx up (country and bluegrass). As we all know, habits can be very hard to change, which is one of the reasons that it can take a lot of study and practice to become an excellent singer. Understanding your body's natural reflexive habits can make some of this work a bit easier.

There is one more significant pitfall to the close proximity of all these articulators: tension in one area is easily passed along to another. If your jaw muscles are too tight while you sing, that hyperactivity will likely be transferred to the larynx and tongue—remember, they all are interconnected through the hyoid bone. It can be tricky to determine the primary offender in this kind of chain reaction of tension. A tight tongue could just as easily be making your jaw stiff, or an elevated, rigid larynx could make both tongue and jaw suffer.

Neurology complicates matters even further. You have sixteen muscles in your tongue, fourteen in your larynx, twenty-two in your throat and palate, and another sixteen that control your jaw. Many of these are very small and lie directly adjacent to each other, and you often are required to contract one quite strongly while its next-door neighbor must remain totally relaxed. Our brains need to develop laser-like control, sending signals at the right moment with the right intensity to the precise spot where they are needed. When we first start singing, these brain signals come more like a blast from a shotgun, spreading the neurologic impulse over a broad area to multiple muscles, not all of which are the intended target. Again, with practice and training, we learn to refine our control, enabling us to use only those muscles that will help, while disengaging those that would get in the way of our best singing.

FINAL THOUGHTS

This brief chapter has only scratched the surface of the huge field of voice science. To learn more, you might visit the websites of the National Association of Teachers of Singing (NATS), the Voice Foundation (TVF), or the National Center for Voice and Speech (NCVS). You can easily locate the appropriate addresses through any Internet search engine. Remember: knowledge is power. Occasionally, people are afraid that if they know more about the science of how they sing, they will become so analytical that all spontaneity will be lost or they will become paralyzed by too much information and thought. In my forty-plus years as a singer and teacher, I've never encountered somebody who actually suffered this fate. To the contrary, the more we know, the easier—and more joyful—singing becomes. ♪

3

VOCAL HEALTH FOR THE BLUES SINGER

Wendy LeBorgne

GENERAL PHYSICAL WELL-BEING

All singers, regardless of genre, should consider themselves as "vocal athletes." The physical, emotional, and performance demands necessary for optimal output require that the artist consider training and maintaining their instrument as an athlete trains for an event. With increased vocal and performance demands, it is unlikely that a vocal athlete will have an entire performing career completely injury free. This may not be the fault of the singer, as many injuries occur due to circumstances beyond the singer's control such as singing through an illness or being on a new medication seemingly unrelated to the voice. ♪

Vocal injury has often been considered taboo to talk about in the performing world as it has been considered to be the result of faulty technique or poor vocal habits. In actuality, the majority of vocal injuries presenting in the elite performing population tend to be overuse and/or acute injury. From a clinical perspective over the past seventeen years, younger, less experienced singers with fewer years of training (who tend to be quite talented) generally are the ones who present with issues related to technique or phonotrauma (nodules, edema, contact ulcers), while more mature singers with professional performing careers tend to present with acute injuries (hemorrhage) or overuse and misuse injuries (muscle tension dysphonia, edema, GERD) or injuries following an illness. There are no current studies documenting use and training in correlation to laryngeal pathologies. However, there are studies that document that somewhere between 35 percent and 100 percent of professional vocal athletes have abnormal vocal fold findings on stroboscopic evaluation. Many times these "abnormalities" are in singers who have no vocal complaints or symptoms of vocal problems. From a performance perspective, uniqueness in vocal quality often gets hired and perhaps a slight aberration in the way a given larynx functions may become quite marketable. Regardless of what the vocal folds may look like, the most integral part of performance is that the singer must maintain agility, flexibility, stamina, power, and inherent beauty (genre appropriate) for their current level of performance taking into account physical, vocal, and emotional demands.

Unlike sports medicine and the exercise physiology literature where much is known about the types and nature of given sports injuries, there is no common parallel for the vocal athlete model. However, because the vocal athlete utilizes the body systems of alignment, respiration, phonation, and resonance with some similarities to physical athletes, a parallel protocol for vocal wellness may be implemented/considered for vocal athletes to maximize injury prevention knowledge for both the singer and teacher. This chapter aims to provide information on vocal wellness and injury prevention for the vocal athlete.

CONSIDERATIONS FOR WHOLE BODY WELLNESS

Nutrition

You have no doubt heard the saying "You are what you eat." Eating is a social and psychological event. For many people, food associations and eating have an emotional basis resulting in either overeating or being malnourished. Eating disorders in performers and body image issues may have major implications and consequences for the performer on both ends of the spectrum (obesity and anorexia). Singers should be encouraged to reprogram the brain and body to consider food as fuel. You want to use high-octane gas in your engine, as pouring water in your car's gas tank won't get you very far. Eating a poor diet or a diet that lacks appropriate nutritional value will have negative physical and vocal effects on the singer. Effects of poor dietary choices for the vocal athlete may result in physical and vocal effects ranging from fatigue to life-threatening disease over the course of a lifetime. Encouraging and engaging in healthy eating habits from a young age will potentially prevent long-term negative effects from poor nutritional choices. It is beyond the scope of this chapter to provide a complete overview of all the dietary guidelines for pediatrics, adolescents, adults, and the mature adult; however, a listing of additional references to help guide your food and beverage choices for making good nutritional choices can be found online at websites such as Dietary Guidelines for Americans, Nutrition .gov Guidelines for Tweens and Teens, and Fruits and Veggies Matter. See the online companion web page on the NATS website for links to these and other resources.

Hydration

"Sing wet, pee pale." This phrase was echoed in the studio of Van Lawrence regarding how his students would know if they were well hydrated. Generally, this rule of pale urine during your waking hours is a good indicator that you are well hydrated. Medications, vitamins, and certain foods may alter urine color despite adequate hydration. Due to the varying levels of physical and vocal activity of many performers, in order to maintain adequate oral hydration, the use of a hydration calculator based on activity level may be a better choice. These hydration calculators are easily accessible online and take into account the amount and level of activity the performer engages in on a daily basis. In a recent study of the vocal habits of musical theater performers, one of the findings indicated a significantly underhydrated group of performers.[1]

Laryngeal and pharyngeal dryness as well as "thick, sticky mucus" are often complaints of singers. Combating these concerns and maintaining an adequate viscosity of mucus for performance has resulted in some research. As a reminder of laryngeal and swallowing anatomy, nothing that is swallowed (or gargled) goes over or touches the vocal folds directly (or one would choke). Therefore, nothing that a singer eats or drinks ever touches the vocal folds, and in order to adequately hydrate the mucous membranes of the vocal folds, one must consume enough fluids for the body to produce a thin mucus. Therefore, any "vocal" effects from swallowed products are limited to potential pharyngeal and oral changes, not the vocal folds themselves.

The effects of systemic hydration are well documented in the literature. There is evidence to suggest that adequate hydration will provide some protection of the laryngeal mucosal membranes when they are placed under increased collision forces as well as reducing the amount of effort (phonation threshold pressure) to produce voice. This is important for the singer because it means that with adequate hydration and consistency of mucus, the effort to produce voice is less and your vocal folds are better protected from injury. Imagine the friction and heat produced when two dry hands rub together and then what happens if you put lotion on your hands. The mechanisms in the larynx to provide appropriate mucus production are not fully understood, but there is enough evidence at this time to support oral hydration as a vital component of every singer's vocal health regime to maintain appropriate mucosal viscosity.

Although very rare, overhydration (hyperhidrosis) can result in dehydration and even illness or death. An overindulgence of fluids essentially makes the kidneys work "overtime" and flushes too much water out of the body. This excessive fluid loss in a rapid manner can be detrimental to the body.

In addition to drinking water to systemically monitor hydration, there are many nonregulated products on the market for performers that lay claim to improving the laryngeal environment (e.g., Entertainer's Secret, Throat Coat Tea, Greathers Pastilles, Slippery Elm, etc.). Although there may be little detriment in using these products, quantitative research documenting change in laryngeal mucosa is sparse. One study suggests that the use of Throat Coat when compared to a placebo treatment for pharyngitis did show a significant difference in decreasing the perception of sore throat.[2] Another study compared the use of Entertainer's Secret to two other nebulized agents and its effect on phonation threshold pressure (PTP).[3] There was no positive benefit in decreasing PTP with Entertainer's Secret.

Many singers use personal steam inhalers and/or room humidification to supplement oral hydration and aid in combating laryngeal dryness. There are several considerations for singers who choose to use external means of adding moisture to the air they breathe. Personal steam inhalers are portable and can often be used backstage or in the hotel room for the traveling performer. Typically, water is placed in the steamer and the face is placed over the steam for inhalation. Because the mucus membranes of the larynx are composed of a saltwater solution, one study looked at the use of nebulized saline in comparison to plain water and its potential effects on effort or ease to sound production in classically trained sopranos.[4] Data suggested that perceived effort to produce voice was less in the saline group than the plain water group. This indicated that the singers who used the saltwater solution reported less effort to sing after breathing in the saltwater than singers who used plain water. The researchers hypothesized that because the body's mucus is not plain water (rather it is a saltwater—think about your tears), when you use plain water for steam inhalation, it may actually draw the salt from your own saliva, resulting in a dehydrating effect.

In addition to personal steamers, other options for air humidification come in varying sizes of humidifiers from room size to whole house humidifiers. When choosing between a warm air or cool mist humidifier, considerations include both personal preference and needs. One of the primary reasons warm mist humidifiers are not recommended for young children is due to the risk of burns from the heating element. Both the warm mist and cool air humidifiers act similarly in adding moisture to the environmental air. External air humidification may be beneficial and provide a level of comfort for many singers. Regular cleaning of the humidifier is vital to prevent bacteria and mold buildup. Also, depending on the hardness of the water, it is important to avoid mineral buildup on the device and distilled water may be recommended for some humidifiers.

For traveling performers who often stay in hotels, fly on airplanes, or are generally exposed to other dry-air environments, there are products on the market designed to help minimize drying effects. One such device is called a Humidflyer, which is a face mask designed with a filter to recycle the moisture of a person's own breath and replenish moisture on each breath cycle.

For dry nasal passages or to clear sinuses, many singers use Neti pots. Many singers use this homeopathic flushing of the nasal passages regularly. Research supports the use of a Neti pot as a part of allergy relief and chronic rhinosinusitis control when utilized properly, sometimes in combination with medical management.[5] Conversely, long-term use of nasal irrigation (without taking intermittent breaks from daily use) may result in washing out the "good" mucus of the nasal passages, which naturally help to rid the nose of infections. A study presented at the 2009 American College of Allergy, Asthma, and Immunology (ACAAI) annual scientific meeting reported that when a group of individuals who were using twice-daily nasal irrigation for one year discontinued using it, they had an increase in acute rhinosinusitis.[6]

Tea, Honey, and Gargle to Keep the Throat Healthy

Regarding the use of general teas (which many singers combine with honey or lemon), there is likely no harm in the use of decaffeinated tea (caffeine may cause systemic dryness). The warmth of the tea may provide a soothing sensation to the pharynx and the act of swallowing can be relaxing for the muscles of the throat. Honey has shown promising results as an effective cough suppressant in the pediatric population.[7] The dose of honey given to the children in the study was two teaspoons. Gargling with salt or apple cider vinegar and water are also popular home remedies for many singers with the uses being from soothing the throat to curing reflux. Gargling plain water has been shown to be efficacious in reducing the risk of contracting upper respiratory infections. I suggest that when gargling, the singer only "bubble" the water with air and avoid engaging the vocal folds in sound production. Saltwater as a gargle has long been touted as a sore throat remedy and can be traced back to 2700 BCE in China for treating gum disease. The science behind a saltwater rinse for everything from oral hygiene to sore throat is that salt (sodium chloride) may act as a natural analgesic (pain killer) and may also kill bacteria. Similar to the effects that not enough salt in the water may have on drawing the salt out of the tissue in the steam inhalation, if you oversaturate the water solution with excess salt and gargle it, it may act to draw water out of the oral mucosa, thus reducing inflammation.

Another popular home remedy reported by singers is the use of apple cider vinegar to help with everything from acid reflux to sore throats. Dating back to 3300 BCE, apple cider vinegar was reported as a medicinal remedy, and it became popular in the 1970s as a weight loss diet cocktail. Popular media reports apple cider vinegar can improve conditions from acne and arthritis to nosebleeds and varicose veins. Specific efficacy data regarding the beneficial nature of apple cider vinegar for the purpose of sore throat, pharyngeal inflammation, and/or reflux has not been reported in the literature at this time. Of the peer-reviewed studies found in the literature, one discussed possible esophageal erosion and inconsistency of actual product in tablet form.[8] Therefore, at this time, strong evidence supporting the use of apple cider vinegar is not published.

Medications and the Voice

Medications (over the counter, prescription, and herbal) may have resultant drying effects on the body and often the laryngeal mucosa. General classes of drugs with potential drying effects include: antidepressants, antihypertensives, diuretics, ADD/ADHD medications, some oral acne medications, hormones, allergy drugs, and vitamin C in high doses. The National Center for Voice and Speech (NCVS) provides a listing of some common medications with potential voice side effects including laryngeal dryness. This listing does not take into account all medications, so singers should always ask their pharmacist of the potential side effects of a given medication. Due to the significant number of drugs on the market, it is safe to say that most pharmacists will not be acutely aware of "vocal side effects," but if dryness is listed as a potential side effect of the drug, you may assume that all body systems could be affected. Under no circumstances should you stop taking a prescribed medication without consulting your physician first. As every person has a different body chemistry and reaction to medication, just because a medication lists dryness as a potential side effect, it does not necessarily mean you will experience that side effect. Conversely, if you begin a new medication and notice physical or vocal changes that are unexpected, you should consult with your physician. Ultimately, the goal of medical management for any condition is to achieve the most benefits with the least side effects. Please see the companion page on the NATS website for a list of possible resources for the singer regarding prescription drugs and herbs. ♪

In contrast to medications that tend to dry, there are medications formulated to increase saliva production or alter the viscosity of mucus.

Medically, these drugs are often used to treat patients who have had a loss of saliva production due to surgery or radiation. Mucolytic agents are used to thin secretions as needed. As a singer, if you feel that you need to use a mucolytic agent on a consistent basis, it may be worth considering getting to the root of the laryngeal dryness symptom and seeking a professional opinion from an otolaryngologist.

Reflux and the Voice

Gastroesophageal reflux (GERD) and/or laryngopharyngeal reflux (LPR) can have a devastating impact on the singer if not recognized and treated appropriately. Although GERD and LPR are related, they are considered as slightly different diseases. GERD (Latin root meaning "flowing back") is the reflux of digestive enzymes, acids, and other stomach contents into the esophagus (food pipe). If this backflow is propelled through the upper esophagus and into the throat (larynx and pharynx), it is referred to as LPR. It is not uncommon to have both GERD and LPR, but they can occur independently.

More frequently, people with GERD have decreased esophageal clearing. Esophagitis, or inflammation of the esophagus, is also associated with GERD. People with GERD often feel heartburn. LPR symptoms are often "silent" and do not include heartburn. Specific symptoms of LPR may include some or all of the following: lump in the throat sensation, feeling of constant need to clear the throat/postnasal drip, longer vocal warm-up time, quicker vocal fatigue, loss of high frequency range, worse voice in the morning, sore throat, and bitter/raw/brackish taste in the mouth. If you experience these symptoms on a regular basis, it is advised that you consider a medical consultation for your symptoms. Prolonged, untreated GERD or LPR can lead to permanent changes in both the esophagus and/or larynx. Untreated LPR also provides a laryngeal environment that is conducive for vocal fold lesions to occur as it inhibits normal healing mechanisms.

Treatments of LPR and GERD generally include both dietary and lifestyle modifications in addition to medical management. Some of the dietary recommendations include: elimination of caffeinated and carbonated beverages, smoking cessation, no alcohol use, and limiting tomatoes, acidic foods and drinks, and raw onions or peppers, to name a few. Also, avoidance of high-fat foods is recommended. From a lifestyle perspective, suggested changes include not eating within three hours of lying down, eating small meals frequently (instead of large meals), elevating the head of your bed, avoiding tight clothing around the belly, and not bending over or exercising too soon after you eat.

Reflux medications fall in three general categories: antacids, H2 blockers, and proton pump inhibitors (PPI). There are now combination drugs that include both an H2 blocker and proton pump inhibitor. Every medication has both associated risks and benefits, and singers should be aware of the possible benefits and side effects of the medications they take. In general terms, antacids (e.g., Tums, Mylanta, Gaviscon) neutralize stomach acid. H2 (histamine) blockers, such as Axid (nizatidine), Tagamet (cimetidine), Pepcid (famotidine), and Zantac (ranitidine), work to decrease acid production in the stomach by preventing histamine from triggering the H2 receptors to produce more acid. Then there are the PPIs: Nexium (esomeprazole), Prevacid (lansoprazole), Protonix (pantoprazole), AcipHex (rabeprazole), Prilosec (omeprazole), and Dexilant (dexlansoprazole). PPIs act as a last line of defense to decrease acid production by blocking the last step in gastric juice secretion. Some of the most recent drugs to combat GERD/LPR are combination drugs (e.g., Zegrid [sodium bicarbonate plus omeprazole]), which provide a short-acting response (sodium bicarbonate) and a long release (omeprazole). Because some singers prefer a holistic approach to reflux management, strict dietary and lifestyle compliance is recommended and consultation with both your primary care physician and naturopath are warranted in that situation. Efficacy data on nonregulated herbs, vitamins, and supplements is limited, but some data does exist.

Physical Exercise

Vocal athletes, like other physical athletes, should consider how and what they do to maintain both cardiovascular fitness and muscular strength. In today's performance culture, it is rare that a performer stands still and sings, unless in a recital or choral setting. The range of physical activity can vary from light movement to high-intensity choreography with acrobatics. As performers are being required to increase their on-stage physical activity level from the operatic stage to the pop-star arena, overall physical fitness is imperative to avoid compromise in the vocal system. Breathlessness will result in compensation by the larynx, which is now attempting to regulate the air. Compensatory vocal behaviors over time may result in a change in vocal performance. The health benefits of both cardiovascular training and strength training are well documented for physical athletes but relatively rare in the literature for vocal performers.

Mental Wellness

Vocal performers must maintain a mental focus during performance and a mental toughness during auditioning and training. Rarely during vocal performance training programs is this important aspect of performance addressed, and it is often left to the individual performer to develop their own strategy or coping mechanism. Yet, many performers are on antianxiety or antidepressant drugs (which may be the direct result of performance-related issues). If the sports world is again used as a parallel for mental toughness, there are no elite-level athletes (and few junior-level athletes) who don't utilize the services of a performance/sports psychologist to maximize focus and performance. I recommend that performers consider the potential benefits of a performance psychologist to help maximize vocal performance. Several references that may be of interest to the singer include: Joanna Cazden's *Visualization for Singers* (Joanna Cazden, 1992) and Shirlee Emmons and Alma Thomas's *Power Performance for Singers: Transcending the Barriers* (Oxford, 1998). ♪

Unlike instrumentalists, whose performance is dependent on accurate playing of an external musical instrument, the singer's instrument is uniquely intact and subject to the emotional confines of the brain and body in which it is housed. Musical performance anxiety (MPA) can be career threatening for all musicians, but perhaps the vocal athlete is more severely impacted. The majority of literature on MPA is dedicated to instrumentalists, but the basis of definition, performance effects, and treatment options can be considered for vocal athletes. Fear is a natural reaction to a stressful situation, and there is a fine line between emotional excitation and perceived threat (real or imagined). The job of a performer is to convey to an audience through vocal production, physical gestures, and facial expression a most heightened state of emotion. Otherwise, why would audience members pay top dollar to sit for two or three hours for a mundane experience? Not only is there the emotional conveyance of the performance but also the internal turmoil often experienced by the singers themselves in preparation for elite performance. It is well documented in the literature that even the most elite performers have experienced debilitating performance anxiety. MPA is defined on a continuum with anxiety levels ranging from low to high and has been reported to comprise four distinct components: affect, cognition, behavior, and physiology. Affect comprises feelings (e.g., doom, panic, anxiety). Affected cognition will result in altered levels of concentration, while the behavior component results in postural shifts, quivering, and trembling. Finally physiologically the body's autonomic nervous system (ANS) will activate, resulting in the "fight or flight" response.

In recent years, researchers have been able to define two distinct neurological pathways for MPA. The first pathway happens quickly and without conscious input (ANS), resulting in the same fear stimulus as if a person were put into an emergent, life-threatening situation. In those situations, the brain releases adrenaline, resulting in physical changes of increased heart rate, increased respiration, shaking, pale skin, dilated pupils, slowed digestion, bladder relaxation, dry mouth, and dry eyes, all of which severely affect vocal performance. The second pathway that has been identified results in a conscious identification of the fear/threat and a much slower physiologic response. With the second neuromotor response, the performer has a chance to recognize the fear, process how to deal with the fear, and respond accordingly.

Treatment modalities to address MPA include psycho-behavioral therapy (including biofeedback) and drug therapies. Elite physical performance athletes have been shown to benefit from visualization techniques and psychological readiness training, yet within the performing arts community, stage fright may be considered a weakness or character flaw precluding readiness for professional performance. On the contrary, vocal athletes, like physical athletes, should mentally prepare themselves for optimal competition (auditions) and performance. Learning to convey emotion without eliciting an internal emotional response by the vocal athlete may take the skill of an experienced psychologist to help change ingrained neural pathways. Ultimately, control and understanding of MPA will enhance performance and prepare the vocal athlete for the most intense performance demands without vocal compromise.

VOCAL WELLNESS: INJURY PREVENTION

In order to prevent vocal injury and understand vocal wellness in the singer, general knowledge of common causes of voice disorders is imperative. One common cause of voice disorders is vocally abusive behaviors or misuse of the voice to include phonotraumatic behaviors such as yelling, screaming, loud talking, talking over noise, throat clearing, coughing, harsh sneezing, and boisterous laughing. Chronic or less than optimal vocal properties such as poor breathing techniques, inappropriate phonatory habits during conversational speech (glottal fry, hard glottal attacks), inapt pitch, loudness, rate of speech, and/or hyperfunctional laryngeal-area muscle tone may also negatively impact vocal function. Medically related etiologies, which also have the potential to impact vocal function, range from untreated chronic allergies and sinusitis to endocrine dysfunction and hormonal imbalance. Direct trauma, such as a blow to the neck or the risk of vocal fold damage during intubation, can impact optimal performance in vocal athletes depending on the nature and extent of the trauma. Finally, external irritants ranging from cigarette smoke to reflux directly impact the laryngeal mucosa and ultimately can lead to laryngeal pathology.

Vocal hygiene education and compliance may be one of the primary essential components for maintaining the voice throughout a career. This section will provide the singer with information on prevention of vocal injury. However, just like a professional sports athlete, it is unlikely that a professional vocal athlete will go through an entire career without some compromise in vocal function. This may be a common upper respiratory infection that creates vocal fold swelling for a short time, or it may be a "vocal accident" that is career threatening. Regardless, the knowledge of how to take care of your voice is essential for any vocal athlete.

Train Like an Athlete for Vocal Longevity

Performers seek instant gratification in performance sometimes at the cost of gradual vocal building for a lifetime of healthy singing. Historically, voice pedagogues required their students to perform vocalises exclusively for up to two years before beginning any song literature. Singers gradually built their voices by ingraining appropriate muscle memory and neuromotor patterns through development of aesthetically pleasing tones, onsets, breath management, and support. There was an intensive master-apprentice relationship and rigorous vocal guidelines to maintain a place within a given studio. Time off was taken if a vocal injury ensued or careers potentially were ended, and students were asked to leave a given singing studio if their voices were unable to withstand the rigors of training. Training vocal athletes today has evolved and appears driven to create a "product" quickly, perhaps at the expense of the longevity of the singer. Pop stars emerging well before puberty are doing international concert tours, yet many young artist programs in the classical arena do not consider singers for their programs until they are in their mid- to late twenties.

Each vocal genre presents with different standards and vocal demands. Therefore, the amount and degree of vocal training are varied. Some would argue that performing extensively without adequate vocal training and development is ill-advised, yet singers today are thrust onto the stage at very young ages. Dancers, instrumentalists, and physical athletes all spend many hours per day developing muscle strength, memory, and proper technique for their craft. The more advanced the artist or athlete, generally the more specific the training protocol becomes. Consideration of training vocal athletes in this same fashion is recommended. One would generally not begin a young, inexperienced singer on a Wagner aria without previous vocal training. Similarly, in non-classical vocal music, there are easy, moderate, and difficult pieces to consider pending level of vocal development and training.

Basic pedagogical training of alignment, breathing, voice production, and resonance are essential building blocks for development of good voice production. Muscle memory and development of appropriate muscle patterns happen slowly over time with appropriate repetitive practice. Doing too much, too soon for any athlete (physical or vocal) will result in an increased risk for injury. When the singer is being asked to do "vocal gymnastics," they must be sure to have a solid basis of strength and stamina in the appropriate muscle groups to perform consistently with minimal risk of injury.

Vocal Fitness Program

One generally does not get out of bed first thing in the morning and try to do a split. Yet many singers go directly into a practice session or audition without proper warm-up. Think of your larynx like your knee, made up of cartilages, ligaments, and muscles. Vocal health is dependent upon appropriate warm-ups (to get things moving), drills for technique, and then cooldowns (at the end of your day). Consider vocal warm-ups a "gentle stretch." Depending on the needs of the singer, warm-ups should include physical stretching; postural alignment self-checks; breathing exercises to promote rib cage, abdominal, and back expansion; vocal stretches (glides up to stretch the vocal folds and glides down to contract the vocal folds); articulatory stretches (yawning, facial stretches); and mental warm-ups (to provide focus for the task at hand). Vocalises, in my opinion, are designed as exercises to go beyond warm-ups and prepare the body and voice for the technical and vocal challenges of the music they sing. They are varied and address the technical level and genre of the singer to maximize performance and vocal growth. Cooldowns are a part of most athletes' workouts. However, singers often do not use cooldowns (physical, mental, and vocal) at the end of a performance. A recent study looked specifically at the benefits of vocal cooldowns in singers and found that singers who used a vocal cooldown had decreased effort to produce voice the next day.[9]

Systemic hydration as a means to keep the vocal folds adequately lubricated for the amount of impact and friction that they will undergo has been previously discussed in this chapter. Compliance with adequate oral hydration recommendations is important and subsequently so is the minimization of agents that could potentially dry the membranes (e.g., caffeine, medications, dry air). The body produces approximately two quarts of mucus per day. If not adequately hydrated, the mucus tends to be thick and sticky. Poor hydration is similar to not putting enough oil in the car engine. Frankly, if the gears do not work as well, there is increased friction and heat, and the engine is not efficient.

Speak Well, Sing Well

Optimize the speaking voice utilizing ideal frequency range, breath, intensity, rate, and resonance. Singers generally are vocally enthusiastic individuals who talk a lot and often talk loudly. During typical conversation, the average fundamental speaking frequency (times per second the vocal folds are impacting) for a male varies from 100 to 150 Hz and 180 to 230 Hz for women. Because of the delicate structure of the vocal folds and the importance of the layered microstructure vibrating efficiently and effectively to produce voice, vocal behaviors or outside factors that compromise the integrity of the vibration patterns of the vocal folds may be considered phonotrauma.

Phonotraumatic behaviors can include yelling, screaming, loud talking, harsh sneezing, and harsh laughing. Elimination of phonotraumatic behaviors is essential for good vocal health. The louder one speaks, the farther apart the vocal folds move from midline, the harder they impact, and the longer they stay closed. A tangible example would be to take your hands, move them only six inches apart, and clap as hard and as loudly as you can for ten seconds. Now, move your hands two feet apart and clap as hard, loudly, and quickly as possible for ten seconds. The farther apart your hands are, the more air you move and the louder the clap, and the skin on the hands becomes red and ultimately swollen (if you do it long enough and hard enough). This is what happens to the vocal folds with repeated impact at increased vocal intensities. The vocal folds are approximately 17 mm in length and vibrate at 220 times per second on A3, 440 on A4, 880 on A5, and more than 1,000 per second when singing a high C. That is a lot of impact for little muscles. Consider this fact when singing loudly or in a high tessitura for prolonged periods of time. It becomes easy to see why women are more prone than men to laryngeal impact injuries due to the frequency range of the voice alone.

In addition to the amount of cycles per second (cps) the vocal folds are impacting, singers need to be aware of their vocal intensity (volume). One should be aware of the volume of the speaking and singing voice and consider using a distance of three to five feet (about an arm's-length distance) as a gauge for how loud to be in general conversation. Using cell phones and speaking on a Bluetooth device in a car generally results in greater vocal intensity than normal and singers are advised to minimize unnecessary use of these devices.

Singers should be encouraged to take "vocal naps" during their day. A vocal nap would be a short period of time (five minutes to an hour) of complete silence. Although the vocal folds are rarely completely still (because they move when you swallow and breathe), a vocal nap minimizes impact and vibration for a short window of time. A physical nap can also be refreshing for the singer mentally and physically.

Avoid Environmental Irritants: Alcohol, Smoking, Drugs

Arming singers with information on the actual effects of environmental irritants so that they can make informed choices on engaging in exposure to these potential toxins is essential. The glamour that continues to be associated with smoking, drinking, and drugs can be tempered with the deaths of popular stars such as Amy Winehouse and Cory Monteith who engaged in life-ending choices. There is extensive documentation about the long-term effects of toxic and carcinogenic substances, but here are a few key facts to consider when choosing whether to partake.

Alcohol, although it does not go over the vocal folds directly, does have a systemic drying effect. Due to the acidity in alcohol, it may increase the likelihood of reflux, resulting in hoarseness and other laryngeal pathologies. Consuming alcohol generally decreases one's inhibitions, and therefore you are more likely to sing and do things that you would not typically do under the influence of alcohol.

Beyond the carcinogens in nicotine and tobacco, the heat at which a cigarette burns is well above the boiling temperature of water (water boils at 212°F; cigarettes burn at over 1400°F). No one would consider pouring a pot of boiling water on their hand, and yet the burning temperature for a cigarette results in significant heat over the oral mucosa and vocal folds. The heat alone can create a deterioration in the lining, resulting in polypoid degeneration. Obviously, cigarette smoking has been well documented as a cause for laryngeal cancer.

Marijuana and other street drugs are not only addictive but can cause permanent mucosal lining changes depending on the drug used and the method of delivery. If you or one of your singer colleagues is experiencing a drug or alcohol problem, research or provide information and support on getting appropriate counseling and help.

SMART PRACTICE STRATEGIES FOR SKILL DEVELOPMENT AND VOICE CONSERVATION

Daily practice and drills for skill acquisition are an important part of any singer's training. However, overpracticing or inefficient practicing may be detrimental to the voice. Consider practice sessions of athletes: they may practice four to eight hours per day broken into one- to two-hour training sessions with a period of rest and recovery in between sessions. Although we cannot parallel the sports model without adequate evidence in the vocal athlete, the premise of short, intense, focused practice sessions is logical for the singer. Similar to physical exercise, it is suggested that practice sessions do not have to be all "singing." Rather, structuring sessions so that one-third of the session is spent on warm-up; one-third on vocalises, text work, rhythms, character development, and so on; and one-third on repertoire will allow the singer to function in a more efficient vocal manner. Building the amount of time per practice session—increasing duration by five minutes per week, building to sixty to ninety minutes—may be effective (e.g., Week 1: twenty minutes three times per day; Week 2: twenty-five minutes three times per day, etc.).

Vary the "vocal workout" during your week. For example, if you do the same physical exercise in the same way day after day with the same intensity and pattern, you will likely experience repetitive strain–type injuries. However, cross-training or varying the type and level of exercise aids in injury prevention. So when planning your practice sessions for a given week (or rehearsal process for a given role), consider varying your vocal intensity, tessitura, and exercises to maximize your training sessions, building stamina, muscle memory, and skill acquisition. For example, one day you may spend more time on learning rhythms and translation and the next day you spend thirty minutes performing coloratura exercises to prepare for a specific role. Take one day a week off from vocal training and give your voice a break. This does not mean complete vocal rest (although some singers find this beneficial), but rather a day without singing and limited talking.

Practice Your Mental Focus

Mental wellness and stress management are equally as important as vocal training for vocal athletes. Addressing any mental health issues is paramount to developing the vocal artist. This may include anything from daily mental exercises/meditation/focus to overcoming performance anxiety to more serious mental health issues/illness. Every person can benefit from improved focus and mental acuity.

SPECIFIC VOCAL WELLNESS CONCERNS FOR SINGERS OF CONTEMPORARY STYLES

General vocal wellness guidelines for all singers hold true for the CCM (contemporary commercial music) singer. Because contemporary singing encompass styles from hip hop, rap, jazz, R&B, and country to Broadway musicals (and everything in between), there is potential increased need for attention to vocal health and wellness. There are a multitude of studies discussing the vocal health and wellness of artists that fall within varying categories of CCM. It is often the slightly abnormal and sometimes pathologic voice that gets hired within the CCM market because of the unique vocal quality. Vocal wellness with a pathologic or abnormal voice includes maintaining flexibility, agility, stamina, power, and consistent performance to meet market demands. If any of the above elements are compromised, the CCM artist is no longer functioning in a vocally healthy manner. Contemporary commercial music singers may or may not have formal vocal training but are required to keep vocally demanding and extensive performing and recording schedules often while touring and/or sleeping in hotels, busses, planes, and trains.

Vocal Wellness Tips

For the CCM artist, the most common presentation in my voice clinic relates to vocal fatigue, acute vocal injury, and loss of high frequency range. Vocal fatigue complaints are generally related to the duration of their rehearsals, recording sessions, "meet and greets," performances, vocal gymnastics, general lack of sleep, and the vocal requirements to traverse their entire range (and occasionally outside of physiological comfort range). Depending on the genre performed, CCM singing includes a high vocal load with the associated risk of repetitive strain and increased collision force injuries. Acute vocal injuries within this population include phonotraumatic lesions (hemorrhages, vocal fold polyps, vocal fold nodules, reflux, and general vocal fold edema/erythema). Often these are not injuries related to problematic vocal technique, but rather due to "vocal accidents" and/or overuse (due to required performance/contract demands). CCM singers are required to connect with the audience from a vocal and emotional standpoint. Physical performance demands—dependent on the subgenre within CCM—may be extreme and at times highly cardiovascular and/or acrobatic. Both physical and vocal fitness should be foremost in the minds of anyone desiring to perform CCM music today and these singers should be physically and vocally in shape to meet the necessary performance demands.

Performance of CCM music requires that the singer has a flexible, agile, and dynamic instrument with appropriate stamina. The singer must have a good command of their instrument as well as exceptional underlying intention to what they are singing as it is about relaying a message, characteristic sound, and connecting with the audience. The singers that perform CCM, must reflect the mood and intent of the composer requiring dynamic control, vocal control/power, and an emotional connection to the text.

All commercial music singers use microphones and personal amplification to their maximal capacity. If used correctly, amplification can be used to maximize vocal health by allowing the singer to produce voice in an efficient manner while the sound engineer is effectively able to mix, amplify, and add effects to the voice. Understanding both the utility and limits of a given microphone and sound system is essential for the singer both for live and studio performances. Using an appropriate microphone can not only enhance the singer's performance, but can also reduce vocal load. Emotional extremes (intimacy and exultation) can be enhanced by appropriate microphone choice, placement, and acoustical mixing; thus, saving the singer's voice.

Not everything a singer does is "vocally healthy," sometimes because the emotional expression may be so intense it results in vocal collision forces that are extreme. Even if the singer does not have formal vocal training, the concept of "vocal cross-training"—which can mean singing in both high and low registers with varying intensities and resonance options—before and after practice sessions and services is likely a vital component to minimizing vocal injury.

FINAL THOUGHTS

Ultimately, the singer must learn to provide the most output with the least "cost" to the system. Taking care of the physical instrument through daily physical exercise, adequate nutrition and hydration, and focused attention on performance will provide a necessary basis for vocal health during performance. Small doses of high-intensity singing (or speaking) will limit impact stress on the vocal folds. Finally, attention to the mind, body, and voice will provide the singer with an awareness when something is wrong. This awareness and knowledge of when to rest or seek help will promote vocal well-being for the singer throughout his or her career.

NOTES

1. W. LeBorgne et al., "Prevalence of Vocal Pathology in Incoming Freshman Musical Theatre Majors: A 10-year Retrospective Study," Fall Voice Conference, New York, 2012.
2. J. Brinckmann et al., "Safety and Efficacy of a Traditional Herbal Medicine (Throat Coat) in Symptomatic Temporary Relief of Pain in Patients with Acute Pharyngitis: A Multicenter, Prospective, Randomized, Double-Blinded, Placebo-Controlled Study," *Journal of Alternative and Complementary Medicine* 9, no. 2 (2003): 285–298.

3. N. Roy et al., "An Evaluation of the Effects of Three Laryngeal Lubricants on Phonation Threshold Pressure (PTP)," *Journal of Voice* 17, no. 3 (2003): 331–342.

4. K. Tanner et al., "Nebulized Isotonic Saline versus Water Following a Laryngeal Desiccation Challenge in Classically Trained Sopranos," *Journal of Speech Language and Hearing Research* 53, no. 6 (2010): 1555–1566.

5. C. Brown and S. Graham, "Nasal Irrigations: Good or Bad?" *Current Opinion in Otolaryngology, Head and Neck Surgery* 12, no. 1 (2004): 9–13.

6. T. Nsouli, "Long-Term Use of Nasal Saline Irrigation: Harmful or Helpful?" American College of Allergy, Asthma and Immunology Annual Scientific Meeting, Abstract 32, 2009.

7. M. Shadkam et al., "A Comparison of the Effect of Honey, Dextromethorphan, and Diphenhydramine on Nightly Cough and Sleep Quality in Children and Their Parents," *Journal of Alternative and Complementary Medicine* 16, no. 7 (2010): 787–793.

8. L. Hill et al., "Esophageal Injury by Apple Cider Vinegar Tablets and Subsequent Evaluation of Products," *Journal of the American Dietetic Association* 105, no. 7 (2005): 1141–1144.

9. R. O. Gottliebson, "The Efficacy of Cool-Down Exercises in the Practice Regimen of Elite Singers," PhD dissertation, University of Cincinnati, 2011.

4

THE MAGIC AND MECHANICS OF SINGING THE BLUES

Darrell Lauer with Eli Yamin

You must have complete freedom.

—B. K. S. Iyengar, yoga master[1]

Many years ago when contemplating marriage, I worried, *What if the magic goes away?* A wise man I knew encouraged me to look up the word "magic." There, I found a Greek root, "magikos." Obviously, the word "magic" comes from this root, but other words come from it as well. One of those words is "mechanic." For many years, I have contemplated the relationship between the magic of things and the mechanics behind them. This contemplation has provided a guideline for me in marriage, music, and many other things in life. Take care of the *mechanics*, and you will find pathways to sustain the *magic*. In this chapter, we apply this idea to blues singing, of which little has been written about. Even the great blues master B.B. King said, "The blues aren't a science; the blues can't be broken down like mathematics. The blues are a mystery, and mysteries are never as simple as they look."[2] There is much more on the mechanics of singing as applied to classical styles, and we draw on these principles where they are relevant while integrating the blossoming pedagogy supporting singers of contemporary commercial music (CCM), which includes American styles such as gospel, country, rock, rhythm and blues, and blues.

Understanding the mechanics of the blues starts with the ears. You can't sing the blues from reading it on the page. The blues is an oral tradition passed down by generous master musicians and storytellers. Every nuance, inflection, tone, and color choice is part of the communicative power of the blues. To sing the blues, you need to know about the African American culture that shaped it—a culture that developed extremely complex systems of communication in coded language during an extended period of enslavement and one that combined many cultures from Africa into a blended tapestry of shared values, mystical practices, and common sense that kept people alive or at least from going crazy under the stress and burden they faced on a daily basis.

The blues is medicinal. As with many effective medicines, its raw elements or *mechanics* are simple yet, when combined in the right proportions, extremely potent: *magic*. The wrong proportions can actually cause an ill effect. This is why it is so critical to listen to the masters and, if possible, study with one or find a way to spend time with someone who has lived the blues. Your range as a singer will be expanded tremendously.

This chapter gives you the fundamentals of how to train your body and voice to make the sounds needed in the blues in a healthy way. Many voice teachers and conductors I have worked with shy away from blues music because they fear that singing these sounds will damage performers' voices. Of course, as with any demanding style of singing, including opera, musical theater, and rock and roll, this is always possible. And so it is true with blues. However, there are many blues singers who enjoy long, successful careers without debilitating vocal issues. Just look at B.B. King, and you will see a man who performed extremely energetic concerts more than three hundred nights a year in different cities for over six decades. He is a great example of someone who knew how to use his voice in an efficient, healthy, and supremely expressive way in the blues idiom. Although B.B. King did not have formal vocal training as such, he wrote in his autobiography that "I admired those who used their whole voice, from the falsetto on down."[3] And about the singers who influenced him: "Blind Lemon [Jefferson] was strong and direct and bone-close to my home . . . Lonnie [Johnson] was different. Where Blind Lemon was raw, Lonnie was gentle. Lonnie was more sophisticated. His voice was lighter and sweeter, more romantic, I'd say. He had a dreamy quality to his singing."[4]

In later chapters, we investigate in detail several master blues singers from the 1920s forward. It is difficult to uncover verifiable information about how these singers learned to sing. However, the best blues singers consistently demonstrate tremendous range and control of their instrument. Some blues singers did, in fact, have voice teachers from a young age in the vibrant gospel music communities they grew up in. Dinah Washington from Chicago and Etta James from Los Angeles are stellar examples of this. At this point, we can only speculate as to what Washington's and James's voice teachers taught them and how they taught them. My best guess is that these teachers possessed a keen awareness of how the voice functions and how to control it in a way that was relatively healthy and free. They nurtured in their students this awareness and enabled them to have the technique they needed to excel as superstar interpreters of the blues. In the case of Washington and James, the foundation they had from gospel and blues allowed them to excel at singing many forms of CCM influenced by the blues, including rhythm and blues, country and western, and pop.

Let us investigate how the voice works and how to best prepare to make the kinds of sounds made by B.B. King, Dinah Washington, Etta James, and other blues masters. Now, there are multiple ways of doing this, and we certainly don't claim to know or be able to explain them all. What we attempt to do here is offer an informed point of view of the mechanics of voice function, strategies to train and heal your voice so that it can remain healthy and free for years of singing. This view encompasses ideas from traditional classical training and more contemporary concepts used to train singers in CCM styles. If you have been singing the blues for some time and have ever had problems such as hoarseness for extended periods of time or limited range, you may find great relief in knowing more about how your voice works and how you can train to make your instrument stronger, more resilient, and flexible to manage the demands of your work and give you the range of expression of your dreams.

HEALTHY VOCAL PRODUCTION FOR SINGING

The same basic technique is used for all genres of vocal music. Healthy vocal production can be achieved through the following:

1. Good posture
2. Efficient breathing technique
3. Minimal tension in the body, including the neck, jaw, tongue, facial muscles, and torso
4. Establishing the three main registers of the voice—falsetto/head, mix, and chest—and learning how to blend these three registers into one seamless connected range
5. Creating various dynamics in all registers in a healthy way
6. Learning to minimize any damage to the voice when using demanding techniques required in the genre, such as growling, nasality, and shouts

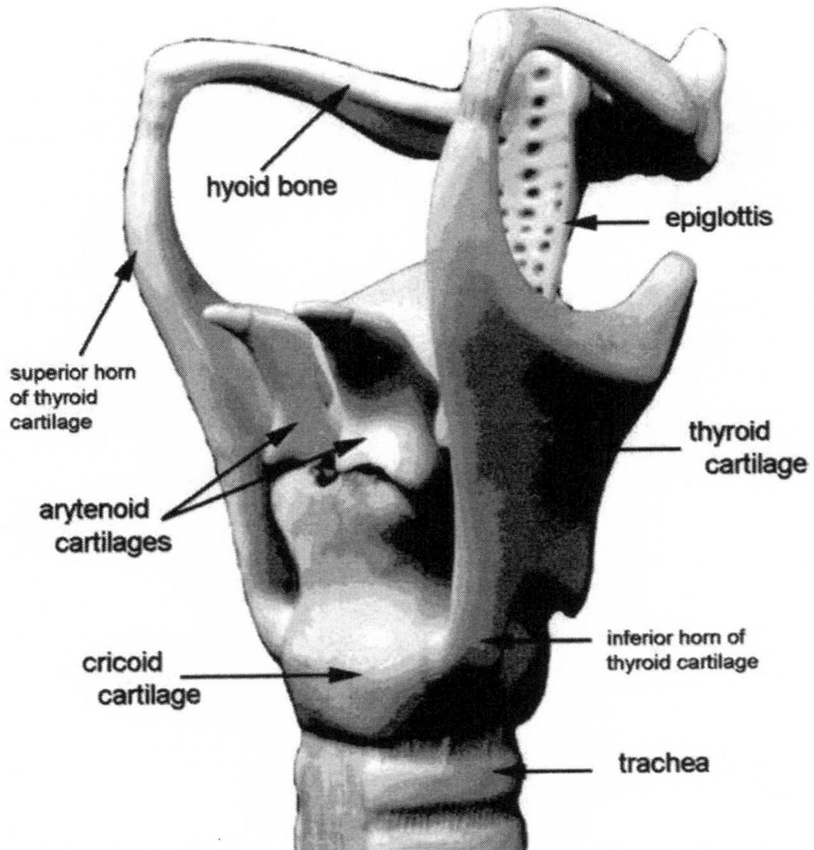

Figure 4.1. Cartilages of the larynx viewed at an angle from the back.
Dr. Scott McCoy

AREAS OF VOCAL PRODUCTION

There are three areas of vocal production:

1. Energy source—breath
2. Sound source—larynx, sometimes called "voice box"
3. Resonators—face, mouth, neck, and throat

VOCAL REGISTERS

Registers are the parts of the voice that make up the entire range of a singer. Each register uses a different combination of muscles in the throat, modes 2 and 3 being the most actively used:

Mode 1—the Pulse or vocal fry—is the lowest register. CCM singers, including blues singers, use the fry effectively for a gravelly and rough effect. It is best used sparingly and should never be the default register because doing so for prolonged periods can cause vocal strain.

Mode 2—the thyroarytenoid (TA)—is the register most people use to speak and is often referred to as the *chest register*. It is one of the primary registers.

Mode 3—the cricothyroid (CT)—is the other primary register and is known as *falsetto* in men or *head register* in both women and men.

Mode 4—the flute, or whistle, register—is the extremely high register, which some high-voiced women can use effectively.

In addition to these four modes, there is something called a *mixed register*, where the singer combines modes 2 and 3. For anyone struggling to sing high notes without strain, learning to sing consistently in *mix* is a lifesaver.

Consciously Engaging Modes 2 and 3 and Blending Them for Healthy Singing

The TA/chest register is usually the most developed register because it is the register most used during speech. However, to sing higher notes without straining, you need to develop the CT/head register by using it regularly. The muscles in the throat are like other muscles: they get stronger if you use them regularly in a healthy manner and weaker if they aren't used or are abused. Training the CT/head muscles takes time and regular exercise. Once you have a well-functioning CT/head register, you can work on blending it with TA/chest for that lifesaving *mix*.

Start practicing in head voice and gradually work your way down while keeping a lightness in the sound. When singing lower pitches, try not to be overly heavy by keeping an awareness of the CT/head voice. This awareness of the high when you are singing low can help you sing the higher pitches with greater ease.

When learning how to blend from CT/head voice register down into TA/chest register, you will most likely find a point where the timbre of the voice changes a lot. This is often referred to as the "break" and can sound like a yodel, which is itself part of blues vocal language. Sometimes you want a yodel, and sometimes you don't. Training your voice can help you have the option to blend seamlessly from one register to another. Noticing the break will establish in your mind where both registers are.

In order to blend from head register into chest, classical singers often train by lightly sliding down the range from the CT/head register until feeling a change where the voice might break. Yawning at this point while keeping the breath flowing has the effect of lowering the middle and back of the tongue and lifting the soft palette, thereby making room in the vocal tract for the air to pass through. Gradually, you can learn to engage the TA/chest register muscles with little or no break or yodel. Doing this with different vowels can help you see which one is the easiest for you. Try different pitches and vowels. Continue working on this transition until the register change is accomplished at any pitch, vowel, or dynamic. This smooth vocal blending of the CT and TA registers takes time and patience.

Another strategy favored by CCM singers is taking the chest register up.[5] The main thing is to minimize tension in the throat and figure out how to use the CT/head register and TA/chest register muscles as efficiently as possible to make the sounds you want to sing the blues. And it is not all about the throat. The throat dwells in the body, and good singing begins with good posture.

GOOD POSTURE

1. The feet are separated shoulder-width apart.
2. The weight of the body is on the balls of the feet.
3. The knees are loose.
4. The buttocks are tucked slightly under.
5. The stomach is hanging out.
6. The sternum/rib cage is elevated as if a string is holding it up.
7. The shoulders are low and relaxed.
8. The head is looking straight out.

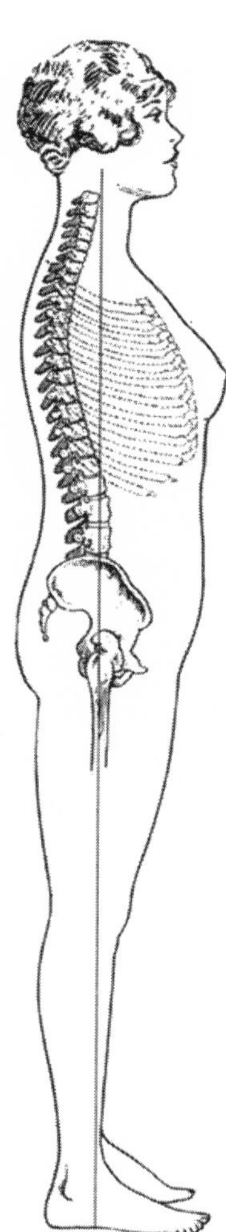

Figure 4.2. (left) Efficient body alignment. ***By Unknown—a catalog, page 18, copyrighted free use, https://commons.wikimedia.org/w/index.php?curid=2904917***

Figure 4.3. (right) Inefficient body alignment. ***By Unknown—a catalog, page 18, copyrighted free use. Retrieved from https://commons.wikimedia.org/w/index.php?curid=2904987***

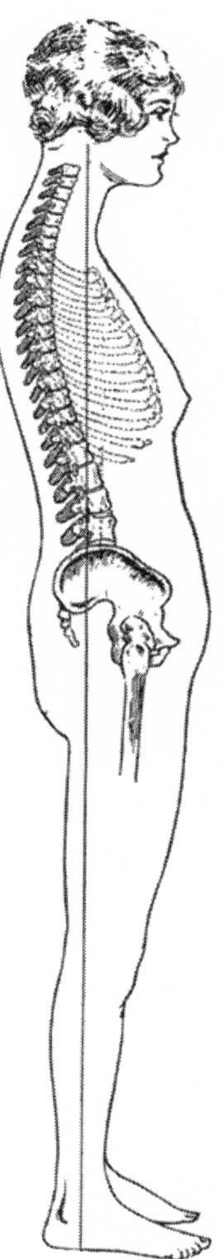

Remember that most of the time, people see you before they hear you. Jazz icon Miles Davis famously hired a young future icon, Herbie Hancock, because he liked his "carriage." It's true that many a job or audition has been lost due to a poor first impression, and the way you carry yourself is a big part of that. Keep the knees loose, shoulders low and relaxed, and the sternum and rib cage elevated.

OPTIMAL BREATHING

Optimal breathing engages the abdominal muscles in the front, back, and sides. These muscles are big and strong and can control the expiration of air more easily over a longer time. While keeping the sternum elevated and the shoulders low and relaxed, *breathe low into your abs only*. Make your inhalation quiet and smooth, regardless of the time that you have to breathe. We want there to be no resistance to air entering the lungs.

When you are not using your voice at all, breathing through the nose with the mouth closed is best. It helps keep your throat moist with warm, filtered air entering your lungs. For singing, breathing through the mouth *and* nose works well because it takes less time.

PRACTICE OPTIMAL INHALATION FOR SINGING

1. Establish good posture then place one hand on your sternum and the other hand directly under your ribs at your side and back. Take an easy full breath and feel which hand moves and where. If the hand under your ribs moves and your hand on your sternum doesn't, then you are on the right track.

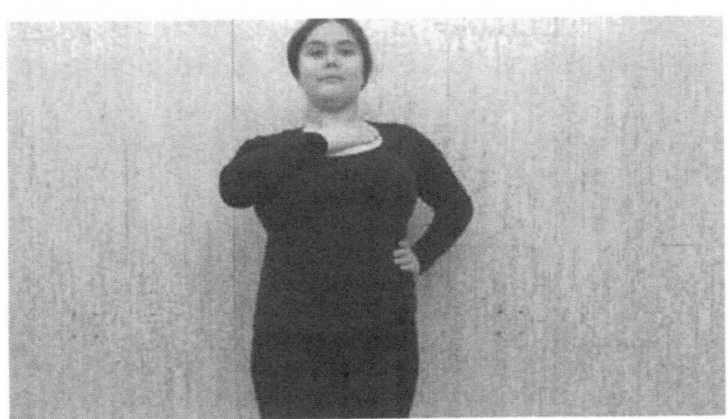

Figure 4.4. Sternum raised. ***Photo by Eli Yamin (Paloma Brooks)***

2. After low, abdominal breathing is established with consistency, check to see if both sides are expanding equally by placing both hands on your side and back under your ribs and taking another easy full breath. Is the expansion in both hands equal? If not, begin concentrating more on the side that has less expansion to even it out.
3. For more work on getting more expansion on both sides of the back, sit in a chair while keeping the sternum elevated and your hands placed on both sides of the lower back. Bend over almost completely and take another easy full breath. See if you feel more expansion in your hands in this position than when you were standing. Notice if one side expands more than the other. If so, try to even it out by taking several more breaths in this position. Gradually, you can work your way up to sitting while continuing to breathe with the hands placed on the back and focusing on maintaining consistent abdominal expansion on both sides. This will improve over time. After establishing balanced breath on both sides, return to step 2 to apply this idea to standing.

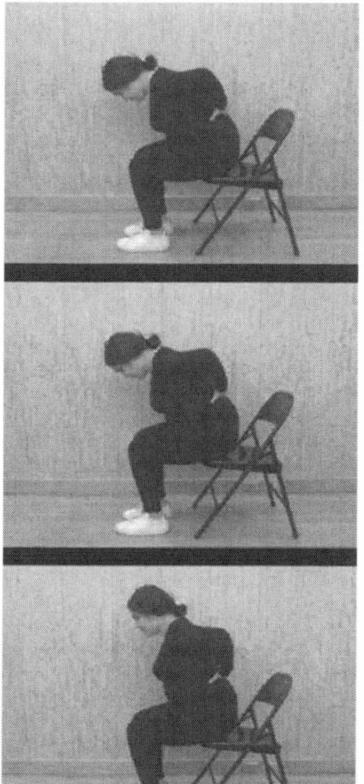

Figure 4.5. Breathing into the back. ***Photos by Eli Yamin***

Optimum breath originates from the sides and back, so make sure you live with this step long enough that this process becomes second nature. In this way, when you are in the heat of performing, you can be focused on expression while receiving the support of optimal breathing.

PRACTICE OPTIMAL EXHALATION FOR SINGING

Having a steady, even flow of air is essential for singing well:

- "s" hiss or lip buzz: To develop a steady, even flow of air over the course of the entire exhalation, practice a loose-lipped *hiss* on the syllable "s," sounding like an old steam radiator. You can also do a *lip buzz*, which is when you vibrate your lips to sound like a purring car engine. It is helpful to start the lip buzz with no pitch and add pitch later. Try placing a finger on opposite sides of the mouth to provide support and keeping the cheeks from puffing out. Keep the lips as relaxed as possible and the airflow steady without wasting air at the beginning.

Our goals here are the following:

1. To be able to maintain steady airflow on an "s" hiss for twenty-five seconds and/or steady airflow on a lip buzz for fifteen seconds.
2. To build stamina by working up to six repetitions of steady airflow without stopping in between. This helps in singing long phrases with greater ease.

ADDITIONAL TIPS TO MINIMIZE TENSION

- Take the correct amount of breath for the phrase that you are going to sing—not too much and not too little. Too much air as well as too little can build up tension in the body.
- Do not pause between the end of the inhalation and the beginning of the exhalation. Any delay in beginning the exhalation can also lead to unnecessary tension. Maintain awareness of this while

you are singing and try to avoid holding your breath. Wherever possible, let one exhalation release freely into the next inhalation without pausing.

SPEAKING

The renowned Oren Brown of the Juilliard School always used to say, "You have one voice whether you use it to speak or to sing. Since you speak much more than you sing you had better learn to use your speaking voice in a healthy manner."[6] He meant that one must do the following:

1. Use an optimum pitch area for speaking pitch—one that will give the most energy for the least amount of effort.
2. Have correct posture and breath.
3. Reduce or minimize any tension in the body.
4. Blend your vocal registers.
5. Use plenty of breath when speaking—no more than four or five words per breath.
6. Refrain from speaking too fast.

In other words, the same principles of good singing in terms of posture, breathing, and register awareness apply to both speaking and singing. Many singers tire their voices through poor speaking habits. One bad habit we singers sometimes have is *talking too much*. You can do your voice a favor by limiting your speech before performances whenever possible. Be careful of trying to speak over loud music after the performance and squeezing your throat. This can cause singing problems. Take care of your voice when speaking and singing. One way to do this is by regularly warming up the speaking voice each morning before speaking.

Why Warm Up the Speaking Voice?

1. When sleeping, the body relaxes and the vocal folds shorten and thicken. That is why most people have a lower speaking voice when they first wake up. Overspeaking in the lowest part of your range can lead to vocal difficulties over time.

2. The breathing muscles have relaxed overnight and may strain to support sound before being warmed up.
3. The muscles of the jaw, neck, abdomen, and tongue might have also tensed during the night, so you need to relax them.

Table 4.1. Phonetic symbols

Symbol	*Examples*
/a/	mama, nana
/ɑ/	father, ponder
/i/	see, me
/I/	it, sit
/ɛ/	Fred, Ed
/o/	so, go
/ɔ/	sought, ought
/u/	sue, shoe
/ʊ/	put, foot
/ng/	sung, flung
/m/	hum, murmur

SPEECH WARM-UP

There are seven steps to this warm-up. After regular practice, the warm-up will take about ten minutes to perform.

Figure 4.6. Establishing good posture and breathing. ***Photo by Eli Yamin (Alex Jones)***

1. Establish good posture.
2. Relax the tongue. The tongue is extremely important in singing and speaking and can cause many problems if not used properly. Here are some tips to relax and control the tongue.

   a. In front of a mirror, slowly extend the tongue out as far as you can without quivering or feeling the need to retract. Then voluntarily retract the tongue while maintaining maximal relaxation. Repeat.
   b. In front of a mirror, place your tongue right behind your teeth. This is the position of the tongue for singing unless you have a consonant that requires the tip to move [d, l, n, t]. See if you can keep the tongue still in this position. If not, keep working on this by relaxing the body and mind until you can.

Figure 4.7. Relaxing the tongue. ***Photo by Eli Yamin***

3. Head roll in two semicircles. Release your head forward and, starting at the bottom, slowly shift the head from side to side, leading with the left ear when going left and the right ear when going right. Do at least two 180-degree semicircles each way. Go only as fast as there is no clicking or discomfort. Do several times a day.

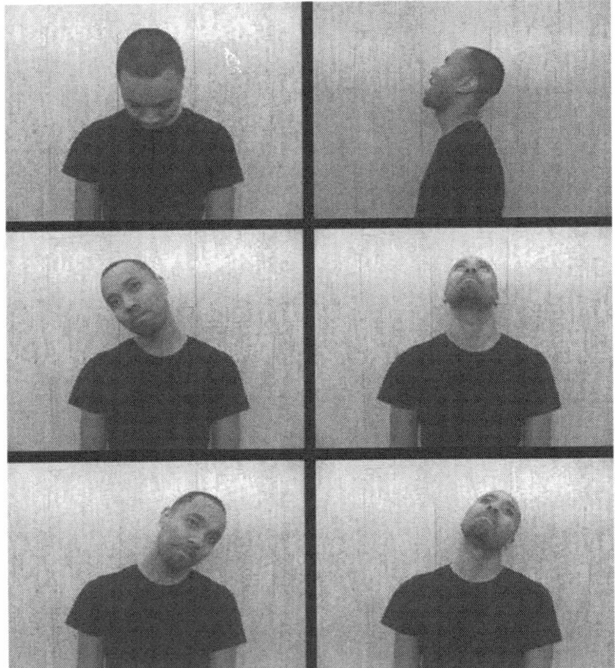

Figure 4.8. Head roll. ***Photos by Eli Yamin***

4. Gentle jaw stretches.

    a. Place the lower part of the palms of your hands by the temporomandibular joint/cheekbones and *slowly* come down the side of the jaw on the jawbone with the hands lowering the jaw while vocalizing a smooth falsetto/head voiced pitch and sliding downward in pitch while the jaw releases. Make the transition from falsetto/head voice to chest voice as smooth as possible with no break. Do this two or three times. The starting pitch should be placed in head voice where there is no strain on the voice and a smooth initiation of the sound. If you can't find falsetto/head, use a light, breathy sound.

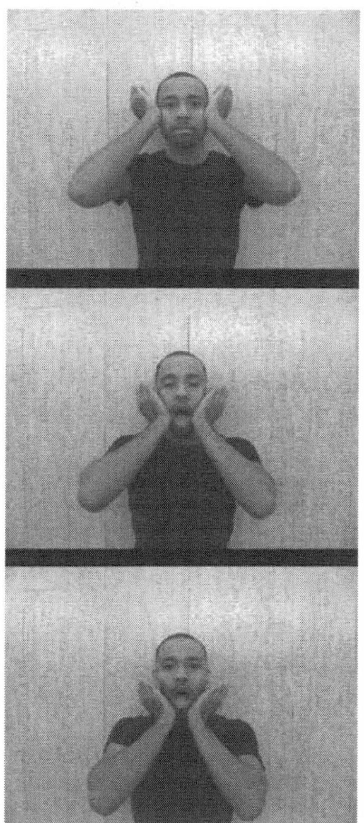

Figure 4.9. Jaw stretch I. ***Photos by Eli Yamin***

b. Move your jaw up and down with fingers holding the chin and *doing all the work*, going only as fast as there is no resistance or tension. Do this for twenty seconds a time and repeat this exercise at least ten times a day.

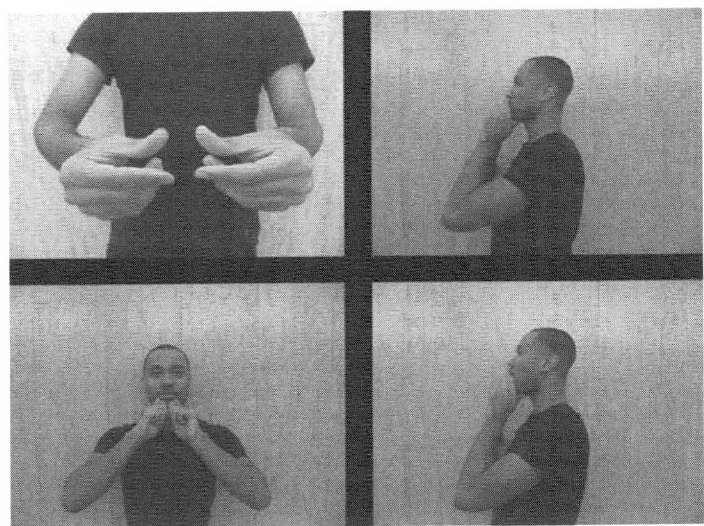

Figure 4.10. Jaw stretch II. ***Photos by Eli Yamin***

c. Let the jaw fall by itself as if surprised and then, with thumbs beneath the chin and doing all the work, push the jaw up slowly with no resistance or tension. Do this for twenty seconds a time and repeat this exercise at least ten times a day. Helpful hint: If you still experience jaw tension, you can check to make sure there is enough space between the upper and lower teeth for the tongue to rest. If not, then try putting tongue between teeth when not speaking. Give yourself a reminder note throughout the day to return to this position.

5. Breathing with abdominal muscles.

    a. Gentle *panting* with no noise and as little intake and exhale of breath as you can at a speed that you can sustain consistently for at least two minutes. This exercise helps keep the abdominal wall free of unnecessary tension.

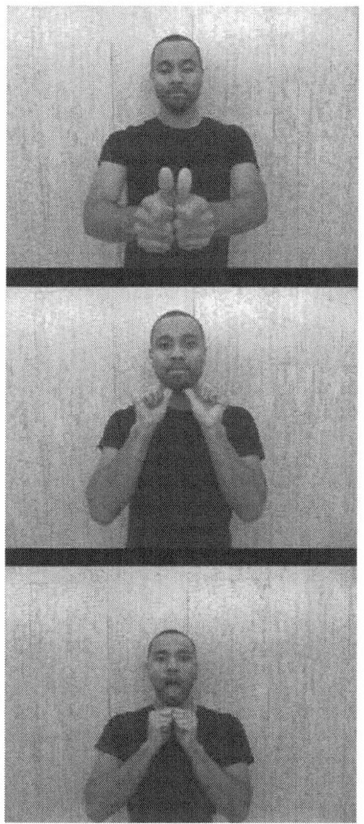

Figure 4.11. Jaw stretch III.
Photos by Eli Yamin

b. Hiss on syllable "s" with steady airflow six times in a row. Gradually build up to being able to sustain this for twenty-five seconds while maintaining the jaw free of tension.

6. Vocalizing.

   a. Using a lip buzz or tongue roll, slide down from falsetto or light, breathy tone to a mixed voice with no break and little effort. Do this two times with a breath in between, then start again in falsetto or light, breathy tone and slide down, up, and down in one breath, again with little effort and no tension in the jaw.
   b. Do the same exercise in the same manner while using a *hum*.
   c. Do the same exercise in the same manner while using the vowels [u], [i], and [a].

7. Speaking.
   a. Say, "My name is," take a breath, and then say your name. Do this in a singsong way using a lot of head voice but also gliding down into a mixed voice, up and down again.
   b. Say, "My address is," take a breath, and then begin your address, taking breaths after street, after city and state, then say the ZIP code. Do this also in a singsong manner, using a lot of head voice but gliding down into a mixed voice, up and down again.
   c. Say, "My telephone number is," take a breath, and say the area code, then a breath, then the first three numbers, then a breath, and then the last four numbers. Do this also in a singsong manner, using a lot of head voice but gliding down into a mixed voice.
   d. Say a short poem, nursery rhyme, prayer, or song text you know from memory. Begin by using the singsong approach described above and gradually work your way toward normal speech by the end. Take many breaths during this exercise with four or five words maximum per breath.

Your voice is now warmed up for speaking.

During the day, if you have not spoken in a while, you can do a shortened version of this warm-up to relocate and condition the speaking voice.

OPTIMAL PITCH RANGE FOR SPEAKING

Speaking in your *optimum pitch range* can help keep your voice in good shape. Many people speak lower than their optimal range, and a few speak higher, which can fatigue the voice and lead to vocal problems. Determine your optimum pitch range by sliding down from your upper middle voice and see where you get a ring or a fuller sound without adding any more breath or trying to increase the intensity. If you have trouble locating this pitch by feel or sensation yourself, record this exercise and listen back to it to see if you can identify an optimal pitch where your voice naturally rings. Find this pitch on a keyboard and remind yourself throughout the day by checking in with a piano or keyboard app on your phone. The more you play this pitch and speak around this pitch, the easier it will be to establish the habit of speaking consistently in this range. Pretty soon, you will feel that your speaking voice is work-

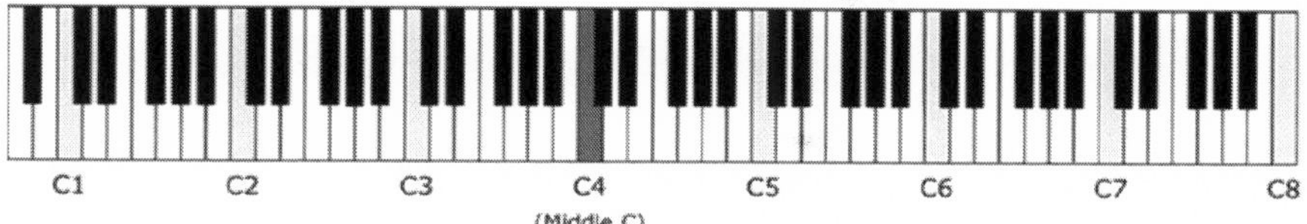

Figure 4.12. Key of pitch numbers. ***Creative Commons***

ing better for you. Since speaking and singing are so closely related, your speech should sound like the type of singing voice you have. If you have a higher voice, your speaking voice should be higher, whereas a lower voice should be lower.

SINGING WARM-UP

After letting the voice rest for a period of time, you can begin a singing warm-up. Some people warm up by singing songs instead of doing any vocal exercises. However, most songs place too heavy a demand on the instrument when not already warmed up. In addition, in a song, there are more things to concentrate on, such as words, rhythm, dynamics, and so on. It is better to do a warm-up like the one outlined here before dealing with the demands of singing a song.

1. Blending registers: head, chest, and mix. Since most people have a more developed chest voice than head voice, it is better to start singing from the top in an easy head voice at a pitch that can be produced without strain and a smooth initiation. If you cannot find the head voice, start with a light, breathy sound at a pitch that causes no strain or tension.

   a. Glide or slide down from the top into middle voice without any break. Do this on all five vowels—[e], [i], [a], [o], and [u]—plus the lip roll and hum.
   b. Glide down on a hum to establish resonance.
   c. Gliding down on a lip trill serves to maintain a good connection with the breath as well as freedom of the jaw and lips and also establishes better resonance.

2. Awaken the entire body. Starting on C3 for lower men or E♭3 for higher men and C4 for lower women or E♭4 for higher women. Work your way up a fifth in half steps, singing m[i], m[e], m[a],

m[o], m[u] on each pitch while loosening up the body. Start by bending over while swinging from side to side with the arms like a heavy elephant for the first three pitches while coming up slowly to a standing posture. Then stretch the elbows from front to back for the next pitch. Then, for the next pitch, extend your arms above your head and make a deep, complete circle. Then reverse. For the next two pitches, you will rotate your shoulders in complete circles, reversing on the second pitch. Then start descending, first with an arm rotation of a backstroke and the next lower pitch coming forward like doing a crawl, as in swimming. The next two pitches have your arms extending over the side of your head, one side for each pitch. Then do a back scratch for the next two pitches, using one arm at a time, and finally do some bouncing or pretending to do a dance of rock and roll. This will then get the entire body warmed up and ready for some good singing.

Figure 4.13. Singing warm-up. ***Photos by Eli Yamin***

3. Relax the tongue. See the section "Speech Warm-Up," step 2.
4. Mix head and chest voice. An exercise to mix the head voice to the chest voice from the top down can be restorative for blues singers. Start with a pitch where it is easy to produce a head voice sound with no strain or tension. Then, as you begin to go down on a five-note pattern, add the chest voice by creating space in the oral cavity and pharynx by lowering the tongue and raising the soft palate. The goal is to make the transition from head to chest voice as smooth as possible. If you can't find your head voice, start with a very light free sound and add some fullness to the mixed sound. Continue with this exercise, with the starting note continuing to be a half step higher until it becomes difficult to do. As you go down the five-note phrase, add as much chest voice as possible without strain or pushing.
5. Bring the chest voice up. On an [o] vowel, start in the lower part of your range and, while keeping some lightness in the low notes, sing this pattern:

   1-5-1-5-1-5-1

   Keep the transition from 1 to 5 smooth, then change to this:

   1-♭3-5-♭3-1-♭3-5-♭3-1

   Finally, while keeping everything smooth, sing this pattern:

   1-♭3-5-5-4-♭3-4-♭3-1

   Do this up several half steps, maintaining a smooth connection between all the notes.

6. Get ready to jump. Since many phrases start from a lower pitch and ascend into higher pitches, it's good to practice this in the form of an exercise. In the same way that a basketball player needs to be ready to jump, so must a singer. One key to success in jumping up to high notes with ease is to be careful not to sing low notes overly heavy. In fact, when singing low notes before high notes, you can actively think of the high notes in the low notes. Keep some lightness in your sound like a great basketball player would in his step. In this way, you will be ready to jump. Practice first singing an interval of a fifth with this idea in mind moving up in half steps. The goal is to feel *no strain or pushing*. Next, do this same exercise and add a flat third to the mix. Then do all five notes. Then increase the exercise to a full octave in the same manner, with first going

from the low note to the octave higher. Then add the flat third and fifth to the exercise without having any strain or tension in the voice or body. You can do this on any vowel of your choice. Many teachers start with an [i] vowel on the lower note and a darker vowel, perhaps an [o] or a darker [a] vowel, for the top note. (See the appendix for vocal exercises.)

7. Get ready for blues effects. Blues singing requires scooping up to pitches. One of the challenges in scooping is to land solidly on the pitch you are scooping up to. Master blues singers like Robert Johnson provide great examples of this throughout their recordings. One strategy you can use to scoop without tiring your voice and landing accurately on the final pitch is to be careful to not bring up too much weight from chest voice as you ascend. Keep some lightness in your low sounds so that you are ready to jump like the basketball player mentioned above. The same can be stated for using the slide, a growl, nasality, and shout in blues singing. In using these techniques, always remember that it will be easier on the voice if the sound is not produced too heavily. Use a microphone to support you wherever possible and keep in mind that you can always change the key of the song to suit your range. You are not obligated to sing the song in the key that other people sing it in. It should be easy and effectively performed in the key that best fits your voice!

YOU ARE A VOCAL ATHLETE

In today's thinking, most otolaryngologists, voice scientists, voice therapists, voice teachers, and vocal performers think that people who give vocal performances should be considered vocal athletes. What does this mean, and why is it important? For the performer, this means that they must consider all of the elements that will contribute to their giving consistent performances over a long period of time and of avoiding vocal damage through abuse of their bodies. This includes the following:

1. What to eat on a daily basis and what to eat before performing and when.

2. How much sleep and rest they should have regularly and on the days leading up to a performance.
3. How much vocal usage they should have during the days leading up to a performance to have maximum strength and little vocal fatigue during their performances.
4. How much and what type of vocal exercising they should have on a regular basis and on the days leading up to the performance and on the day of the performance.
5. What type of a vocal warm-down to do after heavy vocal singing on a consistent basis.
6. What to do to keep their entire bodies in good physical condition.

One of the most frequent questions that I am asked is, What and when should I eat before a performance? My response is that this is an individual decision based on the individual's own body. Some people like to eat right before a performance, while others feel they can't perform well unless they have an empty stomach. Most people do best when singing after a couple of hours of eating a heavy meal of carbohydrates and protein with some vegetables. What this includes is a personal matter. However, some consideration also must include any medical conditions, such as acid reflux, allergies, diabetes, and so on.

Getting enough sleep is extremely important for the performer to do his or her best. Here again, this will vary from individual to individual, but for most people, eight hours is the recommended amount. The performer must, however, be *up and alert at least three hours before the performance* in order for all the vocal preparation to occur properly. And one's eating schedule needs to be added to the mix. Many performers like to take a nap if time permits or just relax while lying down and being quiet on the day of a performance. However, with possible sound checks and media appearances, this might not be possible.

On the day before and on the day of a performance, as little extra vocal usage as possible should be the hard-and-fast rule. Only do what is absolutely necessary with regard to your vocal output. This includes singing and *speaking*. One must remember that the vocal folds are muscles (and small ones at that) and will become fatigued if used too much, leaving the performer with less than an optimal condition for the performance. If there are sets with time off in between, don't speak to everyone during these breaks. Wait until after the entire show is over as much as possible. Also, if the venue is noisy, get away from the noise and speak minimally. If it is absolutely necessary to say anything, get as close as possible to the person and keep the conversation to an absolute minimum. Most performers are very social people and feel uncomfortable not talking to as many people as possible. However, you can tell your friends and colleagues that you have to limit your vocal output beforehand. If there is a house manager or agent there during the performance, they can do a great service to you by keeping people away until afterward.

Vocal exercises on a daily basis are absolutely necessary for the vocal athlete, just as they are necessary for the sporting performer. What this consists of will depend on the exercises that the singer has developed with his or her voice teacher, who should be seen on a regular basis. Obviously, the exercises should develop both the CT and the TA muscles and the blending of these two muscle groups in order to have a smooth transition of the registers and extended range necessary for the type of repertoire that you are doing. This will include doing vocal exercises first and then adding in the repertoire for the performance. There will also be rehearsals with other performers, included in this planning. An hour or two daily should be the maximum output for keeping a healthy voice and having a long career. On the day before and on the day of the performance, this should be curtailed to save vocal life for the performance.

After any strenuous vocal usage, just like a sports athlete, a *vocal warm-down* should be performed as close to the vocal usage as possible. This includes after a vocal lesson, rehearsal, or performance. The warm-down should include reestablishing the CT muscles by themselves and lightening up the entire range in general. When performing, the TA muscles are generally used more and the voice becomes too heavy, making it harder to use after a rest period in a healthy manner. The lower part of the vocal range will become fuller, making it harder to achieve an easy transition into the upper register. Exercises from the top down in both speech-slide and singing-slide should be used in a very gentle manner for a short period of time to achieve the desired result.

Many singers forget or never equate vocal health with being in good physical condition. Never forget that the vocal mechanism is part of the body and that the entire body must be in tip-top shape for maximum efficiency in order to have consistent performances over the long period of a career. Many careers are cut short unnecessarily due to the individual not taking care of his or her health. A consistent physical exercise program should be maintained, which includes some form of aerobic exercise and easy muscle strengthening. Being at the ideal weight is also very important to stay healthy. As you get older, it is more difficult to keep the correct weight. Therefore, it is beneficial to become more disciplined in what you eat and how much. Equally important is maintaining a physical exercise program. Many performers are ravenous after performing and also want to relax by imbibing alcoholic beverages. Then they go to sleep. After a number of such episodes, they have found that they have gained an inappropriate amount of weight, which contributes to poorer health and more difficulty in sustaining this active lifestyle. See yourself as a vocal athlete and take care of your body by developing good eating, drinking, and exercise habits.

LEARNING SONGS

Be careful to learn the song well before trying to sing it. Many technical problems can arise when the singer tries to combine too many elements, such as tune, rhythm, words, and meaning/interpretation, at the same time. It's better to have each one secure before trying to combine them. Remember that it is easier to learn something correctly at the beginning than it is to unlearn something and then retrain your brain to do it correctly. Keep these points in mind:

1. *Speak* the text as a poem *many times* with all the inflections and feeling that you can without singing it. Don't get bound in by the music. The words are the key to singing a song with great feeling, and this holds true for almost any style of singing.
2. Scat the *rhythm* of the words that are set in the song as a simple combination of consonants, such as "ba-ba-da-ba."
3. Learn the tune well until you can hear the song in your head with all the turns, slides, and embellishments before singing it.
4. Sing the tune first on a single vowel, such as [a].

5. Sing the song on the vowels of the words in the song.
6. Sing it with the words.
7. Finally, sing the song with the accompaniment the song is going to have. If you are going to accompany yourself, practice your accompaniment part without singing first until it is second nature. Then gradually add the singing to your accompaniment. When you practice, give yourself time to learn songs by singing them without having to play. Then, when you are ready, play and sing.

AUTHENTIC BLUES SOUND, TECHNICALLY SPEAKING

Dialect

Blues singing started with African Americans in the southern United States. During the Great Migration (1910s through the 1970s), many of these singers arrived in northern cities, such as Chicago, the blues capital, with an African American southern dialect very much intact. You cannot mimic a dialect 100 percent that is not your own without sounding silly. The blues is a personal expression, so it is important that your own voice shine through. However, there are certain parameters derived from African American dialect that are generally accepted as a given no matter what your background is. This means a very relaxed vowel and a tendency to soften consonants or eliminate them entirely when the word will be understood without it. Published transliterations of the dialect of W. C. Handy's "Saint Louis Blues" are good examples of roots-of-blues dialect. Practice saying the words before you sing:

Feelin' tomorrow, lak' I feel today
Feelin' tomorrow, lak' I feel today
I'll pack my bag and make my getaway

"Saint Louis Blues" performed by Bessie Smith ♪

Brightness and Using the Microphone

Another important aspect of blues singing is brightness. Some singers naturally have a bright sound, and others do not. Brighter vowels, like [i] and [e], make bright sounds, and these are generally close to the way vowels sound in regular talking. The vowels are not modified or darkened as they are in classical styles, or, if they are modified, it is by only a very small amount when singing high and loud. Blues singers almost always use a microphone and therefore don't have to sing loud to project their voice into an auditorium or concert hall. With a good sound system in place, you can focus on making contrasts in volume for expression and making more of a song and avoid forcing more sound out to have the audience hear you. Although you can let the sound system do a lot of the work, there are things you can practice to make a bright sound in a relaxed manner.

In addition to using brighter vowels, brightness can increase when there is a sensation of vibration in the areas under the eyes, cheeks, and upper lip—as opposed to having this sensation in the throat and upper chest. It is best to do this by thinking it more than consciously trying to place it there, which can cause unnecessary tension. When training the voice for bright blues singing, establish this upper facial vibration sensation in lower tones and gradually ascend while maintaining the sensation.

For a good example of this bright sound, listen to Joe Williams sing "Every Day I Have the Blues." ♪

Vibrato and Vowel Modification

When singing the blues, you want to make words sound as natural as possible without much vibrato. Some blues artists use vibrato at times, but many don't. When you sing high in your range, you can modify the vowels by making them slightly "darker" to keep your throat relaxed and open and not strained. An example of this is an [i] vowel becoming more of an [I] when going high. We discuss an example of this in chapter 7 with Etta James's performance of her hit "Roll with Me Henry (aka "Wallflower")." Notice how James gradually changes the [i] vowel in "Henry" to [I]. ♪

Gravelly and Strained Sounds

Sometimes for the blues you want to have a strained sound for a particular effect. This can be managed when done intentionally and at moderate volumes whenever possible. Once again, use the microphone to your advantage to amplify the sound you are making so you can go easy on your throat. Avoid making squeezing your throat the default method of singing high. It is not necessary and can cause problems.

The blues singers we analyze in later chapters were masters of singing the full expression of the blues, including gravelly and squeezed sounds, while maintaining balance overall. You will notice in the case of Bessie Smith, Muddy Waters, Dinah Washington, Etta James, and B.B. King that the singer always defaults to a clear tone that is not strained or gravelly. These singers provide great models for keeping your voice healthy when singing the blues.

The Holler

Another technique that is essential in blues singing is the holler. Some blues singers, like Joe Turner, use the holler as the foundation of their style. However, most people would find this style too hard on their instrument and instead use the holler as a special effect to achieve particular emotional impact. Technically, it is good to realize that this is the exception for an effect and not your basic technique for singing.

The holler is done with an open throat and plenty of air with full freedom and relaxation of the jaw, tongue, and chest and abdominal cavities. The vowel is open and relaxed as in speech. The actual sound should not be made at the very extreme of the singer's range, and the dynamic should also not be extreme. Allow the microphone to support healthy execution of this technique. Pick and choose one or two places in the song for this blues technique for hollering, such as toward the end of "Every Day I Have the Blues" sung by Joe Williams. Notice how Williams hollers at the outset and then switches almost immediately into a more intimate sound quality. Williams is another great example of a blues singer who uses the wide range of his voice and maintained a balanced and versatile instrument throughout a prolific career as performer and recording artist.

Belting

Belting can be an effective and expressive way to sing the blues when you want a lot of power. The belter uses only the TA muscles in much of the lower range until the stage is reached where the transition to a mixed register must begin. There are different types of belters. Like all types of voices, some have a heavier belt sound, while others have an ability to carry this belt sound higher in their range than others. It is our opinion that one should stick with the type of belt that is easiest to achieve and not try to change to something that is more difficult. A strict belter has a limited range and can have an obvious shift into his or her head voice. Some people like this "yodel effect." For a smoother transition from chest to head, develop the CT muscles and learn to blend these muscles into the strong TA muscles. This will produce a lighter belt sound in the upper reaches of this register and make a smooth shift into the head voice. The method is the same one used when combining the CT and TA muscles to produce a seamless transition into the more dominant CT register.

ADDITIONAL SINGING TIPS

Making Good Use of the Tongue

Try using the *tongue only* for producing certain consonants and all vowels. It is much more efficient to produce all vowels and certain consonants ([t], [d], [n], [l], [k], [g], and semiconsonant [y]). The tongue can produce these phonemes quicker and can keep the jaw from disturbing the vocal tract. This also can reduce the possibility of creating tension in the jaw. At first, it will be awkward to do this efficiently, but with practice and time, one can get accurate and efficient phonemes while keeping the jaw relaxed and uninvolved. Use a mirror to train yourself to keep the jaw still. You can also lightly hold the jaw to feel whether it is moving. First, work with a single phoneme, such as [l]. Then, when this is easy, add a second phoneme, such as [la], in the first position. Then go through all the vowels with one consonant. Then go to the final position of the consonant. At first, do this slowly and with time increase the speed without sacrificing accuracy. Then go to a text and practice saying it slowly at first and then increasing speed. After this, sing the text on a single pitch. Finally, sing the song.

Maximizing Relaxation When Inhaling and Exhaling

Inhaling with the mouth in the shape of the syllable you will sing makes for more efficient singing. Tension builds up when singing, so it is very important when inhaling to release any tension in the front, back, and sides of the abdomen. Releasing tension during the inhalation is critical; otherwise, tension buildup can cause problems.

Different Ways of Starting the Sound: Onset

The beginning of the sound you make, especially at the top of phrases, is extremely important and is known as *onset*. Series author Trineice Robinson-Martin explains this very well in her book *So You Want to Sing Gospel* (p. 87). Robinson identifies four types of onsets:

Hard
Breathy
Balanced
Gravel

All four types of onsets are used in singing blues.

Hard onset is when sound is initiated abruptly without a smooth flow of air. This draws the vocal folds together quickly and creates a pressed, rough sound. Hard onset is the most strenuous type of onset and can cause damage to the vocal folds in some singers if done repeatedly over time. However, it can also be very expressive if performed in moderation and a limited number of times at the top of one's vocal range.

Breathy onset is where you hear an excessive amount of air before the vocal folds are drawn together to make the sound. The sound tends to be weaker and can be interpreted as more emotionally vulnerable. Naturally, it is expressive for situations that call for this effect. One must realize that to produce this breathy onset, a lot of air is required. Sometimes, this makes singers run out of air at the end of a phrase, causing them to squeeze the throat to get the final notes out. Avoid this by allowing for extra breaths.

Balanced onset is where there is a smooth initiation of the sound and an optimal amount of airflow draws the vocal folds together. There is no noticeable popping or pressed quality in the initiation of tone. Balanced onset is the healthiest way to sing, causing the least amount of fatigue and potential strain. Use this onset most of the time and the others for intentional contrast when the music calls for it.

Gravel onset is also important in blues, and this is accomplished by beginning the sound in a vocal fry and then sliding into a pitched tone. Gravel onset can be very effective for blues expression. Keep your voice healthy by using it a limited number of times while keeping the vocal tract very relaxed, letting the microphone do the work of projecting the sound.

Moving and Singing

Blues singers are often moving when performing. Making facial gestures and even dancing are common. As for faces, one need only watch videos of Muddy Waters, B.B. King, and Son House to see it in action. However, in all three of those singers, you will notice that a contorted facial gesture is never the default. The singer always returns to a position of relaxation. This is essential to keep their instruments balanced. Many blues singers also perform with an instrument while singing. All these things can lead to challenges in maintaining optimal posture for singing. Develop your awareness of this and return to correct posture as soon as possible in each situation. If you are a mover, practice moving while maintaining the best possible alignment of your vocal apparatus located in your upper body. For the singer who plays an instrument simultaneously, similar awareness can be developed. It's best to practice your repertoire singing only and playing instrument only before putting them together in order to maintain the best possible body alignment and vocal awareness.

Make Friends with Your Constrictor Muscles

Another common area of tension in singers is the constrictor muscles. You can find these muscles—*inferior constrictors*—by placing your fingers right under your mandible at the side of your neck and then swallowing. After finding this area, you can massage it to see whether it needs releasing or whether it is loose. Another set of constrictor muscles—*middle constrictors*—are connected to the hyoid bone and can be felt placing a finger right above the larynx and then swallowing. These are the muscles that are used primarily for swallowing and gargling.

Massaging this area as well to see whether it is loose is very important. There is also a third set—*superior constrictors*—located at the top of the vocal tract behind the nose and throat.[7]

Some singers have developed the habit of keeping these muscles tight when not swallowing. This produces a great deal of unnecessary tension and greatly affects the quality of the vocal sound. For the blues, this habit can help achieve edgy and growl effects important to the style. However, if you do this, it is better for your voice to make sure that it does not become your default position. That is the secret to keeping your voice healthy for the next gig, tour, or recording. Habitual constriction of these muscles causes them to tire the vocal fold muscles as well, which can compromise the whole vocal mechanism.

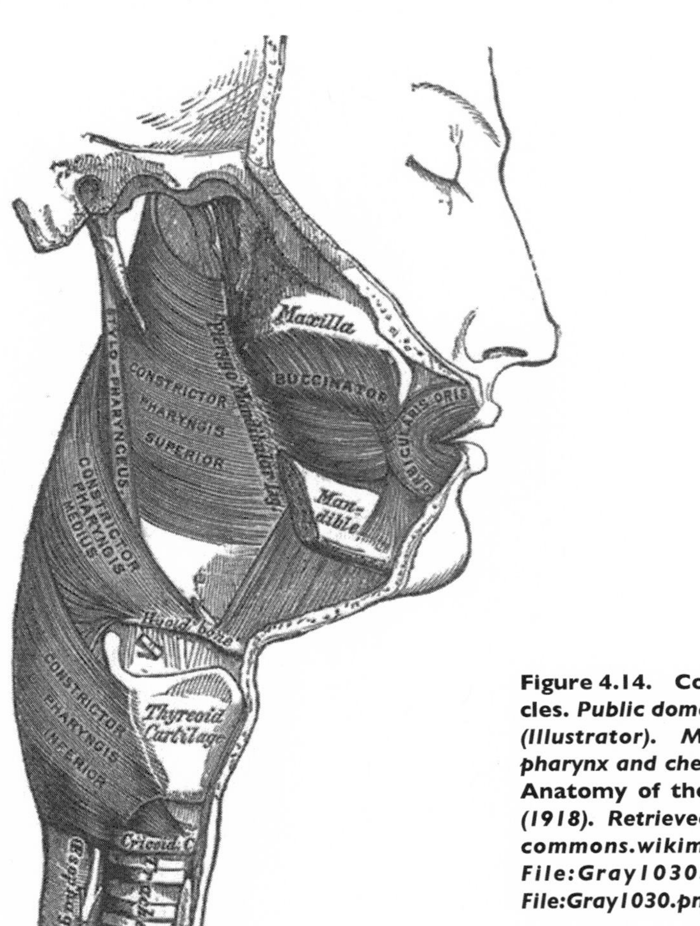

Figure 4.14. Constrictor muscles. ***Public domain/H. V. Carter (Illustrator). Muscles in the pharynx and cheeks. In H. Gray,*** **Anatomy of the Human Body** ***(1918). Retrieved from https://commons.wikimedia.org/wiki/File:Gray1030.png#/media/File:Gray1030.png***

With this healthy voice production in place, you have the technical tools or *mechanics* you need to increase your knowledge and performance of authentic blues singing styles. This is where the *magic* begins.

NOTES

1. Correspondence with Eli Yamin, 2008.
2. B.B. King, with David Ritz, *Blues All Around Me: The Autobiography of B.B. King* (New York: HarperCollins, 1996), 2.
3. King, *Blues All Around Me*, 128.
4. King, *Blues All Around Me*, 22–23.
5. Jeanie LoVetri, Somatic Voicework: The LoVetri Method, level 3 course, taken by Eli Yamin.
6. Oren Brown, correspondence with Darrell Lauer.
7. Trineice Robinson-Martin, *So You Want to Sing Gospel* (Lanham, MD: Rowman & Littlefield, 2017), 100.

5

DEVELOPING AUTHENTIC STYLE CHARACTERISTICS

Early Blues Women

The healing power of the blues was a necessity in the African American community in which it was created. No one could have predicted that this music, which functioned as a survival tool for African Americans, could become a gift to the world with such universal appeal to spawn the development of most other American music styles, including jazz, country, rap, rhythm and blues, bluegrass, rock, and pop. Renowned scholar and activist Angela Davis writes,

> Naming issues that pose a threat to the physical or psychological wellbeing of the individual is a central function of the blues. Indeed, the musical genre is called the "blues" not only because it employs a musical scale containing "blue notes" but also because it names, in myriad ways, the social and psychic afflictions and aspirations of African Americans. . . . Through the blues, menacing problems are ferreted out from the isolated individual experience and restructured as problems shared by the community. As shared problems, threats can be met and addressed within a public and collective context.[1]

Blues heals the world. Yet awareness of its origins and influence remains vague at best. I once told a group of teenage African American boys from Brownsville, Brooklyn, what Chicago bluesman Willie Dixon once said: "The blues is the roots and everything else is the fruits." These young men responded, "Naw, that's not true, what about R&B?"

I said, "What do you think R&*B* stands for?" I was surprised to find that they did not know that the *B* stands for "blues." This is typical in black and white communities around the United States. We don't recognize the parts of America created by black Americans the way we should. Perhaps by teaching the blues with specifics and giving people more opportunities to feel its ingenious healing power, we can change that.

It doesn't take long to feel how the blues is the roots everything else the fruits. Usually, in one session of learning the shuffle beat and singing bluesy call-and-response vocalizations, the reality becomes clear. Blues is the heart of American singing. In this chapter, we explore early blues women and the musical language they codified on the extremely popular records they made in the 1920s. We focus on three seminal blues women: Mamie Smith, Ma Rainey, and Bessie Smith.

A MYSTICAL EQUATION

To sing the blues authentically, we must know about African American culture as it is expressed through language, sound, rhythm, embellishment, sourcing your story, and form. At its core, the blues is a healing song, a *mystical equation* that offers some of the greatest challenges and traumas of life to a process that provides release and relief to the performer and everyone around him or her.

The well-schooled African American musician W. C. Handy wrote about his first encounter with the blues in the Tutwiler Train Station in Clarksdale, Mississippi, around 1903:

> A lean, loose-jointed Negro had commenced plunking a guitar beside me while I slept. His clothes were rags; his feet peeped out of his shoes. His face had on it some of the sadness of the ages. As he played, he pressed a knife on the strings of a guitar in a manner popularized by Hawaiian guitarists who used steel bars. The effect was unforgettable. His song, too, struck me instantly. "Goin' where the Southern cross the Dog." The singer repeated the line three times, accompanying himself on the guitar with the weirdest music I ever heard.[2]

I find it interesting that Handy reports that the music sounds "weird" to his well-trained ears. Handy recognized the source of a unique sound that he could use in the best sense of Western composition tradition as a folk source. In this manner, Handy brilliantly scored compositions that provide a formal structure of the blues, such as "Saint Louis Blues," "Memphis Blues," and "Yellow Dog Blues." These songs, as sheet music and as commercial recordings by numerous artists, shaped the way millions of people first heard the blues and thought about it for generations. Handy possessed a unique and invaluable perspective growing up in the African American community with exposure to folk traditions *and* receiving formal training in Western classical music. Handy's parents had been enslaved, yet he became a world-renowned composer, scholar, performer, entrepreneur, and author—an extraordinary American journey indeed.

ZORA NEALE HURSTON'S CHARACTERISTICS OF NEGRO EXPRESSION[3]

Before we delve deep into Handy's conception of the blues, however, let's consider the context in which Handy and others in the early twentieth century spawned the genre. Author and ethnomusicologist Zora Neale Hurston offers us keys to understanding African American art in her 1933 essay "Characteristics of Negro Expression." Hurston lists 11 characteristics: drama, will to adorn, angularity, asymmetry, dancing, Negro folklore, originality, imitation, absence of privacy, the jook, and dialect.

For many years, I have found these characteristics to be an invaluable lens to help increase perception in listening to and appreciating jazz and blues music. They are an indispensable resource for jazz and blues history courses and individual study. Here we use Hurston's characteristics to frame our discussion of developing authentic style characteristics in singing blues. They are presented in the four style chapters roughly in this sequence:

Chapter 5: Developing Authentic Style Characteristics: Early Blues Women

1. Dialect
2. Will to adorn (embellishment)

3. Asymmetry (syncopation)
4. Drama

Chapter 6: Developing Authentic Style Characteristics: Early Blues Men and Another Woman

5. The Jook
6. Originality
7. Imitation

Chapter 7: Developing Authentic Style Characteristics: Chicago and the Modern Blues Vocal Sound

8. Angularity
9. Folklore
10. Dance

Chapter 8: Making a Soulful Sound

11. Absence of Privacy

Hurston's characteristics are an excellent framework for looking at blues and jazz and all the music influenced by it. As we mine the treasures of early blues music, we can name these characteristics and see a distinct range of aesthetic values that make the blues sound like the blues. Nowhere is the distinct sound of the blues more apparent than in the sound of the *voice*.

DIALECT

Early blues performers came from the southern United States. They spoke a dialect of English that is a key ingredient of the blues sound. When singing the blues, as with any style of music, it's helpful to pay attention to the sound of the vowels, where consonants are dropped or emphasized, and to learn how to make these sounds in a natural and free way. Many African Americans speak today in a dialect that has its roots in the South. During the Great Migration (1910s through the 1970s), millions of African Americans left the South for cities in the North, bringing with them all aspects of southern culture, including food, music, and the way they spoke the English language.[4]

Blues singers sing like they talk. We can look at this from the standpoint of the sound color, or timbre, of their voice and how they use chest, head, and mix voice. We must also investigate the style of language, which is distinctly African American. Some years ago in Oakland, California, there was an uproar over educators wanting to officially acknowledge the way in which many African American students talked. These educators sought to acknowledge African-American Vernacular English (AAVE) as a system of speaking the English language. The debate touched a nerve with many people who criticized what was labeled teaching "Ebonics" as a way of dumbing down American education. Oakland educators always planned to continue to teach American Standard English. Their effort was simply to officially acknowledge AAVE as a legitimate way of speaking with its own system of rules.

Linguist Geoffrey K. Pullum of the University of California, Santa Cruz, who played in a blues/rock band in his early years, well demonstrates this in his article "African-American Vernacular English Is Not Standard English with Mistakes." Pullum asserts that AAVE "has a degree of regularity and stability attributable to a set of rules of grammar and pronunciation, as with any language. It differs strikingly from Standard English, but there is no more reason for calling it bad Standard English than there is for dismissing Minnesota English as bad Virginia speech or the reverse."[5] Becoming familiar with AAVE can be helpful in singing the blues authentically.

Practice

Speak the following lyrics until they sound completely normal to you. Your goal is to embody the language as an insider who knows a specific set of rules where saying "ain't had nothin'" is as natural as saying "I am going to the store":

I ain't had nothin' but bad news,
Now I got those crazy blues.

"Crazy Blues": First Blues Record ♪

An African American composer named Perry Bradford from Atlanta, Georgia, wrote this song. Like W. C. Handy, he was a formally schooled musician and was mesmerized by the richness of the blues-folk tradition. He sourced the blues sounds he heard in the South to create modern compositions for commercial release. This song was recorded by Mamie Smith in 1920 and famously sold more than 75,000 copies in the first month priced a dollar a piece—no small sum in working-class African American communities in the United States at that time. Other songs had been recorded before with the word "blues" in the title, but this recording is widely considered the first blues record. It is the first one recorded by an African American singer, and scholars have noted how hearing a commercial record with someone singing the way people talked in African American communities was a milestone in terms of acknowledgment for African Americans in American society. This commercially released blues recording by Smith proclaimed far and wide the humanity of African Americans as human beings with thoughts and feelings about love just like everyone else.

The lyrics below exemplify AAVE. Chord symbols are shown to help create accompaniment with guitar or piano. Published versions of this song are available, but they don't accurately convey how Mamie Smith actually sang the song in terms of timing of the notes and phrasing, nor do they give the correct harmony. The best way to learn the song is by singing it with the original recording and learning it by ear. Pay particular attention to which vowels are drawn out, indicated in bold print. Notice the bright timbre of her voice and *dialect*. Our discussion on brightness will continue throughout this book.

F
I **can't** sleep at night
I **can't** eat a bite.
C7
'Cause the **man** I love,
F
He **don't** treat me right!
Dmin (quicker)
He makes me feel so blue,

Dmin(+7)
I don't know what to do;
Dmin7
Sometimes I'm sad inside
G7
And then begin to cry,
C
'Cause my best friend
F
Said his **last** goodbye.

F C7
There's a change in the oc**ean**,
F F7
Change in the **deep** blue sea, my baby;
B♭
I tell you folks there,
F
Ain't no **change** in me,
C7 F
My **love** for that **man** will **always** be!

F
Now I got the crazy blues
B♭ F
Since my baby **went** away;
F D7
I ain't got no time to lose,
G7 C7
I must find him today!

F Bo7/F
Now the doctor's gonna do all **that** he can,
B♭6/F
But what you're gonna need
F
Is the undertaker man!
F Dmin F D7
I ain't had nothin' but bad news,

G7 **C7** **F**
Now I got the crazy blues!

F6 (walkup)
Now I can read his letters,
F **F7**
I sure can't read his mind!
B♭
I thought he's lovin' me,
F
He's leavin' **all** the time!
C7 **F**
Now I see my poor love was blind!

F6
I went to the railroad,
F7
Set my head **on** the track,
B♭
Thought about my daddy,
F
I gladly **snatched** it back!
C7
Now my babe's gone
F
And gave **me** the sack!

F **F7**
Now I've got the crazy blues
B♭ **F**
Since my baby went away!
F **D7**
I ain't had no time to lose,
G7 **C7**
I must find him today!
F
I'm gonna do like a Chinaman,
Bo7/F
Go and get some hop,

B♭6/F
Get myself a gun
F
And shoot myself a cop!
F Dmin F D7
I ain't had nothing but bad news,
G7 C7 F
Now I've got the crazy blues!
C+7 F
The blues!

WILL TO ADORN

One of Hurston's characteristics is *will to adorn*. This relates to the idea of embellishment, and a great deal of authenticity is established in blues singing when the singer draws from a well of embellishments established by masters of the genre.

Practice

Let's take the first couple of stanzas of "Crazy Blues." Listen carefully to how Mamie Smith embellishes the melody. Take a pencil and draw a line over words and/or syllables where you hear her do some kind of embellishment (see figure 5.1).

"I can't sleep at night

I can't eat a bite.

'Cause the man I love,

He don't treat me right!"

You probably made a mark on the first two occurrences of "can't." Especially the second one, I hear a scoop up to the pitch. Perhaps indicated like this...

The word "Cause" has a bend in it as well which could be indicated like this...

The last word in the fourth line, "right," has a marvelous, idiomatic blues shape to it like this....

Figure 5.1. Markings in text

As we explore more blues repertoire, we will develop a vocabulary of idiomatic blues embellishments. In this way, we will see how different singers use similar vocabulary to indicate the style and establish authenticity. For singers who are new to singing the blues style, practicing these embellishments along with a recording such as "Crazy Blues" by Mamie Smith is a great way to develop an ear for more embellishments and establish your own storehouse of possibilities. This way, when you approach singing any blues song, you will have ideas to draw from that make you sound authentic in the style—like you belong, not corny or trite.

MA RAINEY (1886–1939)

Gertrude "Ma" Rainey is considered the mother of the blues. Born in the South, based in Chicago, she made 92 sides between 1923 and 1928 and influenced countless blues artists, including Koko Taylor, who said, "I always said I would like to be like these people I'm hearing on these records. . . . What these women did—like Ma Rainey—they was the foundation of the blues. They brought the blues up from slavery up to today."[6] Rainey sang blues on tour as early as 1902 and was a celebrity long before she started recording.[7]

In 1924, Ma Rainey recorded her composition "See See Rider Blues." A young trumpeter from New Orleans named Louis Armstrong accompanied her. In 2004, "See See Rider Blues" was inducted into the Grammy Hall of Fame and in 2018 The Blues Foundation inducted "See See Rider" into the Blues Hall of Fame as a "classic of blues recording."

"See See Rider" is a standard in blues repertoire today and a great song to study for learning to sing the blues. Most people leave out the verse in the beginning and start with the chorus, which starts just before the one-minute mark on the original recording. ♪

Practice

Again, listen carefully to one stanza of the song and pay close attention to which notes she emphasizes in a fuller speech quality and which words she embellishes. You could spend all day with "Law'd, law'd, law'd." Listen to it over and over again and sing it with her. Do your best to embody the feeling. She is not merely singing words to fill in space. She is truly invoking mercy to give comfort to her as the song's protagonist but also to everyone who hears the song. Once again, take a pencil and mark embellishments you hear in the following verse.

> See See Rider, see what you have done. Law'd, law'd, law'd,
> made me love you, now your gal's done come.

Which notes did you mark as embellished? (See figure 5.2.)

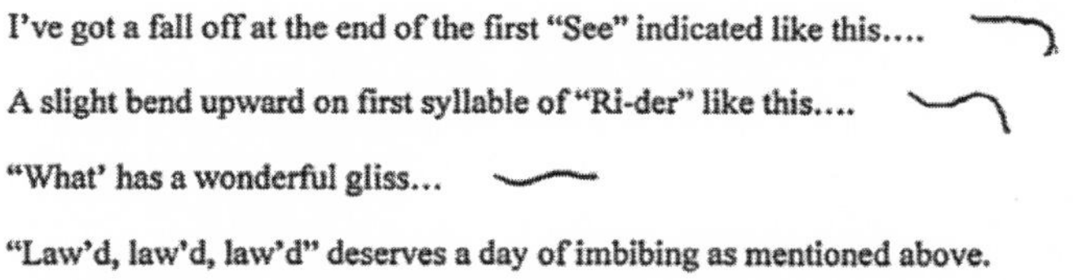

I've got a fall off at the end of the first "See" indicated like this....

A slight bend upward on first syllable of "Ri-der" like this....

"What' has a wonderful gliss...

"Law'd, law'd, law'd" deserves a day of imbibing as mentioned above.

Figure 5.2. Markings in text

Seems to me that the long notes in the next line, "love" and "gal's," are pretty straight. This is important to note because if everything is embellished, the embellishments lose their significance. There needs to be straight notes present for contrast.

The word "made" in the last line is bent and the rest of the line is straight. Happy practicing.

ASYMMETRY (SYNCOPATION)

Zora Neale Hurston names *asymmetry* as another "characteristic of Negro expression" and discusses its presence in African sculpture and carvings as well as in the literature of Langston Hughes and in dancers like Bojangles and Snake Hips. In music, this idea is expressed through the use of syncopation, accenting the unexpected beats. Noted musician and scholar Gunther Schuller observes that Bessie Smith, in particular, breaks up words and melodic patterns in unexpected and often asymmetrical ways through the use of syncopation.[8]

BESSIE SMITH (1894–1937)

Bessie Smith towers above all the blues singers recording in the 1920s. She earned the title of empress of the blues. Not only did she project her entire personality into the music, but she also consistently exhibited phenomenal vocal control in terms of timbre and pitch. She possessed an "extreme sensitivity to word meaning and the sensory, almost physical feeling of a word. Her diction is second to none. She was the first singer to value diction, not for itself, but as a vehicle for conveying emotional states . . . never at the expense of musical flow."[9] Audiences could understand every word. And with her natural, speechlike tone quality, they could easily relate to her and the stories she told in her songs.

Smith started her career as an entertainer at a young age dancing with her brother in the streets of Chattanooga, Tennessee, for change before getting cast in a traveling tent show while still in her teens. These tent shows were places African American women could earn an independent living, and in the process, create enduring art. Ma Rainey starred in the first show that young Bessie traveled with, no doubt inspiring her and possibly acting as her mentor. By the time these women started recording in the 1920s, they had spent years honing their craft in front of audiences and had developed extraordinary abilities to engage people emotionally and intellectually through the sound of their voice and the stories they told.

Leading blues singer and Grammy Award winner Catherine Russell says,

> It's a difficult thing to analyze with your head because it's not Bach. It comes from shout-singing—people sang in very loud places unamplified. So those singers had to get over whatever was going on in the venue. Whether it was a brothel, a bar, people are fighting in the corner, all the things that were going on in the club. They were singing over that. Plus, it does come from field hollers and work songs where the people are working with their bodies so the voice . . . like if you listen to prisoners when they're singing as they work. They are singing in rhythm as they build the railroads. It's a thing that's connected to the body. So, it's not something you *think* so much about. It just comes from how you are feeling at the moment as opposed to something that's written down on paper.

> It's storytelling. So, if you are not connected to the story you are telling, it's very difficult to sing anything and convince yourself or anybody else. So, all of this early blues is storytelling. And people also have to understand your words. So, clarity and diction are important. Bessie Smith's diction was excellent.[10]

"Jailhouse Blues" by Bessie Smith ♪

The story, the sound of your voice, and the importance of diction: keep this in mind as you listen to "Jailhouse Blues" recorded by Bessie Smith in 1923. Notice the embellishment traits that form the essence of her style. Gunther Schuller writes,

> "Thirty days in jail with my back turned to the wall," the importance of the words in the sentence determines the degree of embellishment each receives. Almost every word is emphasized by an upward scoop or slide, but each one differently. The words "thirty," "jail," and "wall"—the three main words of the sentence—are also those most modified by slides. "Thirty" starts with a relatively fast upward slur from approximately E♭ to G♭. "Days" slides more slowly from the blue flat third to the major third, G♮. The next word, "in," is a slightly flat G, in preparation for a large major-third upward scoop on "jail": the most important word, ergo the strongest embellishment.[11]

Catherine Russell emphasizes the need for an open throat; a full, deep breath at the beginning of phrases for support; and a strong connection to the entire body from head to toe to make this sound effectively. She likens it to the physical demands of singing in an operatic style:

> Bessie Smith doesn't use much embellishment in her singing. She uses the words and a strong chest dominant voice from the beginning right through to the end of the note. The energy in the note does not diminish. This is the similarity with opera technique. The two styles of singing are similar in the intensity of vocal production for the full length of the note, use of vibrato and intention of storytelling. The opera "Porgy and Bess," although written by the Gershwins, is a good example of blending classical, the Spiritual "style" and the blues.[12]

Speaking of opera, none other than Louis Armstrong spoke of hearing opera growing up in New Orleans. He proudly announced to historian Phil Schaap that "I had *records*," including the great turn-of-the-century tenor Enrico Caruso.

Bessie Smith recorded with Louis Armstrong on many occasions, and one of their most famous collaborations is the 1925 recording of "Saint Louis Blues" published by W. C. Handy in 1914 and inducted into the Grammy Hall of Fame in 1993.

"Saint Louis Blues" by W. C. Handy (1914) sung by Bessie Smith ♪

Origins The composer of "Saint Louis Blues" is W. C. Handy. Born in Alabama, he received a formal Western-style music education including sight singing and classical theory. In the black church, he loved baptismal and burial hymns that were typically accompanied by vocalized moans and chanted prayers.[13] This hybrid musical background gave him the ideal skill set to integrate the folk forms of the blues he heard as a musician traveling throughout the South with formal structures that he knew Western-trained musicians could relate to. And so, with an early hit in 1912 that he wrote, "The Memphis Blues," Handy set out to write his masterpiece in 1914. He actually rented an apartment away from his growing family in downtown Memphis to focus his attention on creating what would become one of the biggest blues hits of all time, "Saint Louis Blues."

Story This song is a prime example of the importance of *story*telling in the blues. Handy writes,

> A flood of memories filled my mind. First, there was the picture I had of myself, broke, unshaven, wanting even a decent meal, and standing before the lighted saloon in St. Louis without a shirt under my frayed coat. There was also from that same period a curious and dramatic little fragment that till now had seemed to have little or no importance. While occupied with my own miseries during that sojourn, I had seen a woman whose pain seemed even greater. She had tried to take the edge off her grief by heavy drinking, but it hadn't worked. Stumbling along the poorly lighted street, she muttered as she walked, "Ma man's got a heart like a rock cast in de sea."

> The expression interested me, and I stopped another woman to inquire what she meant. She replied, "Lawd, man, it's hard and gone so far from her she can't reach it." Her language was the same down-home medium that conveyed the laughable woe of lamp-blacked lovers in hundreds of frothy songs, but her plight was much too real to provoke much laughter. My song was taking shape. I had now settled upon the mood.[14]

Melody In chapter 1 on the origins of the blues, we discussed the strong connection between spirituals and the blues, and Handy points to this in his reference to the melody of "Saint Louis Blues" when he says, "My aim would be to combine ragtime sophistication with a real melody in the spiritual tradition."[15]

Form This song has three distinct sections, and as such, it is a great piece to learn about both the most common blues form of 12 bars as well as other forms and movements in blues.

A Section You can see hear the AAB lyric format of repeating the first line and then answering it in the second. Notice how the AAVE is transliterated in the originally published lyric:

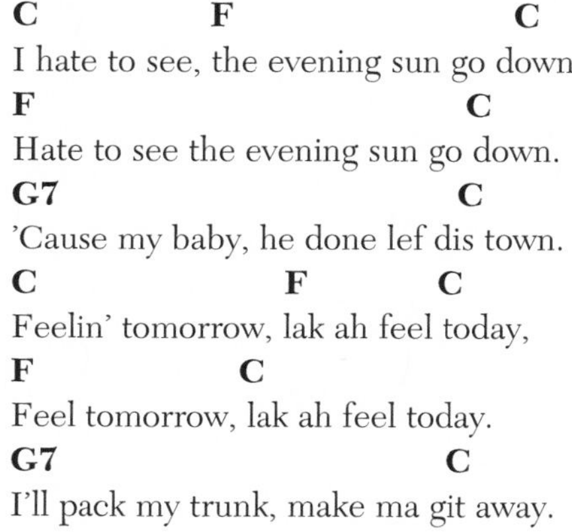

C F C
I hate to see, the evening sun go down.
F C
Hate to see the evening sun go down.
G7 C
'Cause my baby, he done lef dis town.
C F C
Feelin' tomorrow, lak ah feel today,
F C
Feel tomorrow, lak ah feel today.
G7 C
I'll pack my trunk, make ma git away.

B Section In this section, a habanera rhythm is employed for a brilliant contrast with the swing of the A section. Handy credits the dancers he had played for in Dixie Park, Memphis, as "convincing him that there was something racial in their response to this rhythm. . . . Indeed, the very word 'tango,' as I now know, was derived from the African 'tangana,' and signified this same tom-tom beat."[16] Handy had actually traveled to Cuba many years prior to composing this song and, like other

American composers, embraced the rhythms he heard. This section is 16 bars long and introduces the character of "Saint Louis Woman" as the source of the problem that the protagonist of the song is up against. The harmony shifts from major to minor:

Cmin **G7**
St. Louis woman, wid her diamon' rings,
Cmin
Pulls dat man roun' by her apron strings.
Cmin **G7**
Twant for powder, an' for store-bought hair,
Cmin **G7**
De man ah love would not gone nowhere, no where.

C Section This section returns to a 12-bar form in the major mode but does not employ the typical AAB lyric format often used. Instead, the narrative is brilliantly continued within the 12-bar structure:

C7
Got de St. Louis Blues jes as blue as ah can be,
F7 **C7**
Dat man got a heart lak a rock cast in the sea,
G7 **F** **C**
Or else he wouldn't have gone so far from me

Further Comments about the Composition This song succeeds on so many levels. The published lyrics embrace AAVE to poetically reveal a story that contains anguish and release with many engaging images along the way. The use of the 12-bar form in the A and C sections gives the composition unity. However, the varied structure of lyrics (abc) in the C section makes for an appealing contrast. The middle section, with its shift to the minor mode habanera beat and extended 16-bar form, provides an extra level of intrigue compositionally and well serves the narrative.

Handy packs so much blues information into this composition! It is the perfect format for any student of the blues to study, imbibe, and share with others. Now let's reflect on how American masters Bessie Smith and Louis Armstrong interpret the song.

Bessie Smith's Performance of "Saint Louis Blues" with Louis Armstrong on Trumpet The first thing you notice is Bessie's powerful voice. As Catherine Russell points out, "Open throat, full breath." She also uses a good amount of vibrato in this performance. Her diction, as always, is crystal clear, and you can feel her telling you the *story* of the song as if it were written for her. She is singing with complete commitment to the lyric as her personal experience. Unlike other songs we have examined, she does not embellish many notes here. Maybe that's because Louis Armstrong is providing all the embellishment needed!

DRAMA

Although the movie is completely fiction, the 2015 HBO Film *Bessie*, with Queen Latifah as Bessie Smith, offers some precious moments imagining how early blues women may have interacted with each other and the world around them as well as the magic of their music. There is a scene where Ma Rainey advises young Bessie Smith, "The blues is not about people knowing you. It's about you knowing people." And here is where *drama* begins.

"Backwater Blues" by Bessie Smith ♪

This sentiment is masterfully reflected in Bessie Smith's composition "Backwater Blues," recorded in 1927. Although initially inspired by an earlier flood, this song became emblematic for victims of the historic Great Mississippi Flood of 1927, which displaced hundreds of thousands of southerners from their homes, mostly African American. Bessie's delivery and the words she wrote spoke directly to their hearts and helped them cope with the emotional devastation of this disaster of epic proportions.

Form The form is a standard 12-bar structure with AAB "lyric" structure, meaning that the first line of each verse is repeated and then answered by the third line.

Practice Notice the rhythmic drive in Bessie's delivery and how she works with and against the masterful piano accompaniment of

James P. Johnson. Through repeated listenings, learn to sing the lyrics exactly with Bessie to get a sense of her timing.

You will also see clearly that each time she repeats the first line of the lyric, she changes it by emphasizing and/or drawing out a different word so that the listener can go deeper with her into the story of the song. This is further demonstration of asymmetry, described earlier as one of Zora Neale Hurston's characteristics of Negro expression.

Verse 5 of "Backwater Blues"

Then I **went** and stood upon some high old lonesome hill.
Then **I** went and stood upon some high old lonesome hill.
I looked down on the house where I used to live.

REVIEW

In this chapter, we have identified basic parameters of blues singing and introduced Zora Neale Hurston's characteristics of Negro expression as a framework for understanding. We explored how Bessie Smith delivers *drama* through her original song "Backwater Blues." Mamie Smith demonstrated *will to adorn* and helped us develop our storehouse of blues embellishments. Bessie Smith, Mamie Smith, and Ma Rainey exemplified use of African American *dialect*, and composer W. C. Handy well demonstrated this dialect in the way he composed lyrics for his classic blues composition "Saint Louis Blues." We also saw how Bessie Smith uses diction and phrasing to demonstrate *asymmetry*.

In this chapter, we began a discussion of blues form by introducing the most common 12-bar form using "aab" lyric structure as demonstrated in Bessie Smith's "Backwater Blues." We also discussed some common variations on the form, such as the 16-bar B section of "Saint Louis Blues" and an alternate lyric structure for the 12-bar blues that uses three different lines of lyrics "abc," such as the C section of "Saint Louis Blues" and some of the verses of "See See Rider" by Ma Rainey.

Many resources on the blues overemphasize the form as the essential defining characteristic of the idiom. This book makes the case that *the blues is defined by the sound of the singer*. Even when the blues is played instrumentally, its authenticity is gauged by how well the musician embodies the vocal qualities of the blues through his or her instrument.

Our effort in *So You Want to Sing the Blues* is to provide as many resources as possible for the modern singer to embody the spirit of the blues by expanding his or her knowledge of vocal tools for the blues, including timbre, rhythm, phrasing, embellishment, diction, and emphasizing the power of story.

For all her accomplishments singing early blues styles in modern times, Catherine Russell speaks in reverent tones about an out-of-print book she got from her mother called *African-American Spirituals* by Hansonia Caldwell and how much she learned from it. She cites "Swing Low, Sweet Chariot" as a good bridge between classical and the blues. Russell actually started out singing in classical-style choirs and got interested in the blues later because that is where she found the most work opportunities. Satisfying commercial demand has been a driving force of the blues since its beginnings, and the blues have provided a good living for many artists who apply themselves to it.

There are many other blues women of note and heaps of wonderful songs with poignant stories, double entendre, and all kinds of entertaining twists and turns. Sippie Wallace, Trixie Smith, Clara Smith, Victoria Spivey, Alberta Hunter, and Lil Green are a few more for you to check out. We are fortunate to live in a time when so many of these records can be heard by the simple click of the mouse. Some of the sheet music is available, but the more you learn by ear, the better.

NOTES

1. Angela Davis, *Blues Legacies and Black Feminism* (New York: Random House, 1998), 33.
2. W. C. Handy, *Father of the Blues: An Autobiography* (New York: Da Capo, 1941),74.
3. Zora Neale Hurston, "Characteristics of Negro Expression," 1933; Robert O'Meally, *The Jazz Cadence of American Culture* (New York: Columbia University Press, 1998), 298.
4. Isabel Wilkerson, *The Warmth of Other Suns* (New York: Vintage, 2010).
5. Geoffrey K. Pullum, "African-American Vernacular English Is Not Standard English with Mistakes," in *The Workings of Language*, ed. Rebecca S. Wheeler (Westport, CT: Praeger, 1999), 45.
6. *Wild Women Don't Have the Blues* (videocassette).

7. Eileen Southern, *The Music of Black Americans: A History* (New York: Norton, 1997), 372.

8. Gunther Schuller, *Early Jazz, Its Roots and Musical Development* (New York: Oxford University Press, 1968), 233.

9. Schuller, Early *Jazz, Its Roots and Musical Development*, 229.

10. Catherine Russell, interview with the author, 2016.

11. Schuller's essay in Chris Albertson and Gunther Schuller, *Bessie Smith: Empress of the Blues* (New York: Schirmer, 1975), 29.

12. Catherine Russell, interview by the author, 2016.

13. William Ferris, *W. C. Handy's Blues—An Anthology* (Jackson: University of Mississippi Press, 1990).

14. W. C. Handy, *Father of the Blues: An Autobiography* (New York: Da Capo, 1941), 119.

15. Handy, *Father of the Blues*, 120.

16. Handy, *Father of the Blues*, 97.

6

DEVELOPING AUTHENTIC STYLE CHARACTERISTICS

Early Blues Men and Another Woman

As much as the blues can be about everyday life, the blues helps us transcend it. Much has been made about the blues and the supernatural. These myths persist because the blues offers a sense of renewal. The feeling is so strong that it's easy to see why many people attribute it to being beyond human power. Let the wonder continue but let us not forget that the great early blues women and men were hardworking artists who constantly cultivated and refined their ability to connect with, entertain, and heal the audiences they came into contact with. They did this through drawing on great traditions and practices of the past and adapting and innovating to keep current with a demanding public for whom the blues was a lifeline. In this way, so-called Negro folklore was not just some old-fashioned, irrelevant thing but something real and present—still in the making and demonstrating the great adaptability of African Americans. Zora Neale Hurston writes,

> Nothing is too old or too new, domestic or foreign, high or low, for his use. God and the Devil are paired and are treated no more reverently than Rockefeller and Ford. . . . The Angel and the apostles walk and talk like section hands. And through it all walks Jack, the greatest culture hero of the South; Jack beats them all—even the Devil, who is often smarter than God.[1]

ROBERT JOHNSON (1911–1938)

Today, the most famous of the Delta blues singers is Robert Johnson, crowned king of the Delta blues several decades after his death. Championed by rock stars like Keith Richards and Eric Clapton in the 1960s, Johnson is rightly admired for brilliantly connecting the dots of Mississippi Delta blues, weaving folk/country elements that he learned in person from observing elder masters like Son House with virtuoso/city music traditions that he picked up from hit records by Leroy Carr, Lonnie Johnson (no relation), Tampa Red, Kokomo Arnold, and Peetie Wheatstraw.

Robert Johnson also carries a mystique because of his somewhat mysterious death at the young age of twenty-seven and some of the lyrics of his songs dealing with the Devil. Like Zora Neale Hurston says, "Negro folklore is not a thing of the past. It is still in the making." These elements are part of Johnson's artistry as they are for other great artists of the period, such as Skip James ("Devil Got My Woman"), Charley Patton ("Devil Sent the Rain"), and Peetie Wheatstraw ("Devil's Son-in-Law").

Let's look at some of Robert Johnson's tunes and, like the great trumpeter Clark Terry says, *imitate* so that we can assimilate some of his wide early blues palette. We follow this with a sample of some of the artists who influenced him, such as Blind Lemon Jefferson and Leroy Carr, and then close the chapter with a look at some of his peers who outlived him, namely, Memphis Minnie and Big Bill Broonzy, who continued to perform and record for decades after Johnson's death.

"Come On in My Kitchen" sung by Robert Johnson ♪

Robert Johnson's "Come On in My Kitchen" captures a lot of the magic of early blues. Musician and author Elijah Wald writes,

> There is only one other player in early blues who recorded anything this moodily soulful, the sort of music that sounds as if the singer is somewhere off alone, absorbing all the world's sorrows and transforming them into a perfectly formed, deeply personal gem of poetic wisdom. That was Skip James, and it is no surprise that the first full verse Johnson sings is taken from James's masterpiece, "Devil Got My Woman": "The woman I love, stole her from my best friend / But he got lucky, stole her back

again." The two songs have nothing else in common, as far as words and melody go, but that one couplet alerts us to a kinship that gave Johnson the most moving, spiritual—I want to say unearthly, except that is also desperately human—strain in his music.[2]

There are two takes of this song recorded by Johnson, and we are focusing on the first take, issued by Columbia Records on "King of the Delta Blues Singers" in 1961.

Analysis After the plaintive guitar introduction, Johnson establishes a steady beat of quarter-note chords on the guitar. He begins the vocal with a hum, and imbibing the sound of this hum is one of the most direct ways to bring the soul of the blues into your body. Listen again and again and sing along. Experiment with the timbre of your voice. What kind of tone color can you get? How many hums have you got? You can hear that Robert Johnson has a least two: one that is reserved—internal—and one that is bright—nearly brassy. Changes in timbre are key in blues singing, and you want to develop a wide variety of choices to sound authentic. Notice Johnson's phrasing of the hum. Where does he get louder and softer? Where does he vary the pitch and add vibrato? You will find every possible musical variation in his work and that's what makes it so enduring. Every time you listen, you can find something new both in his voice and in his guitar.

From the hum emerges the lyric:

Mmm-mmm-mmm-mmm-mmm-mmm-mmm-mmm-mmm-mmm
Mmm-mmm-mmm-mmm-mmm-mmm-mmm-mmm-mmm-mmm

You better come on in my kitchen . . .

[Notice how he sits this lyric inside the steady beat of the guitar.]

well, it's goin' to be rainin' outdoors

["Well" is a bit raspy, and the other words are clear and dead-on pitchwise.]

Iconic American composer and bandleader Duke Ellington explains that syncopation—accenting the "off" beats—is effective only when the downbeat is strong. The same is true for pitch variation when singing the blues. If every pitch is wavy, then the pitch-varied notes won't be as meaningful. This performance by Robert Johnson well demonstrates his ability to hit pitches dead-on when he wants to and make slides and bends of the pitch for contrast.

This is illustrated in the second verse by the way he sings the words *lucky* and *back*:

Ah, the woman I love, took from my best friend
Some joker got **lucky**, stole her **back** again
You better come on in my kitchen . . .

Notice how he bends the pitches. It sounds like what he's doing on the guitar with his lead lines too. It is interesting to note how the guitar imitates the voice and vice versa. Even if you don't play guitar, you can think of the guitar as you refine your ability to sing the blues. Along the lines of pitch bends, when the left hand on the guitar fretboard bends a string, the pitch bends. When this is released, the pitch goes back to the originally tuned note. This is what you want to cultivate in your singing. Be able to bend a note for emphasis and then return to the original pitch. You always need to be able to go home.

"Come On in My Kitchen" is a great song to learn because it carries so much beauty in its compact 8-bar form. We will see this form again later in Leroy Carr's "How Long—How Long Blues?" "Come On in My Kitchen" also reminds me of the 8-bar form standard "Sittin' on Top of This World" first recorded by the Mississippi Sheiks in 1930. It is no secret that blues musicians borrow musical information from each other. This can be verses of lyrics, melodic fragments, or whole tunes reappropriated with new names and/or personal flourishes. It is the new combination of variations that each individual brings to the song and his or her interpretation that makes it stand out. And, of course, serving your audience and making them feel good or release some kind of strong emotion is the primary goal.

Speaking of his friend Robert Johnson, whom he traveled and played with, musician Johnny Shines recalled,

> His guitar seemed to talk—repeat and say words with him like no one else in the world could. . . . One time in St. Louis we were playing one of the songs that Robert would like to play with someone once in a great while,

> "Come On in My Kitchen." He was playing very slow and passionately, and when we had quit, I noticed no one was saying anything. Then I realized they were crying—both women and men.[3]

MISSISSIPPI DELTA AND THE JOOK

The Mississippi Delta produced some of the most influential blues musicians of all time, including Son House, Robert Johnson, and Muddy Waters. The Delta was and is a particularly fertile area in northwestern Mississippi. You can still see acres and acres of cotton growing there. After the Civil War, many black families gravitated to the Delta for farming opportunities. Some worked on plantations, like the famous Dockery Farm in Cleveland, Mississippi, where early Delta blues man Charley Patton used to play, inspiring countless musicians to follow him. Even though African Americans were free from slavery, life continued to present tremendous challenges, as harsh racial discrimination was the rule rather than the exception. Farming was hard enough, but then, adding to that the burden of ridiculously unfair sharecropping arrangements with landlords and herculean obstacles for black people to own land, to quote a classic blues song, if "they call it stormy Monday" (slavery), you better believe that "Tuesday" (sharecropping) "is just as bad."

As it had during slavery, music played a critical role in helping African Americans survive the challenges they faced. Black communities of the Delta depended on music and strongly supported talented musicians who emerged in their midst. Working people bought records by artists who reflected their culture and story in song, and they went to *jook* joints and other gathering places to hear music live whenever possible and to dance. Zora Neale Hurston explains,

> Jook is the word for a Negro pleasure house. It may mean a bawdy house. It may mean the house set apart on public works where the men and women dance, drink and gamble. Often it is a combination of all these. . . . Musically speaking, the Jook is the most important place in America. For in its smelly, shoddy confines has been born the secular music known as blues, and on blues has been founded jazz. The singing and playing in the true Negro style is called "jooking."[4]

When country blues singers like Robert Johnson would play the *jook*, they would typically play one tune for fifteen minutes or so while people danced, mixing and matching verses as the particular time called for. They might make up some verses to go with verses they had made up before or learned from other people. The main thing was to keep the groove going so that the party never stopped. Naturally, having a variety of vocal styles and capabilities to support this kind of entertaining would be an asset. Robert Johnson's recordings, though honed down to the three minutes available at the time for a single side of a record, offer a stunning example of variety both instrumentally and vocally.

"Walkin' Blues" by Robert Johnson ♪

Robert Johnson learned "Walkin' Blues" directly from his mentor Son House. Elijah Wald explains,

> Johnson's debt to House is clear in his vocal approach, which is rougher and stronger than on his more commercial sides. . . . He did not have House's awesome power as a singer. . . . He mixes a conversational flavor with the Delta growl, and adds some well-placed falsetto.[5]

This song became a theme for Delta blues men clear into the late 1970s, when Sunnyland Slim opened his show at Morgen's Liquors at 61st and Calumet on the South Side of the Chicago, but more on that later.[6]

Robert Johnson idolized Son House in his youth, coming to hear him play regularly before he could gather any kind of respect as a musician himself.[7] He deeply absorbed House's approach so that after an extended period of practicing and imbibing the lessons he learned from House, Johnson emerged being able to pay a strong tribute to his mentor with several songs he learned from him.

If you compare Son House's 1930 recording of "Walking Blues" ♪ with Robert Johnson's from 1937, you will hear similarities as well as significant differences. Take the opening line, "I woke up this morning." In the key of B major, Son House begins the melody of the fifth (F♯) and descends E, D (using minor third), to the root (B). This is a good example of how blues melodies use the minor third over a major third in the chord. This dissonance is part of what makes the blues sound. In

Robert Johnson's version, however, the melody of the first line is quite different and much more difficult to imitate. He starts the melody on the root (B), hits the third (D♯) ascending to the higher octave (B), then down to the minor third (D) with a bend up through the fourth (E) and flat fifth (F) and back down those notes, landing on the root (B). It can make you jump out of your seat if you really learn it. And where the heck did he come up with that?

It reminds me of the East Asian Indian tradition of learning a raga from a guru (teacher). In short, a raga is a particular sequence of pitches ascending and descending designed to evoke a particular mood. Certain musical phrases are closely identified with the raga and used in a spontaneous, improvisatory fashion by the performer. The traditional mode of studying this music dictates that you spend a great deal of time, as much as an entire year, learning one raga from your guru, playing call-and-response and mastering idiomatic phrases in order to imbibe the spirit of the raga into the fabric of your being. Once you have taken the time to do this thoroughly, the raga literally lives in your being and is free to come out in unexpected ways. Perhaps this is what Robert Johnson did in some sense with Son House. We can never know for sure. But the truth of the matter is that Johnson's opening melody of "Walkin' Blues" is a challenge to learn to sing and well worth the effort.

After the opening line, Johnson settles into a nasal timbre. If you have been singing mostly classical music, this sound will be quite new. It can be achieved without straining by activating the muscles in the face. Use the syllable "aah" as in "cat" and create some exercises to activate these muscles. Then start to add the words "feel round for my shoes."

When Johnson gets to "old walkin' blues," he adds what some folks call the "Delta growl." It's a raspy sound and can be challenging to achieve without tightening the throat but can be done relatively easefully with practice engaging mode 1, the fry register. Many singers lost and lose their voices trying these techniques. You have to find a way to sing these styles easefully if you are a professional singer or at least someone who can count on their voice to work well day after day. Fortunately, the artists we have on record found their way to easeful singing. Otherwise, they would never have been able to keep up with the amount of singing they needed to do to make a living. This is particularly true in the 1930s, when most of the jobs did not provide a microphone.

Imagine singing for many hours in a jook joint for people dancing and carrying on without a mic. You better believe the singers who survived figured out how to use their voices efficiently to make the sounds they wanted to make in the Delta. And you can too!

As much of a genius as he was, Robert Johnson was not a major influence in the development of black singing in his time. His influence came decades after his death. As a matter of fact, the twenty-nine sides he recorded in 1936 and 1937 remained in relative obscurity until the 1960s and beyond. There were others who made multiple hit records in the late 1920s and 1930s and were widely known in the black community. These singers establish the lineage of blues singing through this period. Let's check some of them out.

BLIND LEMON JEFFERSON (1893–1929)

Blind Lemon Jefferson made more than one hundred sides in the 1920s, struck a new mold for a modern recording artist with his voice and guitar, and became widely known. He started performing on the street in his native Texas and drew such large crowds that he was invited to record in Chicago for Paramount Records. As a blind or partially blind man, he made a good living as a professional musician and influenced a generation of blues artists.

As one of the earliest male blues guitar/singer stars, you can hear the field holler roots of the blues in Blind Lemon Jefferson's vocal style. Mississippi Delta blues man Honeyboy Edwards put it like this:

> When the people were slaves, they'd holler 'cause it make the day go 'long and they wouldn't worry about what they were doing, and that's what the blues come from. Then in the twenties, like, they named it the blues, with Mama Rainey and all, Ida Cox, Bessie Smith, Blind Lemon Jefferson, Lonnie Johnson.[8]

In addition to the field hollers, Blind Lemon drew from the popular women vocalists who preceded him. In 1926, singer, pianist, and songwriter Victoria Spivey initiated a tradition of songs evoking a black snake. She recorded "Black Snake Blues," and Blind Lemon Jefferson recorded his "Black Snake Moan" shortly after.

"Black Snake Blues" sung by Victoria Spivey ♪

In addition to evoking the image of the black snake, there are melodic similarities between the two songs with Jefferson clearly borrowing material from Spivey. "Black Snake Moan" by Jefferson uses a moan to great effect. Listen to the first and second verses and see if you can emulate his moan. ♪

"Black Snake Moan" sung by Blind Lemon Jefferson ♪

I, I ain't got no mama now (×2)
. . . Mm, mm, black snake crawlin' in my room (×2)
. . . Ohh, oh, that must have been a bed bug
you know a chinch can't bite that hard

What did you discover? I find that each verse has a different moan tone color based on the words "I," "Mmm," and "Oh." You can make a warm-up out of it. Take each syllable and do a bend. Have fun with this:

I
Mm
Oh

LEROY CARR (1905–1935)

Blues vocalists of the 1920s and 1930s were stylistic pioneers in many respects. In addition to the bends, moans, drawn-out notes, and expanding the palette of the timbre of the voice, great strides were made using the availability of a microphone to sing in a more intimate style. Leroy Carr was the leader of the pack in this regard and was possibly the most influential male blues singer and songwriter of the first half of the twentieth century. He was nothing like today's common stereotype of the early blues man. Elijah Wald explains,

> An understated pianist with a gentle, expressive voice, he was known for his natty suits and lived most of his life in Indianapolis. His first record, "How Long—How Long Blues," in 1928, had an effect as revolutionary

> as Bing Crosby's pop crooning, and for similar reasons. Previous blues stars, whether vaudevillians like Bessie Smith or street singers like Blind Lemon Jefferson, had needed huge voices to project their music, but with the help of new microphone and recording technologies, Carr sounded like a cool city dude carrying on a conversation with a few close friends.[9]

I have always known Leroy Carr as a songwriter and love to perform his classic "How Long—How Long Blues."

"How Long Blues" sung by Leroy Carr ♪ / "How Long Blues" sung by Jimmy Rushing with Count Basie ♪

I learned the song from the Count Basie recording featuring vocalist Jimmy Rushing. When researching this book, I discovered just what a tremendous influence Leroy Carr was for all the male blues singers following him. When you listen to his recordings, you can hear how everyone from Robert Johnson to Charles Brown to B.B. King and Ray Charles drew from the well of Carr. For an interesting comparison, check out Carr's original recording of "How Long Blues" and Jimmy Rushing's interpretation with Count Basie.

"When the Sun Goes Down" sung by Leroy Carr ♪

One of Leroy Carr's most famous tunes is "When the Sun Goes Down." Carr's original recording of the song presents the poetic lyric in his intimate, one-to-one kind of style. It's like talking to a friend. And you can approach singing the blues this way. Musically, the main thing you have to deal with is fitting the lyrics in a flowing way into the steady quarter note played, in this case, by the piano. One way to practice this is by keeping a steady beat with your hand in your lap and saying the lyrics in rhythm until you can get them to fit comfortably. Do not underestimate the challenge of this exercise. On first listen, you might think Carr is placing the words in an arbitrary manner, virtually speaking them and letting the rhythms fall where they will. In fact, on close listening and imitating, you will find there are specific rhythmic details that, when mastered, enhance the sense of the "intoxicating" effect of the music. What we are

Figure 6.1. "When the Sun Goes Down," verse 1 transcription. *Transcribed by Eli Yamin*

talking about is music with a heightened sense of mastery of the art of syncopation. Composer Scott Joplin said in his treatise on ragtime, "Most pianists have discovered syncopations are no indication of light or trashy music, and to shy bricks at 'hateful ragtime' no longer passes for musical culture. To assist amateur players in giving the 'Joplin Rags' that weird and intoxicating effect intended by the composer is the object of this work."[10] I would maintain, as for Joplin twenty to thirty years before, so it is for songwriter Leroy Carr. The intoxicating effects of syncopation are baked into his songs in such an effortless way that you may not realize how much art is there. Check it out (see figure 6.1).

Pitchwise, this melody is very circumscribed. The brilliance of the composition is how Carr uses limited pitches and rhythm to create musical interest and story. It's worth noting how this blues melody *does not use a blues scale*. Sadly, the blues scale is overtaught in blues curricula today. Understanding rhythm and timbre is more important to authentic performance, as we can see in Leroy Carr's performance of his classic composition.

Notice how the melody begins on beat 4 before the downbeat and the eighth notes are swung. In measures 3 and 4, we see a great example of polyrhythm where you have the steady 4/4 in the left hand of the piano and the use of eighth-note and quarter-note triplets in the melody. Bar 6 adds the duple rhythm of sixteenth notes immediately followed by another quarter-note triplet. Being able to effortlessly switch between duple and triple rhythms in a variety of configurations is one of the secrets of sounding authentic as a blues and jazz singer. It is one of the essential ingredients of African American music and noted in Zora Neale Hurston's work as "asymmetry." Bar 9 begins with two eighth notes followed by an eighth-note triplet with four sixteenths inside of it. The rhythmic variety is quite striking if you really deal with it—a far cry from monotonous eighth-note melodies and improvisations common today.

As twenty-first-century musicians, we are fortunate to have tremendous technology at our fingertips and piles of books on improvisation. In some ways, these tools hamper us from connecting with the idiosyncratic, asymmetrical aspects of American music. Spending time with these blues recordings and learning to sing along with them, if only in bits and pieces, has the potential to revolutionize your capacity as a musician. You will be more flexible, free, expressive, and honest. This is one of the gifts the blues keeps giving.

The fourth verse consists of nonsense syllables and is another opportunity to create some fun blues-imbibing exercises. Notice how Carr switches from head/falsetto to chest and back so effortlessly. Using falsetto is common among blues men and allows them to extend their expressive range and keep their instrument balanced all at once. I wonder if it is also in some way a nod to the great blues women who pioneered the art of blues singing in the 1920s.

MEMPHIS MINNIE (1897–1973)

Memphis Minnie started recording in 1929 but was performing the blues back in 1915. She would spit tobacco wearing a chiffon gown and always defied expectations as far as women musicians were concerned. An exceptional guitarist from Mississippi, she performed in

Figure 6.2. "When the Sun Goes Down," verse 4 transcription. *Transcribed by Eli Yamin*

Memphis and later Chicago, where she had a significant influence on a generation of musicians. Her guitar style was widely imitated, and she recorded two hundred songs performing steadily through the 1930s and 1940s. The iconic poet Langston Hughes wrote about her performance in Chicago at the tail end of 1942:

> Midnight. The electric guitar is very loud, science having magnified all its softness away. Memphis Minnie sings through a microphone and her voice—hard and strong anyhow for a little woman's—is made harder and stronger by scientific sound. The singing, the electric guitar, and the drums are so hard and so loud, amplified as they are by General Electric on top of the icebox, that sometimes the voice, the words, and melody get lost under sheer noise, leaving only the rhythm to come through clear. The rhythm fills the 230 Club with a deep and dusky heartbeat that overrides all modern amplification. The rhythm is as old as Minnie's most remote ancestor.[11]

Her voice is powerful and modern, and listening to her song "If You See My Rooster, Please Run Him on Back Home," you could imagine her tearing up the rhythm-and-blues charts today.

"If You See My Rooster, Please Run Him on Back Home" sung by Memphis Minnie ♪

E♭
If you see my rooster
E♭7+9
Please run him on back home [guitar riffs]
A♭7
If you see my rooster
E♭7+9
Please run him on back home [guitar riffs]
B♭7 A♭7
I haven't found no eggs in my basket, weeee—
E♭ B♭ E♭
Since my rooster been gone

Analysis Notice the steady beat that is the foundation of this song. You won't be able to sing the syncopations and achieve the polyrhythmic feel of the melody without it. On this recording, the steady beat is achieved through the solid combination of guitar by Memphis Minnie and piano by Black Bob. This guitar/piano combination was popular in blues of the 1920s and 1930s. Other famous duos include Leroy Carr and Scrapper Blackwell as well as Tampa Red and Georgia Tom. On this Memphis Minnie recording from 1936, in addition to guitar and piano, there is also some kind of percussion going on emphasizing beats 2 and 4. This could be someone's foot or an actually designated percussionist.

Form This is a standard 12-bar blues form for AAB lyric structure.

The Melody and Voice Sounding easy and straightforward, close examination of the melody will reveal that Minnie is effortlessly singing two octaves and brilliantly rendering thirds multiple ways. In addition to presenting the major and minor third, she masterfully employs the African melodic concept of "flexible pitch areas." Some of the phrases use a lowered third in the higher octave with the raised third in the lower octave. Notice where she slides the pitches and the use of head voice as well as powerful chest. This is the kind of flexibility most of the great blues singers aspire to, and it's a good way to keep your instrument balanced as well as give yourself great melodic opportunities. The melody is based on a minor pentatonic scale of 1, ♭3, 4, 5, ♭7 with the variations of the third mentioned above. When the chords move to the IV dominant seventh, the third of the melody is flatted on top but raised on the bottom, a fascinating and enduring way of presenting blues melody that gives emotional clarity and ambiguity simultaneously. This is part of what makes the blues so modern. It has devices built into it that are simultaneously clear and obscure, offering the artist myriad options in expressing the complicated feelings of modern life.

The lyric seems playful enough. "If you see my rooster, please send him back on home." And in life, sometimes you just have to laugh to keep from crying. In fact, Minnie is talking about her lover, perhaps husband, who has been running around with other women, an ideal and often-drawn-on subject for the blues.

Led Zeppelin demonstrated their awareness of Memphis Minnie when they recorded her song "When the Levee Breaks" in 1971, just a couple years before she passed away. It's striking how much it does not sound like Minnie's recording, and this is testimony to the creativity of interpretation. However, a strong case can be made that hard-rock singers like Robert Plant and Ozzy Osbourne were in fact greatly influenced by powerful black women singers like Memphis Minnie and later Aretha Franklin and Tina Turner.[12]

BIG BILL BROONZY (1893–1958)

By his own account, Big Bill Broonzy famously lost a blues contest to Memphis Minnie in Chicago in 1933. In the best spirit of competition, Minnie and Broonzy became friends and collaborators, performing together throughout the years.

Big Bill Broonzy is one of the most prolifically recorded blues men from Mississippi. He was introduced to the New York folk and jazz crowd at the famous Carnegie Hall Concert of 1936 "From Spirituals to Swing" produced by John Hammond. Robert Johnson couldn't be found, so they got Big Bill to fit the bill. Although he had had extensive experience as a recording artist in Chicago prior to the concert, he readily stepped into the role of country legend and brought his artistry to millions of homes through his recordings and live performances over the years. He wrote his own songs while championing others, and, as demonstrated above, he did not overlook the importance and accomplishments of women blues artists as many others have.

I find his recording of Bessie Smith's "Backwater Blues" interesting to compare to the original.

"Backwater Blues" sung by Big Bill Broonzy ♪/ "Backwater Blues" sung by Bessie Smith ♪

There are several ways in which Broonzy modernizes the song. In fact, Broonzy's performance, recorded in 1951, sounds like it could easily have been performed last week, whereas Bessie's style is harder to conjure today.

Bessie Smith's original recording has seven verses, and Broonzy's remake has a tight four. Broonzy draws out syllables like "yes," "Lord," "up," and "aw." He adds personalized comments like "yes" and "Lord" and "I declare" in various places. He adds what I will call here a *whoa-back*, a vocal inflection that signifies blues immediately with a quick sforzando reach up to the minor third, fifth, and/or octave above the melody note. We hear the same effect when Robert Johnson sings "Some joker got lucky, stole her back again" in "Come On in My Kitchen." In Broonzy's "Backwater Blues," you can hear this whoa-back effect on the words "rained" and "in" in the first verse; "high," "went," and "high" in the third verse; and "thundered" in the fourth verse.

Broonzy further modernizes the song by using a wider range of dynamics in his vocal delivery. This would not have worked in the large theaters that Bessie Smith was performing in the 1920s. Here, Broonzy provides a great example of using the technique of *delivering the song as if you were speaking to a friend*, introduced by Leroy Carr some twenty years before. To enhance this effect, Broonzy has personalized the lyrics, shortened the number of verses, chosen particular notes to make long, and added whoa-backs to certain words. Another wonderful detail of Broonzy's performance is the way he sings "down" as a vocal fall in the fourth verse. Although it is an extremely literal way of interpreting the lyric, it is executed with such subtlety and grace that you could miss it if you don't really tune in. There are many details here that are worth repeated listening, and the recording is so clear that you can observe with ease and imitate with practice.

REVIEW

In this chapter on early blues men and another woman, we have introduced the idea of singing the blues as if you were talking with a friend with great attention paid to the *rhythm*. We touched on the importance of *Negro folklore* and the *jook* in the development of the art form and expanded our knowledge of vocal timbre when singing blues. Our vocabulary of embellishments has expanded with the introduction of the *whoa-back*. Zora Neale Hurston identifies *originality* as one of the eleven characteristics of Negro expression, and the blues singers we have covered so far bear this out. Whereas *imitation* is critical to the development of blues singing and of the blues singer, finding your own unique combination of elements of what has come before that ultimately serve the message that *you* want to communicate is what blues singing is all about. Learning the nooks and crannies of these different blues singers expands your palette, gives you more tools to choose from, and gets you exposed to a wide range of possibilities. You may be surprised how well techniques made famous by Leroy Carr or Memphis Minnie can work for you. I guarantee that your time studying and emulating these artists will serve you well in developing a deeper sense of blues singing and a more original, multidimensional approach to the art. And as we have said before, *the blues is the roots, everything else is the fruits*. This means that the more blues in your singing, the deeper you will sing other styles drawn from it, such as rock and roll, rhythm and blues, and jazz.

NOTES

1. Zora Neale Hurston, "Characteristics of Negro Expression," 1933; Robert O'Meally, *The Jazz Cadence of American Culture* (New York: Columbia University Press, 1998), 298.
2. Elijah Wald, *Escaping the Delta* (New York: HarperCollins, 2004), 142.
3. Pete Welding, "Ramblin' Johnny Shines," *Living Blues*, no. 22, July–August 1975, 29.
4. Hurston, "Characteristics of Negro Expression"; O'Meally, *The Jazz Cadence of American Culture*, 298.
5. Wald, *Escaping the Delta*, 159.
6. Robert Palmer, *Deep Blues* (London: Penguin, 1981), 147.

7. Wald, *Escaping the Delta*, 158.

8. David "Honeyboy" Edwards, interview with Elijah Wald, 1997.

9. Elijah Wald, "Leroy Carr—The Bluesman Who Behaved Too Well," *New York Times*, July 17, 2004.

10. Scott Joplin, "School of Ragtime," in *44 Original Ragtime Hits* (Naples, FL: Ashley Publications, 1987).

11. Langston Hughes, "Music at Year's End," *Chicago Defender*, January 9, 1943.

12. In 2016, Tamar-Kali made a strong case for this on the panel she led at the Apollo Theater in Harlem, *Live Wire: Mothers of Invention*, which looked at the blues and gospel origins of rock and roll and the groundbreaking female icons and innovators at their heart: Ma Rainey, Bessie Smith, Memphis Minnie, Sister Rosetta Tharpe, and Big Mama Thornton.

7

DEVELOPING AUTHENTIC STYLE CHARACTERISTICS

Chicago Blues and the Modern Blues Vocal Sound

Whereas the blues originates in the South, the modern sound takes shape in the North and follows the trajectory of the Great Migration, when thousands of African American families relocated from the South to the North in search of a better life. Many families from Mississippi landed in Chicago, and this had a transformational impact on the development of blues music. Without Chicago blues, there would be no Bo Diddley, Chuck Berry, Rolling Stones, or the Beatles. Chicago blues forms the cornerstone of American music.

Perhaps if this transition from the South to North was an easy one, the blues would have lost its relevance. It was not easy. Blues as an experience of hardship was ever present as migrant African Americans dealt with challenges of discrimination, lack of decent housing, low wages, overcrowding, and more in their new homes. Some of these challenges—and the music made in the face of them—are depicted in a 1972 film called *Chicago Blues* featuring Dick Gregory, Willie Dixon, Muddy Waters, Buddy Guy, Junior Wells, and others. In the film, Muddy Waters says,

> For the type of blues I sing, you must pay the cost out there. You don't just get up and walk the streets getting you whatever you want whenever you get ready and can sing the blues like myself, Lightning Hopkins, John Lee Hooker, even on down to B.B. King. Plus, you gotta go to church to get this particular thing in your soul.[1]

What is it about the blues as it manifested in Chicago in the 1950s that caused the spark of a global life for the art form? Again, I turn to Zora Neale Hurston's seminal article "Characteristics of Negro Expression" for clues. She writes,

> After adornment, the next most striking manifestation of the Negro is *angularity*. Everything that he touches becomes angular. In all African sculpture and doctrine of any sort we find the same thing. Anyone watching Negro dancers will be struck by the same phenomenon. Every posture is another angle. Pleasing, yes. But an effect achieved by the very means which a European strives to avoid. The pictures on the walls are hung at deep angles. Furniture is always set at an angle. I have instances of a piece of furniture in the middle of a wall being set with one end nearer the wall than the other to avoid the simple straight line.[2]

ANGULARITY

"Avoid simple straight lines. . . . Every posture is another angle. . . . Everything that he touches becomes angular"—these are important clues in understanding how to approach the blues and sound authentic.

It makes me think of the way Thelonious Monk dances. There is wonderful film footage of this iconic American composer and pianist performing with his quartet in the Clint Eastwood film *Straight, No Chaser*. Monk often gets up from the piano during the saxophone solo and dances. He does this fantastic *angular* move with one elbow or another. It's never regular, always surprising, and at odd angles. When he sits at the piano, he maintains this angular approach. I find Zora Neale Hurston's commentary important because it gives context to these artistic choices. They are not whimsical per se, simply the result of artistic eccentricity. They are in fact part of an artistic tradition that succeeded in shifting the center of Western music traditions from European cultural frameworks to American ones. And the primary innovators were African Americans who synthesized the most unique and enduring characteristics of their culture into universally expressive art.

WILLIE DIXON (1915–1992)

One such innovator was the bassist, composer, vocalist, arranger, and record producer Willie Dixon. Born in Vicksburg, Mississippi, in 1915, Dixon grew up with poetry, Bible verses, and the culture of the black American South. Like W. C. Handy before him, he found a way to encapsulate his impressions of the culture into compositions that could give generations of singers songs that had impact and enjoyed great popularity. Dixon's songs used irregular forms—angular you might say. He preferred to shy away from the regular 12 bars. Nonetheless, he is considered one of the blues' top songwriters and helped establish the vocalist as the defining factor of what is blues.

In addition to this, Dixon was a gifted record producer who knew how to organize musicians to perform their best in the studio and onstage. His ability to cast his songs with the right singer allowed him to drive the essential message of the song home to the listener while establishing a persona of the artist him- or herself that left an indelible impression on the audience. Great singers like Muddy Waters, Howlin' Wolf, Little Walter, and Koko Taylor established their voices for eternity when performing Willie Dixon songs. These artists played other material as well with great success. However, there is no other blues artist of this period who was so prolifically involved with so many blues stars. Clearly, Willie Dixon possessed the keys to the blues kingdom, and we can learn a lot about singing the blues from learning his songs and listening to the artists he worked with. In addition to Waters, Wolf, Walter, and Taylor, there is Sonny Boy Williamson, Lowell Fulson, Jimmy Witherspoon, Bo Diddley, Buddy Guy, Jimmy Rogers, Robert Nighthawk, Albert King, Junior Wells, Otis Rush, and Chuck Berry. Willie Dixon writes,

> The average person wants to brag about themselves because it makes that individual feel big. "The gypsy woman told my mother/Before I was born"—that shows I was smart from the beginning, "Got a boy child coming/Gonna be a sonuvagun"—now I'm here. These songs make people want to feel like that because they feel like that at heart, anyway. They just haven't said it so you say it for them.

Like the song, "I Just Wanna Make Love to You," a lot of times people say this in their minds or think it. You don't have to say it but everybody knows that's the way you feel anyway because that's how the other fella feels. You know how you feel so you figure the other fella feels the same way because his life is just like yours.

To know the blues is to know a feeling and understanding within people that puts you in the position of other people by feeling and understanding the plight that they're involved in. You don't always get the experience in the blues from the life you live because sometimes these things are built into a certain individual.[3]

MUDDY WATERS (1913–1983)

Enter Muddy Waters, Willie Dixon's greatest interpreter. Muddy Waters was born in rural Mississippi and moved to Chicago in his late teens. The city's blooming black community embraced him and kept him active musically, almost immediately hiring him to play house parties while he worked at a factory during the day. This arrangement did not last long, as Muddy's talent and dedication led him to the studios of the fledgling Chess Records label. Once there, Muddy scored many hits. In 1948, "Rollin' Stone," "I Can't Be Satisfied," and "I Feel Like Going Home" secured his position as a major blues performer. His recordings featured other musicians who went on to legendary status, including producer/musician Willie Dixon, who wrote many of his big hits; Little Walter; Otis Spann; and, later, Junior Wells, James Cotton, and Buddy Guy. Additional classics by Muddy Waters include "Honey Bee," "She Moves Me," "I'm Your Hoochie Coochie Man," "I Just Wanna Make Love to You," "I'm Ready," "Got My Mojo Working," and "Mannish Boy." Many of these songs have been covered by famous rock groups, and both the rock group the Rolling Stones and *Rolling Stone* magazine took their names from Muddy's first hit, "Rolling Stone."[4]

There is a famous story about when the Beatles first came to the United States and first asked to see Muddy Waters. A reporter asked, "Muddy Waters—where's that?" To which Paul McCartney replied, "Don't you know your own famous people here?" We must never let this happen again.

As for the songs Willie Dixon wrote for Muddy Waters, it's hard to know where Dixon's art ends and Waters's begins. Dixon wrote songs so perfect for Waters that it was like Duke Ellington writing for his baritone saxophonist and friend/soul mate, Harry Carney. You couldn't have one without the other. Listening to Muddy Waters's recording of "I Just Wanna Make Love to You," you hear Muddy's gorgeous, full baritone, sounding like a preacher. His strong intention comes across with authority and strength. The song's lyrics give him the opportunity to simultaneously assert his power and tenderness as a lover (no small feat) while rejecting the remaining psychological bonds of slavery:

I don't want you to be no slave
I don't want you to work all day
I don't want you to be true
I just want to make love to you[5]

Willie Dixon wrote,

> A man don't have to be starving to know how it feels to starve. All he's got to do is know how it feels to miss one or two meals and he knows that other fella is in much worse shape. But if a person don't have no feeling, no imagination or understanding, you can't create feeling with him because he doesn't hear what you say.[6]

This idea of the singer and songwriter possessing a keen understanding of the individual listener's experience is key to success as a blues singer. The giants of the blues have magnificent voices, and there's no getting around that. Train your voice to sing with the fullest tone with the greatest ease. But to sound authentic, get inside the mind and heart of your listener and don't hesitate to use your imagination to do it.

"I Just Want to Make Love to You" sung by Muddy Waters ♪

I don't want you to be no slave
I don't want you to **work** all day
I don't want you to be **true**
I just want to make love to you

Analysis Vocally, this is a good example of using a gravelly onset to a clear tone found in the first two lines on the word "I." Listen carefully to how Waters bends the words "work" in the second line and "true" in the third line. Finally, in the fourth line, observe how short he makes "make" and comes in sweet and tender on "love to you." Very effective. Continue to listen carefully to the song and pick out details that grab you. Then imitate and assimilate.

Another seminal Muddy Waters/Willie Dixon work is "Hoochie Coochie Man." Muddy Waters didn't believe in voodoo per se, but he understood the community he was singing for in Chicago. Initially, they were black southerners who had relocated to the city for better work opportunities and, it was hoped, less racism. With their gains, there was also a loss of some of the country Negro *folklore* ways, including voodoo magic, some of which represented an echo of African culture lost during the horror of slave times.

"Hoochie Coochie Man" brought this into the present in a positive light. Muddy Waters's strength and confidence as a singer delivered the message so that it could give actual power to the listener. The big surprise was that this song actually held the capacity to extend its empowerment beyond the immediate needs of the black community and to the world at large. Countless modern-day rock-and-roll heroes had their worlds turned upside down by Muddy Waters. And "Hoochie Coochie Man" was a big part of that. Notice how the references to Negro folklore, an important characteristic of Negro expression cited by Zora Neale Hurston—voodoo magic-black cat bone, mojo, John the Conqueror root—mix seamlessly with assertions about Waters's prowess as a lover and strength as a man. It has become an anthem for everyone who has ever felt weak, defeated, challenged, or disillusioned. Listen and sing this song, and *you will be healed.*

"Hoochie Coochie Man" sung by Muddy Waters ♪

Analysis Muddy sings the verses with an open sound and storytelling delivery. His virtuosity as a singer comes to the fore in the chorus when he says,

> You know I'm here.
> Eeeeeeeverybody knows I'm here [gravelly onset in beginning to clear tone]

> Well you know the Hoochie Coochie Man [lighter on higher notes]
> Eeeeeverybody knows I'm here [gravelly onset in beginning to clear tone]

Notice how the loudest notes Muddy sings are comfortably in his chest range; when he goes higher, he lightens into a full chest mix. This is a key skill for the endurance and longevity of the blues singer. The loudest and highest note is a G sung on the words "Everybody knows." Keep the mouth open on the [e] and [o] vowels and make the consonants with subtle tongue movements without closing the mouth.

Muddy Waters said,

> Ain't too many left that play the real deep blues. There's John Lee Hooker, Lightnin' Hopkins—he have the Texas sound, and Texas blues is very, very good blues—and, let's see, who else? Ain't too many more left. They got all these white kids now. Some of them can play good blues. They play so much, run a ring around you playin' guitar, but they cannot vocal like a black man. Now B.B. King plays blues, but his blues is not as deep as my blues. He play higher class of peoples—they call 'em urban blues. Bobby "Blue" Bland, the same thing. Albert King play a little deeper blues than they do, Otis Rush is deeper. . . . I don't want to put down nothin' that'll make anybody mad, but it's the truth. There ain't too many left sings the type of blues that I sing.[7]

And I imagine Beethoven felt the same way. "Ain't too many left that can play what I play. Do what I do." This is the nature of genius. One like no other. As for the issue of race, "white kids now . . . cannot vocal like a black man." Indeed, it's true for the most part because the voice is harder to imitate than an instrument. However, tell that to the many people who first heard Elvis Presley and thought he was black or Chuck Berry and thought he was white. Muddy grew up in a particular community, rural Mississippi, where people talk a certain way. His sound is a combination of the instrument bestowed on him at birth, the sounds he heard growing up, and the time he invested in developing his voice. You can't match that. Instead, you can listen carefully to the way Muddy Waters sang and see if there are particular details that you can tease out and make your own. Embrace your sound—"I am a man," or "I am a woman"—while being informed by the giants who came before you.

Blues master B.B. King writes,

> Muddy [Waters] might have been the most magnificent of all the bluesmen to come out of Mississippi. John Lee Hooker is sure enough unique and still stands as one of the great poets of the blues. But Muddy became a father figure to generations of musicians, black and white. Muddy became an institution. I've loved Muddy my whole life. Loved his shouting, his songwriting, his wailing guitar. Back in Indianola [Mississippi], we knew that he'd gone to Chicago, where he established a whole school that he'd rule for five decades. Some went to the South Side before Muddy and some went after; there was Big Bill Broonzy and Memphis Slim and Memphis Minnie and Big Maceo and Little Walter and Howlin' Wolf and Junior Parker and dozens more. But no one had Muddy's authority. He was the boss of Chicago and the reason some call Chicago the sure-enough home of the blues.[8]

DINAH WASHINGTON (1924–1963)

Like Muddy Waters and Willie Dixon, singer and pianist Dinah Washington was born in the South and moved to Chicago. Born Ruth Jones, Dinah was four years old when her family arrived on Chicago's South Side. There were 17 black churches in the town they came from: Tuscaloosa, Alabama. In Chicago's black community where the family settled, there were more than 130 Baptist churches alone! Dinah's family joined St. Luke, one of the better-known such churches, where there could be as many as four different choirs, including a gospel choir, which was fairly new. This is the community that Thomas Dorsey—the father of gospel music—provided his original compositions, combining the musical language of blues and spirituals to praise God. Dinah's mother, Alice, dove deep into service as a musician in the church community, and young Dinah Washington was surrounded by these sounds throughout her youth. She excelled as both a pianist and a singer and began performing around Chicago as a teenager. Her first known public performance, on April 28, 1940, probably included songs by Thomas Dorsey, including the classic "Take My Hand, Precious Lord." Dinah went on to accompany one of Dorsey's close collaborators, Sallie Martin, and was influenced heavily by Roberta Martin, another seminal Chicago singer and gospel pianist/composer.[9]

Declaring to her mother on more than one occasion, "I want to be a showgirl," Dinah Washington's extraordinary voice and musicianship caught the ear of Lionel Hampton, and in 1942, Dinah was hired as his band's singer. She made her first recordings with "Hamp," as he was widely known, as a teenager and soon was being introduced as the queen of the blues. By the 1950s, Dinah Washington had so many hits in different styles that her title expanded to the all-encompassing queen of the jukebox or simply queen. Her versatility as a singer and ability to put her own unique stamp on a wide variety of material are unmatched. Musical icon Quincy Jones described her way with a song in his 2001 autobiography, saying that she "could take the melody in her hand, hold it like an egg, crack it open, fry it, let it sizzle, reconstruct it, put the egg back in the box and back in the refrigerator and you would've still understood every single syllable."

It's important to note that Dinah's path to this level of artistry started with gospel, then blues, then everything else. She is a great example of Willie Dixon's famous saying that "the blues is the roots everything else is the fruits." Let's look at one of Dinah Washington's early hits with Lionel Hampton, "Blow Top Blues" from 1945, and in so doing uncover some of the fundamentals of modern blues singing.

"Blow Top Blues" sung by Dinah Washington ♪

IIII've got bad news baby, and you're the first to know
Yeeeees I've got bad news baby and youuuuu're the **first** to know
IIIII discovered this morning, that my top is **about** to go[10]

Analysis Sound—Dinah's sound is bright as can be. Some of this is simply the nature of her voice. However, additional brightness can be achieved by using bright vowels like [a], [e], and [i]. You can also cultivate the sensation of vibration in the areas under the eyes, cheeks, and upper lip—as opposed to having the feeling of vibration in the throat and upper chest.

Rhythmic feel—Notice where Dinah is phrasing off the beat. The accompaniment on this recording offers a very steady quarter-note background. Listen carefully to where Washington places her melody notes behind the downbeat of the quarters. In order to do this, one must master the feeling of swing that was everywhere at the time of this recording. Swing is based on the mastery and rendering of two simultaneous rhythms: duple and triple.

Mastering Swing Phrasing Clark Terry of the Count Basie and Duke Ellington bands offered us a tool he called the "doo-dle-laa" to help students absorb this concept. While walking in place in a moderate tempo in duple time, you can practice saying "doo-dle-laa" with each step, making sure each syllable of "doo" "dle" "laa" is even, thus rendering the eighth-note triplet. Once this is established, put a gentle accent on the last syllable of the triplet, "laa." This is generally where Dinah is placing her melody notes.

As a further expression of this duple/triple polyrhythm, you can hear Dinah phrase in quarter-note triplets as in the second line, "**Yeeees, I've got** bad news baby, and you're the first to know."

Embellishment—In addition to rhythmic variation and elongating certain notes, we find a particular melodic embellishment that became one of Dinah Washington's aural signatures. In the repetition of the first line, you can hear the embellishment on the words "first" and "about." Here she adds a grouping of four sixteenth notes consistently. Let's call it the *Washington mordent*. You will hear this embellishment in many of Dinah Washington's famous records. The precise execution of it in service of the blues demonstrates the wide variety of blues vocal approaches that are possible, depending on the strengths of the performer. Whereas Memphis Minnie displayed phenomenal control of pitches and bent them to suit her interpretation of the blues, Dinah uses the bent note but also adds this almost classical-sounding embellishment. It still sounds bluesy because it is phrased within the context of swing rhythm and a tonal environment that includes bent notes. However, the clarity of each note of the embellishment is striking and demonstrates the tremendous control, variety, and subtlety of Dinah Washington's vocal arsenal.

In the second verse, the first line has "out" stretched and the pitch waved. The first word of this verse, "Yes," gets a special emphasis. We find the Washington mordent on both renderings of the word "out" as well as "thing." Noted producer and musician Leonard Feather is credited as the composer of this song. He penned other blues hits for Dinah Washington, including her first hit, "Evil Gal Blues." In a perfect world,

Washington would receive cocomposer credit since what she does vocally with these songs gives them their status as blues-beyond-a-doubt classics for all time.

Dinah Washington recorded extensively for Mercury Records and became a huge star before her life was cut short at age thirty-nine by an accidental overdose of diet pills. The material she recorded was wide ranging, and she was often presented with large ensemble backing, including strings and big bands. Other blues songs she recorded are the aforementioned "Evil Gal Blues," "Salty Papa Blues," "Postman Blues," "Mean and Evil Blues," "Early in the Morning," and the supremely comical "Long John Blues." She brought a bluesy feeling to many other songs she recorded, especially tracks like "Please Send Me Someone to Love" and even the ballad "It Isn't Fair."

ETTA JAMES (1938–2012)

Etta James is considered one of the greatest soul singers of all time. We don't necessarily think of her first as a blues singer because like Dinah Washington, whom she looked up to, she had great success with a wide variety of material. Also, like Washington, Etta James was raised in black church music, then shifted to blues, then branched out from there. In many ways, this is the quintessential pathway for an American singer and can serve as a model for enhancing one's skills as an interpreter of American music today. Etta James wrote in her autobiography *Rage to Survive*,

> No matter how pop or schmaltzy a song, I can't help but put a gospel and blues hurting on it. I think that's what I have in common with Dinah [Washington]—and Billie [Holiday] too. I always had the feeling that Dinah was tricking. I knew she was really a blues singer, but she was always righteous, even when she sang pop; she could bend any material into her own unique and gorgeous shape. That's what I wanted.[11]

Etta James grew up in California and got her primary musical education with Professor James Earle Hines at St. Paul Baptist Church in Los Angeles. Many gospel stars of the day visited on a regular basis, inspiring young Jamesetta, as she was then known. These artists included Sister

Rosetta Tharpe and the Sallie Martin Singers. Stories abound about Etta James's lessons with James Earle Hines, and, as with any private teaching scenario, it's hard to know exactly what transpired in the lessons. However, Etta James clearly held Hines in high regard and learned some important fundamentals of singing with support. As she describes,

> Now every Tuesday Mama would trot me over to Professor Hines for voice lessons. I also took piano lessons from his wife, but I wasn't much on practicing. Singing was the only thing that suited my impatient nature. I didn't mind that Professor Hines was strict. I responded to his demands. He was good for me. He didn't treat me like some kid or little girl; he took me seriously. He taught me to sing from my stomach, not my throat. He says, "Don't back off those notes, Jamesetta. Attack 'em, grab 'em, claim those suckers, sing 'em like you own 'em." He called it dynamic singing. Talk about confidence! Professor Hines gave me enough confidence to last a lifetime.[12]

Etta James continued her training as a teenage professional singer on the road with Johnny Otis's band, whom she greatly admired. She writes,

> He's a guru, a man with encyclopedic knowledge and appreciation of black music. He sees its wholeness, from gospel to blues to jazz. Johnny says things like, "Lightnin' Hopkins and Max Roach aren't first cousins"—referring to the country blues singer and bebop drummer—"they're blood brothers."[13]

This background proved valuable to young Etta James as she made her first hit record at the age of 18, "Roll with Me Henry." A spin-off of Hank Ballard's "Work with Me Annie," Etta took Hank's melody, wrote new lyrics, brought her own attitude and tremendous confidence, and established herself as a star. As with most blues, the song has a strong beat, and in this case, the bass plays in two with a consistent backbeat in the snare drum. The feel definitely suggests the shuffle rhythm, the foundation of the blues, though most would hear it as early rock and roll, a subtle difference to be sure. The recording is from 1953, the dawn of the rock-and-roll age.

"Roll with Me Henry" sung by Etta James ♪

Analysis Everything James sings in this song sits inside of the shuffle rhythm. The bass player being in two leaves space for Etta to swing inside of the shuffle, which suits the song well since it's a suggestive song about *dance* (one of Hurston's characteristics) or lovemaking:

You gotta roll with me Henry [i]
Roll with me Henry
Roll with me Henre [E]
Roll with me Henre [E]
Roll with me **Henre [E]** [blended with backup singers]
You better roll while the rollin' is on
Roll on, roll on, roll on

Once again, as with Dinah Washington, James presents an extremely bright sound. This is highly effective for blues, especially in the transition to blues/rock, where more electric instruments are used and the voice needs to be heard over them. Naturally, using a microphone is critical with this music, but even with a mic, a darker-sounding voice does not generally blend well with these instruments. For Etta James, a bright vocal timbre is key.

Next, I call your attention to the word "Henry." Singers always need to be careful with the vowel [i] as in the name Henry. This vowel can easily end up squeezing the throat, leading to unnecessary tension. Etta James is no exception. Her early training guides her to introduce the word "Henry" with a solid [i] sound, the second "Henry" partially modified, and the third fully modified to [E] as if saying "Henre." She does it so naturally that one hardly notices it, and this is one of the great tricks of our trade—finding ways to modify vowels in scarcely noticeable ways to keep the throat relaxed. The [E] vowel is also a better vowel to blend with the backup singers, a tight-knit group called the Peaches, which Etta sang backup with for Johnny Otis.

After the second verse, there is a bridge where James uses the sound "Aahoo" and "oowee" to great effect. I like to use these sounds as a blues warm-up.

"Tough Lover" sung by Etta James ♪

For an up-tempo blues, check out "Tough Lover" from 1956. It starts with a bluesy moan. Then the lyric begins,

I've got the lover that moves me so
He sho' knows how to rock and roll
Cause he's a tough lover, **yeah yeah**
He's a tough lover, wooooo
He's a **tough** lover, yeah yeah
He's a tough lover, **uhuh**.

Analysis For the classical singer, the growl on "yeah yeah" will be alarming. For the blues singer, this is a staple like bread and butter. It is always helpful, though, to observe closely how a master blues singer like Etta James handles this. Notice that the growl is never the default; she always defaults back to a more pure balanced tone. This is extremely helpful—*absolutely necessary* in fact for most people. In this song, the voice is further balanced by the head voice "woooo" an octave above the melody. This device was a staple of early rock-and-roll singing vocabulary. It hails from the blues. You certainly can hear it in many Mississippi Delta blues singers. In addition to the expression it adds, it is a good way to help keep the voice balanced.

Etta James moved to Chicago and made hits for Chess Records as their first female soul star. "At Last" is one of those big hits, as were several other standards she recorded with her classic blues sensibility. She recorded Willie Dixon's "Spoonful" in 1960. It features the same kind of shuffle rhythm over a two feel in the bass that Etta found so effective in "Roll with Me Henry." Etta James's voice is more mature now and notices all the different shadings of the notes she sings.[14]

These shadings are tremendously apparent in her recording of the Willie Dixon tune "I Just Want to Make Love to You." This song makes a great comparison to the Muddy Waters version we discussed earlier:

"I Just Want to Make Love to You" sung by Etta James ♪

I don't want you to be no slave
I don't want you to work all day

But I don't want you to be **true**
I just want to make love to you

Love to you
Hooo
Love to you

Analysis Like Muddy Waters, Etta James sings the first word "I" with a gravelly onset then to balanced onset for the opening two lines of the song. With both Waters and James recording it this way, we can consider that is the way it is *supposed to be*. However, in a departure from the Waters interpretation of the song, it is interesting to note how light James gets on the words "I just want to make love to you" and the following "Love to you. Hooo. Love to you." This is a fantastic contrast that effectively communicates the depth of the song. It is a command. It is also a seduction. Etta James can evoke both with the timbre of her voice simultaneously.

An American icon who carried the classic sounds of her blues lineage up until her death in 2012, Etta James told the *Los Angeles Times* in 1992,

> A lot of people think the blues is depressing, but that's not the blues I'm singing. When I'm singing blues, I'm singing life. People that can't stand to listen to the blues, they've got to be phonies.[15]

HOWLIN' WOLF (1910–1976)

> It was a darkness. It was a "broodingness." It was a man who had seen the bottom of the abyss and was telling you about it.
>
> —Ray Manzarek, The Doors[16]

Born in 1910 in rural Mississippi, Howlin' Wolf moved to Chicago after a stint in Memphis and then military service during World War II. He stood six feet three, wore size 16 shoes, and was known for the professional respect he showed his band members. Wolf played guitar and harmonica, but it was his *voice* that distinguished him as a towering figure in American music—a voice that, to use B.B. King's words, "seemed like a sword *that'd pierce your soul*."[17]

Once again, we find in Howlin' Wolf a great blues singer who started out singing in the Baptist church. His vocal tone is mostly gravelly, but he regularly uses falsetto to provide a wide range of expression in his songs. Like Muddy Waters, Howlin' Wolf recorded mostly for the Chicago-based Chess Records label, and much has been made of a rivalry between them. We will investigate two of his big hits starting with his first from 1951, "Moanin' at Midnight."

"Moanin' at Midnight" sung by Howlin' Wolf ♪

Analysis This song is built on one chord in E major/minor. It holds so many characteristics that define the blues. You've got the steady beat and a dronelike accompaniment with strong African roots. Then the voice enters on a wordless moan/hum, using head voice and slides in a supremely expressive and haunting way. Spend some time really studying and imbibing what Wolf does with this moan/hum in the opening and closing. The more you listen, the more you will realize the seemingly infinite dimensions of it. In recorded interviews with Willie Dixon, Dixon demonstrates a similar kind of seemingly otherworldly hum. These men could express the infinitely beyond in the sound of their voice. The opening hum of "Moanin' at Midnight" is followed by a harmonica and guitar riff. This kind of call-and-response between the voice and the instruments continues. The lyrics are very simple but tremendously effective in concert with the other blues devices present of call-and-response, driving rhythm, and moanful vocal slides. Howlin' Wolf speaks directly to the listener with a personal story. He makes you feel that you are in the room with him. "Yeah somebody knocking on my door." Who could it be? The harmonica and guitar reply. Then again, "Yeah somebody knocking on my door." Notice how he emphasizes *some*body. Once again, who could it be? says the guitar and harmonica. Then the vulnerability of the singer comes through: "Well I'm so worried, don't know where to go." More commentary from harmonica and guitar. Then again "Well I'm so worried, don't know where to go." Harp/guitar. Finally, "Well somebody callin' me, callin' on my telephone." This is something that could happen to anyone and be just about anything. Who's on the telephone? The landlord? A crazy, thwarted lover? The devil himself? It's all open to interpretation. There are more moans in head voice, providing a stark contrast to the gravelly presentation of the spoken lyrics. This stands out in the recordings we have listened to as a magnificent distillation of blues moves. I don't recommend any of us try to imitate Howlin' Wolf exactly. Unlike Dinah Washington, this is not a voice easily evoked without some kind of tension on the vocal cords. However, you can see in the architecture of this piece many blues elements that can realized in different ways. In his song "Smokestack Lightning," some of these same devices are present.

"Smokestack Lightning" sung by Howlin' Wolf ♪

Howlin' Wolf had performed "Smokestack Lightning" in one form or another at least by the early 1930s when he was performing with Charley Patton in small Delta communities.[18] The song's hypnotic effect is based on a characteristically African drone accompaniment based on one chord evoked through a repeated guitar riff contributed by Hubert Sumlin. "Smokestack Lightning" draws on earlier blues, such as Tommy Johnson's "Big Road Blues" (1928, Victor 21279), the Mississippi Sheiks' "Stop and Listen Blues" (1930, OKeh 8807), and Charley Patton's "Moon Going Down" (1930, Paramount 13014).[19] It has been covered by many others, including the Grateful Dead, Bob Dylan, Aerosmith, and Etta James.

Analysis Once again, we find Howlin' Wolf balancing his extraordinary declamatory vocal style with a heavily nuanced use of falsetto.

Ah-oh, smokestack lightnin'
Shinin' just like gold
Why don't ya hear me cryin'?
A-whooo-hooo, oooo
Whooo

The melody opens with two-note holler on D4 and E4, then down an E minor seventh chord, D, B, G, E. With a piano and possibly guitar playing an E dominant seventh accompaniment using E, G♯, B, and D, the melody notes forming E minor establish the rub with the major third of the E7. This establishes the characteristic flexible pitch area around the third. Guitar and piano players can think of this chord as an E7 with a raised ninth. Hubert Sumlin's guitar riff provides the focus of the accompaniment supported by the backbeat of the drums and the bass in two. The riff is like this:

Smokestack Lightning Guitar Riff

Hubert Sumlin

Figure 7.1. Hubert Sumlin guitar riff on "Smokestack Lightning." ***Transcribed by Eli Yamin***

This song is a great example of the blues "yell." Contemporary blues artist Shemekia Copeland told interviewer LaFrae Sci that "my daddy told me, 'you have to learn how to yell.'"[20] "Smokstack Lightning" is a great example of it, and for a version of it performed by a woman in the same key, listen to Etta James from her 2004 Grammy Award–winning recording "Blues to the Bone." ♪

B.B. KING

There are many places besides Chicago and Mississippi that have made essential contributions to the blues, such as Texas, Memphis, New Orleans, Kansas City, and Detroit. Basically, wherever a black community gathered in the twentieth century, there was blues. We have focused on Chicago because of its dominating influence on the blues we hear today both in contemporary blues and in the rock and roll it gave birth to.

B.B. King is not from Chicago but was born outside of Indianola, Mississippi, and launched his career from Memphis, Tennessee. In 1971, when he won his first Grammy Award for Best Male R&B Vocal Performance for "The Thrill Is Gone," he had been working as a blues man for thirty years. In 1956, he played more than 340 shows.

As a singer, B.B. King is a great model for how to keep your voice healthy and strong for the long haul. Phyl Garland of *Ebony* magazine characterized King's presentation like this:

> His approach is so smooth, his fire so controlled, that each performance comes across a little like a triumph of dramatic as well as of musical art.

> His sense of taste is so infallible that he is one of the very few around who can cry out in all passion while retaining his "cool." And this is why he is considered a master.[21]

This description depicts King's expression onstage and his exceptional balance of smoothness and controlled fire. Balancing these elements in your voice as a blues singer is essential to keeping your instrument in good health. Let's listen and discuss one of King's early important recordings to see how he expresses this on record.

"Three O'Clock Blues" sung by B.B. King ♪

> Now here it is three o' clock in the morning
> Can't even close my eyes
> Whoah three o'clock in the morning
> Can't even close my eyes
> Well I can't find my baby
> Lord and I can't be satisfied

Analysis The range of this song is ideally suited for the high tenor, and you can hear King effortlessly mixing tones up to a B♭4 in the regular part of the melody and a variation to a D♭5. The form is a 12-bar blues in the key of B♭. The melody is based on a B♭ minor pentatonic scale with the notes B♭, D♭, E♭, F, A♭. Notice how King uses dynamics to effortlessly mix the higher notes. The phrases are asymmetrical with embellishments in groups of five. When singing in the upper part of your range, it is important to keep the throat relaxed. You can do this by entering the note on falsetto, then increasing the volume to mix with the tongue released downward. Before trying this, make sure the melody is internalized on the [u] vowel. Then practice the melody lightly with the words and be careful to keep the mouth open without excessive movement of the jaw. Most of the sound should come through on the vowels with the mouth and throat open. King provides a great example of this. With the help of YouTube, you can slow the recording down to make sure you get the nuances of the melody. I have provided a transcription below of verse 1 to help get you started if you find musical notation helpful. Notice carefully which notes of the melody are bent and which ones are fixed in pitch.

Figure 7.2. B.B. King's rendition of "Three O'Clock Blues," verse 1. *Transcribed by Eli Yamin*

B.B. King got this song from one of his heroes, Lowell Fulson, who made a recording in 1948, and it's interesting to compare the two performances.

"Three O'Clock in the Morning" sung by Lowell Fulson ♪

Analysis Fulson's version is in the key of A♭, a whole step down from King's. Whereas the melody is fundamentally the same and Fulson's feeling is strong, he is not the virtuoso singer King is and therefore does not hold the notes as long. Of course, it is not necessary to be a virtuoso singer to sing the blues. The feeling is what is most important, and Lowell Fulson is in the top tier of blues people for all time. As a singer, though, King must be considered at the top of the heap according to what he could do with his voice throughout his tremendous range.

B.B. King grew up on a farm in Mississippi. He was very close with his mother, but she died when he was just nine years old. His upbringing was catch-as-catch-can after that. He spent time with his birth father and other relatives. In many ways, he raised himself from the age of ten. His autobiography poetically describes his early years, his fascination with music, girls and women, and the evolution of his work ethic on the farm. He started out plowing behind a mule and later became a tractor driver, allowing him to be exempt from military service overseas during World War II. His story is truly exceptional in terms of how he kept plugging away playing the blues while the music changed around him. While some of his peers and younger, like Little Richard and Chuck Berry, became megastars of rock and roll, King kept playing mostly black clubs with his big band. He valued the musicians working for him and took on the huge overhead costs this required. Finally, in the late 1960s, his star rose with the blues revival spurred by English rockers shining more light on their blues heroes. King's "Live at the Penitentiary and Famous Door" inspired me greatly growing up in the suburbs of New Jersey and will inspire many more for years to come. In his later years, King recorded famous duets with Eric Clapton, Elton John, Sheryl Crow, John Mayer, and Gloria Estefan. He toured more than one hundred nights a year well into his seventies, sang "Sweet Home Chicago" with President Barack Obama at the White House in 2012, and died at the age of eighty-nine.

His greatest hit is the one he won his first Grammy award for: "The Thrill Is Gone." Even though it is technically a minor blues form in 12 bars, it somehow transcends the genre. Perhaps it is the strings or simply the great wisdom of experience of the voice of B.B. King. ♪

CONCLUSION

In this chapter, we traced the blues vocal line from Mississippi to Chicago through blues icons Willie Dixon and Muddy Waters. Their work is *angular* in Zora Neale Hurston's sense of it because it avoids straight lines while dealing with themes of hardship head-on. The blues became modern in this period because it combined this angular approach to music with dealing with the hardships of life in a modern sense—all this while retaining a connection to its rich lineage. In Hurston's framework, there are references to *folklore* by Muddy Waters in "Hoochie Coochie

Man" and to *dance* in Etta James's "Roll with Me Henry." In Dinah Washington, we have the arrival of a tremendously refined voice who could sing any style on any day. Emerging from the rich gospel academy of Chicago, Washington gives us a model of how to apply refined vocal virtuosity to the blues. B.B. King gives us a male point of view on virtuosity with his high tenor on "Three O'Clock in the Morning." King lamented the persistent myth of the "primitive" blues man: no shoes and raggedy clothes. King would have none of this in his presentation. He was all class and gave this to the world in more than sixty years of performances and recordings all over the world.

We have presented the fundamentals of blues vocal language; the next question is, what do you do with it?

NOTES

1. *Chicago Blues* (documentary, produced and directed by Harley Cokeliss, 1970).
2. Zora Neale Hurston, "Characteristics of Negro Expression," 1933; Robert O'Meally, *The Jazz Cadence of American Culture* (New York: Columbia University Press, 1998), 298.
3. Willie Dixon with Don Snowden, *The Willie Dixon Story: I Am the Blues* (New York: Da Capo, 1990), 85.
4. *The Rolling Stone Encyclopedia of Rock & Roll*, 3rd ed. (New York: Simon and Schuster, 2001).
5. Song lyrics, "I Just Want to Make Love to You," Willie Dixon.
6. Willie Dixon, *The Willie Dixon Story*, 85.
7. Robert Palmer, *Deep Blues* (London: Penguin, 1981), 260.
8. B.B. King with David Ritz, *Blues All Around Me: The Autobiography of B.B. King* (New York: HarperCollins, 1996), 106–7.
9. Nadine Cohodas, *Queen: The Life and Music of Dinah Washington* (New York: Pantheon, 2004), 12–23.
10. "Blow Top Blues" lyrics by Leonard Feather.
11. Etta James and David Ritz, *Rage to Survive: The Etta James Story* (New York: Villard, 1995), 103.
12. James and Ritz, *Rage to Survive*, 19.
13. James and Ritz, *Rage to Survive*, 46.
14. Etta James discography, http://www.45cat.com/artist/etta-james.

15. Peter Keepnews, "Etta James" (obituary, *New York Times*, January 20, 2012).

16. Ray Manzarek, "The Blues of Howlin' Wolf," *Morning Edition*, National Public Radio, 2004, https://www.npr.org/templates/story/story.php?storyId=3249069.

17. B.B. King, quoted in James Segrest and Mark Hoffman, *Moanin' at Midnight: The Life and Times of Howlin' Wolf* (New York: Pantheon, 2004), introduction.

18. Segrest and Hoffman, *Moanin' at Midnight*, 20, 126.

19. David Evans, *Big Road Blues: Tradition and Creativity in the Folk Blues* (Berkeley, CA: Da Capo, 1982), 274.

20. LaFrae Sci interview with Shemekia Copeland, 2017.

21. Henry Pleasants, *The Great American Popular Singers* (New York: Simon and Schuster, 1974), 318.

8

MAKING A SOULFUL SOUND AND WRITING YOUR OWN BLUES

Our favorite blues singers have all different kinds of voices, from high to low and from small to gigantic, but they have one thing in common: *soulfulness*. Although the term is used frequently to describe all kinds of things, including people, experiences, food, and music, we seldom hear a straight definition. When you think of a soulful person, whom do you think of—a friend, a mentor, a family member, a singer you like? What do they have in common?

Soulful is full of feeling—genuine expression of emotion. It is often linked with generosity. Some of the most soulful people I have met are supremely generous. They are ready and willing to put the community before themselves.

Zora Neale Hurston's final characteristic of Negro expression is "absence of privacy," and she relates it to a communal style of living going back generations. Perhaps this emphasis on community helps produce more generosity and soulfulness.

There is certainly a spiritual dimension to this as well, and many spiritual leaders naturally embody soulfulness. But in music, blues music in particular, what do we mean?

I think that *honesty*, as in willing to share something intimate and important to you about yourself, is a big part of it. To sum up, I offer you this:

Soulfulness is *honesty* and *offering*.

Let's turn to three master drummers for more clues. Drum master Elvin Jones said,

> It's the honesty you apply to your playing that makes music enjoyable. The style of the music has little to do with it. It's only honesty [that] makes it beautiful.

I witnessed my mentor, drummer Walter Perkins, express soulfulness every day. He was the kind of person who lit up a room when he entered it. Growing up playing drums in Chicago with Muddy Waters, Memphis Slim, and Howlin' Wolf, his shuffle beat made the blues feel good for everyone both on and off the bandstand. He created a platform for other artists and members of the community to shine, and as another master drummer, Art Blakey, said, "wash[ed] away the dust of everyday life."

So, how do we get to this as singers and establish and maintain our blues sound?

In addition to applying principles of healthy singing and authentic style characteristics described in the earlier chapters, a good part of your success in singing blues depends on the songs you choose to sing and your ability as a storyteller.

STANDARD REPERTOIRE

Many blues singers start out singing other people's songs, and there are some blues standards most folks know. Catherine Russell offers this list:

1. "Sweet Home Chicago"
2. "Stormy Monday Blues"
3. "Every Day I Have the Blues"
4. "Big Boss Man"
5. "Dust My Broom"
6. "Born Under a Bad Sign"
7. "Got My Mojo Workin'"
8. "Route 66"

9. "Baby What You Want Me to Do"
10. "Help Me"
11. "How Long Blues" (8-bar blues)
12. "Trouble in Mind" (8-bar blues)
13. "I'm Ready"
14. "See See Rider"
15. "A Good Man Is Hard to Find"

WRITING YOUR OWN BLUES

Writing your own blues can be a great way to source your own story to make a personal statement. You can start with a typical 12-bar blues and write in the AAB lyric format of making a statement, repeating it, and giving an answer. Think carefully about what you are talking about and choose a topic that has personal significance. As you develop as a songwriter, you may want to veer away from the 12-bar structure and explore other forms, including 8 and 16 bars, but also riff-based structures or even verse and chorus. As we have maintained throughout this book, the vocal approach you bring, combined with the nature of the accompaniment, will be what truly identifies your song as a blues or something else.

BLUES SONGWRITING IN THE MODERN ERA

Writing blues songs is personal and communal. The blues are almost always in the first person, yet the best songs somehow touch a nerve with a community of folks who agree: "Yeah, that happened to me too." This is the circle of the blues. We have discussed many blues performers who were also well-known songwriters, including Bessie Smith, Willie Dixon, Muddy Waters, Howlin' Wolf, Robert Johnson, and Leroy Carr. A good example of blues songwriters for the late twentieth and early twenty-first centuries must include performers like Mose Allison, Taj Mahal, Alvin Youngblood, Bonnie Rait, Corey Harris, and Shemekia Copeland (interpreting songs by John Hahn and Oliver Wood).

GEORGE JACKSON (1945–2013)

There are some well-known blues songwriters who have songs that supersede their personal fame, such as George Jackson from Indianola, Mississippi, who wrote "Down Home Blues." Originally recorded in 1982 by Z.Z. Hill, "Down Home Blues" has been covered by many others, including Etta James, Big Nick Nicholas, Denise LaSalle, James Cotton, and Junior Wells.

"Down Home Blues" by George Jackson (born in Mississippi, 1945–2013) sung by Z.Z. Hill ♪

You said your party's jumping
And everybody's having a good time
And you know what's going through my mind
Do you mind if I get comfortable and kick off these shoes
While you fixing me a drink play me some of them down-home blues

Other famous songs by George Jackson are "One Bad Apple," "Old Time Rock and Roll," and "The Only Way Is Up."

MOSE ALLISON (1927–2016)

Mose Allison wrote many songs drawn from his roots growing up in rural Mississippi. A distinctive pianist who arrived in New York in the 1950s to find many great pianists, he retreated to his father's farm in Mississippi to find his own voice. He found it by adding singing his own songs to his act. This led to a successful career spanning more than fifty years performing and recording his songs along with standards and blues by other folks, including fellow Mississippian Willie Dixon. Mose Allison songs have been covered by many other artists, such as The Who, Van Morrison, Bonnie Raitt, Elvis Costello, The Clash, and Diana Krall.

"Ever Since the World Ended" by Mose Allison and sung by Mose Allison ♪

Ever since the world ended, I don't go out as much
People that I once befriended no longer seem to stay in touch

Things that used to seem so splendid
Don't really matter today
It's just as well the world ended
It wasn't working anyway

Other famous songs by Mose Allison are "Parchman Farm," "Your Mind Is on Vacation," and "I Don't Worry About a Thing."

Willie Dixon blazed the trail for blues songs, taking different forms other than the typical 12 bars. Again, we maintain it is the singer's approach and the accompaniment that most define the blues. One of today's leading performers of original blues songs is Shemekia Copeland.

SHEMEKIA COPELAND (1979–)

Born in New York in 1979, Shemekia Copeland's father was the famous blues man Johnny Copeland. Steeped in the blues tradition, Shemekia Copeland brings an extremely personal approach to the blues through her singing and fruitful and prolific collaboration with songwriters John Hahn and Oliver Wood. Hahn and Wood craft songs based on conversations with Copeland and provide her with material that allows her to bring a completely fresh approach to the blues based on her life experiences and astute observations of life in the twenty-first century. Copeland is a virtuoso singer who knows exactly how to put her talent and skill as a vocalist in the right place to effectively deliver the story of the song she is singing. You can see all of this on the knockout filmed version of her song "Ghetto Child" from a performance in October 2017 in Poland.

"Ghetto Child" sung by Shemekia Copeland ♪

Copeland told interviewer LaFrae Sci,

> I try to make the music contemporary, you know. I'm over relationship things . . . the songs about, my man so sad, I'd rather go blind than to see you walk away from me. All are great songs, but I prefer to empower women in a different type of way. Don't get me wrong. I love, love-songs.

> I just think that being contemporary is taking music to another level. And in order to do that, we got to be willing to try different things.

She cites the following examples:

"Ain't Gonna Be Your Tatoo" sung by Shemekia Copeland ♪
"Crossbone Beach" sung by Shemekia Copeland ♪
"Drivin' Out of Nashville" sung by Shemekia Copeland ♪

BLUES HISTORY IS MODERN INSPIRATION

There are so many great blues songs that have not been touched in years. Find the ones that move you, and you might have a hit like Taj Mahal did when he remade a song written by Henry Thomas in the nineteenth century called "Fishin' Blues." ♪

Listen to these artists and find others to avail yourself of the great treasures of blues music and the endless possibilities.

EARLY BLUES WOMEN

Alberta Hunter
Bessie Smith
Carrie Smith
Clara Smith
Ethel Waters
Ida Cox
Lil Green
Ma Rainey
Mamie Smith
Memphis Minnie
Sippie Wallace
Trixie Smith
Victoria Spivey

EARLY BLUES MEN AND COUNTRY BLUES WOMEN

Arthur "Big Boy" Crudup
Big Bill Broonzy
Blind Lemon Jefferson
Blind Willie McTell
Charley Patton
Elizabeth Cotten
Etta Baker
Henry Thomas
John Cephas and Phil Wiggins
Kokomo Arnold

Leadbelly
Leroy Carr
Mississippi Fred McDowell
Mississippi John Hurt
Reverend Gary Davis
Robert Johnson
Robert Lockwood Jr.
Robert Nighthawk
Skip James
Son House
Sonny Boy Williamson I
Tampa Red

MODERN BLUES

Albert Collins
B.B. King
Big Joe Turner
Big Mama Thornton
Bo Diddley
Bobby Blue Bland
Dinah Washington
Elmore James
Esther Phillips
Etta James
Freddie King
Howlin' Wolf
Hubert Sumlin
Irma Thomas
James Cotton
Jimmy Reed
Jimmy Rushing
Jimmy Witherspoon
Joe Williams
John Lee Hooker
Junior Parker
Junior Wells
Koko Taylor
Lightnin' Hopkins
Little Walter
Louis Jordan
Magic Sam
Muddy Waters
Otis Rush
Otis Spann
Percy Mayfield
Pinetop Perkins
Ruth Brown
Sister Rosetta Tharpe
Sonny Boy Williamson II (aka Rice Miller)
Sunnyland Slim
T-Bone Walker
Willie Dixon

CONTEMPORARY BLUES

Alvin Youngblood Heart
Anson Funderburg
Bill "Howlin' Mad" Perry
Bobby Rush
Bonnie Raitt
Buddy Guy
Charlie Musselwhite
Chris Thomas King

Christone "Kingfish" Ingram
Corey Harris
Derek Trucks
Guy Davis
Jeff Healey
Joe Louis Walker
John Hammond Jr.
Johnny Adams
Johnny Copeland
Johnny Winter
Jr. Mack
Keb Mo'
Kenny Neal
King Solomon Hicks
Luther Allison
Maria Muldaur
Otis Taylor
R. L. Burnside
Robben Ford
Robert Cray
Shemekia Copeland
Snooks Eaglin
Son Seals
Stevie Ray Vaughan
Susan Tedeschi
Taj Mahal
Z.Z. Hill

9

USING AUDIO ENHANCEMENT TECHNOLOGY

Matthew Edwards

In the early days of popular music, musicians performed without electronic amplification. Singers learned to project their voices in the tradition of vaudeville performers with a technique similar to operatic and operetta performers who had been singing unamplified for centuries. When microphones began appearing on stage in the 1930s, vocal performance changed forever since the loudness of a voice was no longer a factor in the success of a performer. In order to be successful, all a singer needed was an interesting vocal quality and an emotional connection to what he or she was singing. The microphone would take care of projection.[1]

Vocal qualities that may sound weak without a microphone can sound strong and projected when sung with one. At the same time, a singer with a voice that is acoustically beautiful and powerful can sound harsh and pushed if he or she lacks microphone technique. Understanding how to use audio equipment to get the sounds a singer desires without harming the voice is crucial. The information in this chapter will help the reader gain a basic knowledge of terminology and equipment commonly used when amplifying or recording a vocalist as well as providing tips for singing with a microphone.

THE FUNDAMENTALS OF SOUND

In order to understand how to manipulate an audio signal, you must first understand a few basics of sound including frequency, amplitude, harmonics, and resonance.

Frequency

Sound travels in waves of compression and rarefaction within a medium, which for our purposes is air (see figure 9.1). These waves travel through the air and into our inner ears via the ear canal. There they are converted via the eardrums into nerve impulses that are transmitted to the brain and interpreted as sound. The number of waves per second is measured in Hertz (Hz), which gives us the frequency of the sound that we have learned to perceive as pitch. For example, we hear 440 Hz (440 cycles of compression and rarefaction per second) as A4, the pitch A above middle C.

Amplitude

The magnitude of the waves of compression and rarefaction determines the amplitude of the sound, which we call its "volume." The larger the waves of compression and rarefaction, the louder we perceive the sound to be. Measured in decibels (dB), amplitude represents changes in air pressure from the baseline. Decibel measurements range from zero decibels (0 dB), the threshold of human hearing, to 130 dB, the upper edge of the threshold of pain.

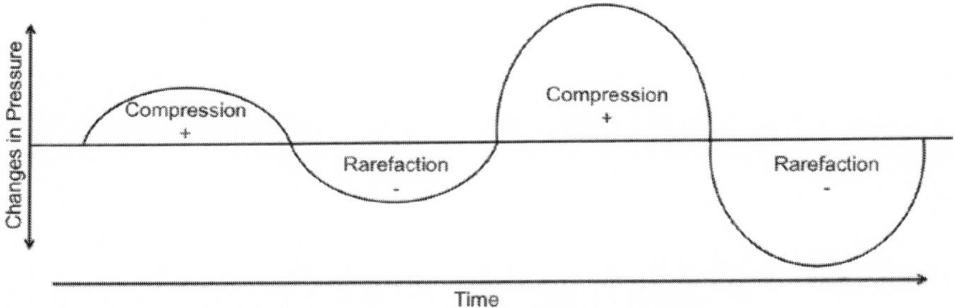

Figure 9.1. Compression and rarefaction. ***Creative Commons***

Harmonics

The vibrating mechanism of an instrument produces the vibrations necessary to establish pitch (the fundamental frequency). The vibrating mechanism for a singer is the vocal folds. If an acoustic instrument, such as the voice, were to produce a note with the fundamental frequency alone, the sound would be strident and mechanical like the emergency alert signal used on television. Pitches played on acoustic instruments consist of multiple frequencies, called overtones, which are emitted from the vibrator along with the fundamental frequency. For the purposes of this chapter, the overtones that we are interested in are called harmonics. Harmonics are whole number multiples of the fundamental frequency. For example, if the fundamental is 220 Hz (A3), the harmonic overtone series would be 220 Hz, 440 Hz (fundamental frequency times two), 660 Hz (fundamental frequency times three), 880 Hz (fundamental frequency times four), and so on. Every musical note contains both the fundamental frequency and a predictable series of harmonics, each of which can be measured and identified as a specific frequency. This series of frequencies then travels through a hollow cavity (the vocal tract) where they are attenuated or amplified by the resonating frequencies of the cavity, which is how resonance occurs.

Resonance

The complex waveform created by the vocal folds travels through the vocal tract, where it is enhanced by the tract's unique resonance characteristics. Depending on the resonator's shape, some harmonics are amplified and some are attenuated. Each singer has a unique vocal tract shape with unique resonance characteristics. This is why two singers of the same voice type can sing the same pitch and yet sound very different. We can analyze these changes with a tool called a spectral analyzer as seen in figure 9.2. The slope from left to right is called the spectral slope. The peaks and valleys along the slope indicate amplitude variations of the corresponding overtones. The difference in spectral slope between instruments (or voices) is what enables a listener to aurally distinguish the difference between two instruments playing or singing the same note.

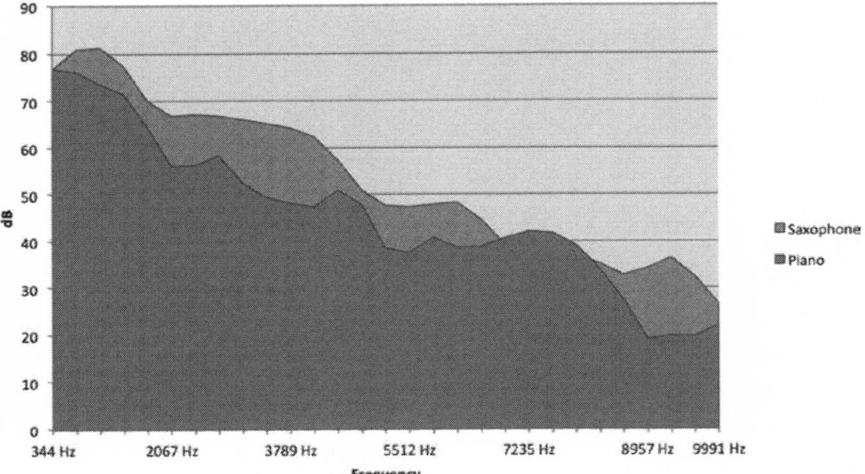

Figure 9.2. The figure above shows two instruments playing the same pitch. The peak at the far left is the fundamental frequency, and the peaks to the right are harmonics that have been amplified and attenuated by the instrument's resonator, resulting in a specific timbre. ***Matthew Edwards***

Because the throat and mouth act as the resonating tube in acoustic singing, changing their size and shape is the only option for making adjustments to timbre for those who perform without microphones. In electronically amplified singing, the sound engineer can make adjustments to boost or attenuate specific frequency ranges, thus changing the singer's timbre. For this and many other reasons discussed in this chapter, it is vitally important for singers to know how audio technology can affect the quality of their voice.

SIGNAL CHAIN

The signal chain is the path an audio signal travels from the input to the output of a sound system. A voice enters the signal chain through a microphone, which transforms acoustic energy into electrical impulses. The electrical pulses generated by the microphone are transmitted through a series of components that modify the signal before the speakers transform it back into acoustic energy. Audio engineers and producers understand the intricacies of these systems and are able to make an infinite variety of alterations to the vocal signal. While some engineers strive to replicate the original sound source as accurately as possible, others use the capabilities of the system to alter the sound for artistic effect. Since more components and variations exist than can be discussed in just a few pages, this chapter will discuss only basic components and variations found in most systems.

Microphones

Microphones transform the acoustic sound waves of the voice into electrical impulses. The component of the microphone that is responsible for receiving the acoustic information is the diaphragm. The two most common diaphragm types that singers will encounter are dynamic and condenser. Each offers advantages and disadvantages depending on how the microphone is to be used.

Dynamic Dynamic microphones consist of a dome-shaped Mylar diaphragm attached to a free-moving copper wire coil that is positioned between the two poles of a magnet. The Mylar diaphragm moves in response to air pressure changes caused by sound waves. When the diaphragm moves, the magnetic coil that is attached to it also moves. As the magnetic coil moves up and down between the magnetic poles, it produces an electrical current that corresponds to the sound waves produced by the singer's voice. That signal is then sent to the soundboard via the microphone cable.

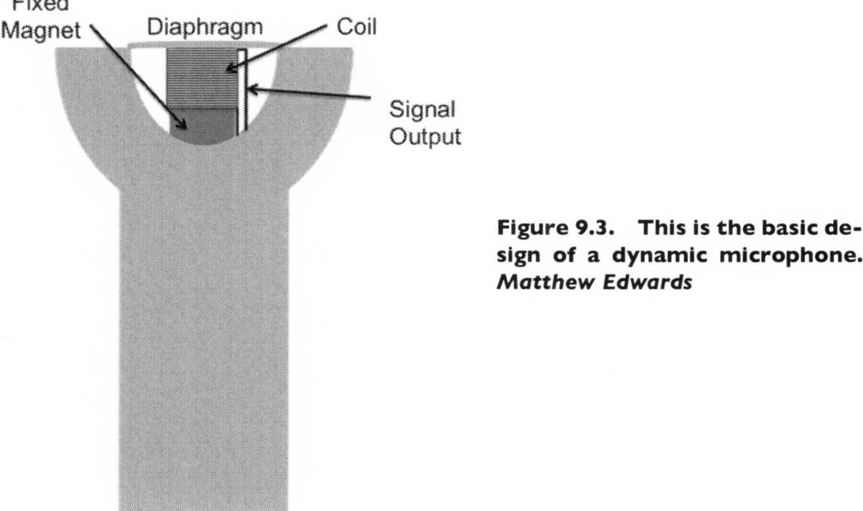

Figure 9.3. This is the basic design of a dynamic microphone. ***Matthew Edwards***

The Shure SM58 dynamic microphone is the industry standard for live performance because it is affordable, nearly indestructible, and easy to use. Dynamic microphones such as the Shure SM58 have a lower sensitivity than condenser microphones, which makes them more successful at avoiding feedback. Because of their reduced tendency to feedback, dynamic microphones are the best choice for artists who use handheld microphones when performing. ♪

Condenser Condenser microphones are constructed with two parallel plates: a rigid posterior plate and a thin, flexible anterior plate. The anterior plate is constructed of either a thin sheet of metal or a piece of Mylar that is coated with a conductive metal. The plates are separated by air, which acts as a layer of insulation. In order to use a condenser microphone, it must be connected to a soundboard that supplies "phantom power." A component of the soundboard, phantom power sends a 48-volt power supply through the microphone cable to the microphone's plates. When the plates are charged by phantom power, they form a capacitor. As acoustic vibrations send the anterior plate into motion, the distance between the two plates varies, which causes the capacitor to release a small electric current. This current, which corresponds with the acoustic signal of the voice, travels through the microphone cable to the soundboard where it can be enhanced and amplified.

Electret condenser microphones are similar to condenser microphones, but they are designed to work without phantom power. The anterior plate of an electret microphone is made of a plastic film coated with a conductive metal that is electrically charged before being set into place opposite the posterior plate. The charge applied to the anterior plate will last for ten or more years and therefore eliminates the need for an exterior power source. Electret condenser microphones are often used in head-mounted and lapel microphones, laptop computers, and smartphones.

Recording engineers prefer condenser microphones for recording applications due to their high level of sensitivity. Using a condenser microphone, performers can sing at nearly inaudible acoustic levels and obtain a final recording that is intimate and earthy. While the same vocal effects can be recorded with a dynamic microphone, they will not have the same clarity as those produced with a condenser microphone.

Frequency Response Frequency response is a term used to define how accurately a microphone captures the tone quality of the signal. A "flat response" microphone captures the original signal with little to no signal alteration. Microphones that are not designated as "flat" have

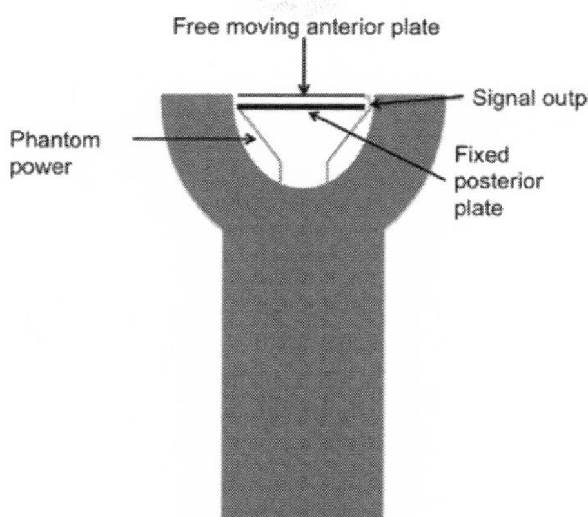

Figure 9.4. This is the basic design of a condenser microphone. *Matthew Edwards*

some type of amplification or attenuation of specific frequencies, also known as cut or boost, within the audio spectrum. For instance, the Shure SM58 microphone drastically attenuates the signal below 300 Hz and amplifies the signal in the 3 kHz range by 6 dB, the 5 kHz range by nearly 8 dB, and the 10 kHz range by approximately 6 dB. The Oktava 319 microphone cuts the frequencies below 200 Hz while boosting everything above 300 Hz with nearly 5 dB between 7 kHz and 10k Hz (see figure 9.5). In practical terms, recording a bass singer with the Shure

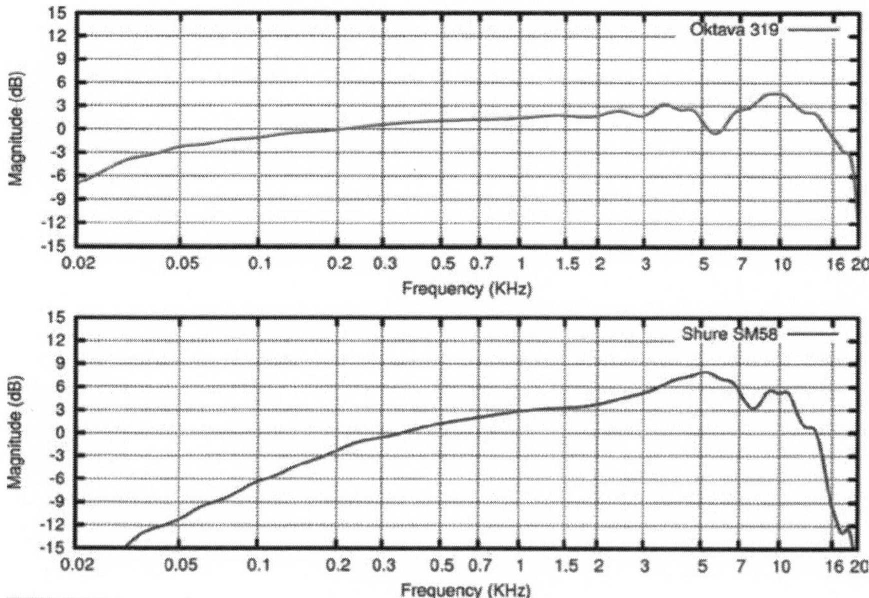

Figure 9.5. Example frequency response graphs for the Oktava 319 and the Shure SM58. *Wikimedia Commons*

SM58 would drastically reduce the amplitude of the fundamental frequency while the Oktava 319 would produce a slightly more consistent boost in the range of the singer's formant. Either of these options could be acceptable depending on the situation, but the frequency response must be considered before making a recording or performing live.

Amplitude Response The amplitude response of a microphone varies depending on the angle at which the singer is positioned in relation to the axis of the microphone. In order to visualize the amplitude response of a microphone at various angles, microphone manufacturers publish polar pattern diagrams (also sometimes called a directional pattern or a pickup pattern). Polar pattern diagrams usually consist of six concentric circles divided into twelve equal sections. The center point of the microphone's diaphragm is labeled 0° and is referred to as "on-axis" while the opposite side of the diagram is labeled 180° and is described as "off-axis."

Although polar pattern diagrams appear in two dimensions, they actually represent a three-dimensional response to acoustic energy. You can use a round balloon as a physical example to help you visualize a three-dimensional polar pattern diagram. Position the tied end of the balloon away from your mouth and the inflated end directly in front of your lips. In this position, you are singing on-axis at 0° with the tied end of the balloon being 180°, or off-axis. If you were to split the balloon in half vertically and horizontally (in relationship to your lips), the point at which those lines intersect would be the center point of the balloon. That imaginary center represents the diaphragm of the microphone. If you were to extend a 45° angle in any direction from the imaginary center and then drew a circle around the inside of the balloon following that angle, you would have a visualization of the three-dimensional application of the two-dimensional polar pattern drawing.

The outermost circle of the diagram indicates that the sound pressure level (SPL) of the signal is transferred without any amplitude reduction, indicated in decibels (dB). Each of the inner circles represents a –5 dB reduction in the amplitude of the signal up to –25 dB. Figure 9.7 is an example.

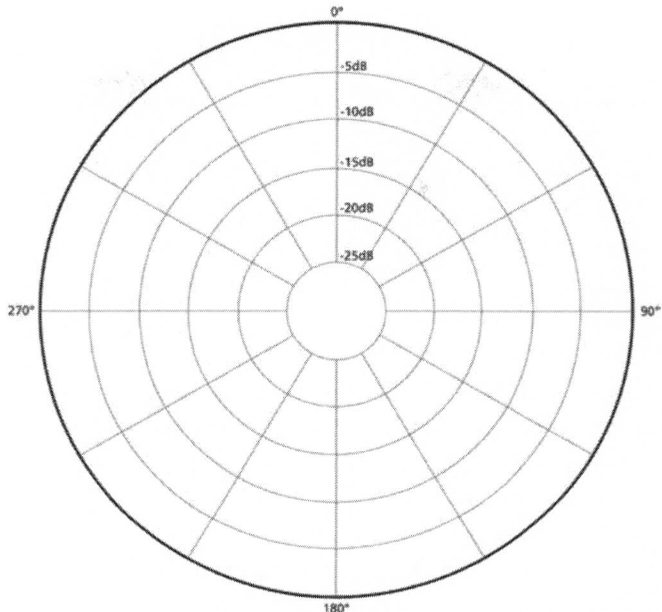

Figure 9.6. An example of a microphone polar pattern diagram. ***Wikimedia Commons***

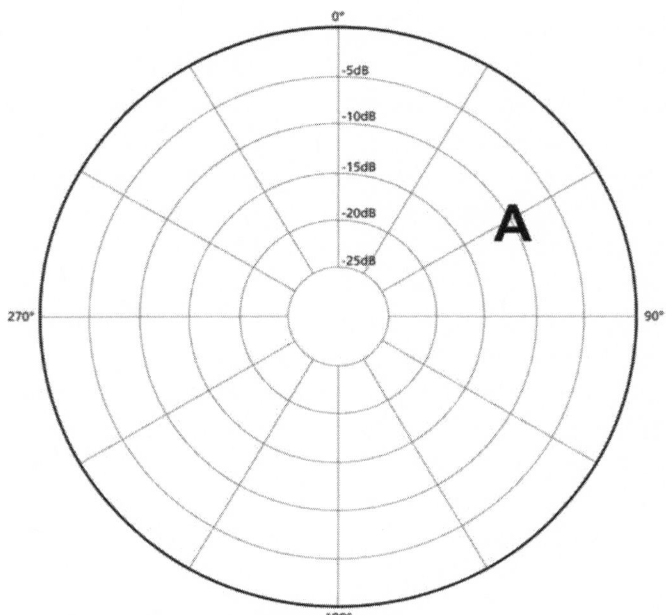

Figure 9.7. If the amplitude response curve intersected with point A, there would be a −10 dB reduction in the amplitude of frequencies received by the microphone's diaphragm at that angle. ***Wikimedia Commons***

Figures 9.8, 9.9, and 9.10 show the most commonly encountered polar patterns.

When you are using a microphone with a polar pattern other than omnidirectional (a pattern that responds to sound equally from all directions), you may encounter frequency response fluctuations in addition to amplitude fluctuations. Cardioid microphones in particular are known for their tendency to boost lower frequencies at close proximity to the sound source while attenuating those same frequencies as the distance between the sound source and the microphone increases. This is known as the "proximity effect." Some manufacturers will notate these frequency response changes on their polar pattern diagrams by using a combination of various lines and dashes alongside the amplitude response curve.

Sensitivity While sensitivity can be difficult to explain in technical terms without going into an in-depth discussion of electricity and electrical terminology, a simplified explanation should suffice for most readers. Manufacturers test microphones with a standardized 1 kHz tone at 94 dB in order to determine how sensitive the microphone's diaphragm will be to acoustic energy. Microphones with greater sensitivity can be placed farther from the sound source without adding excessive noise to the signal. Microphones with lower sensitivity will need to be placed closer to the sound source in order to keep excess noise at a minimum. When shopping for a microphone, the performer should audition several next to each other, plugged into the same soundboard, with the same volume level for each. When singing on each microphone, at the same distance, the performer will notice that some models replicate the voice louder than others. This change in output level is due to differences in each microphone's sensitivity. If a performer has a loud voice, they may prefer a microphone with lower sensitivity (one that requires more acoustic energy to respond). If a performer has a lighter voice, they may prefer a microphone with higher sensitivity (one that responds well to softer signals).

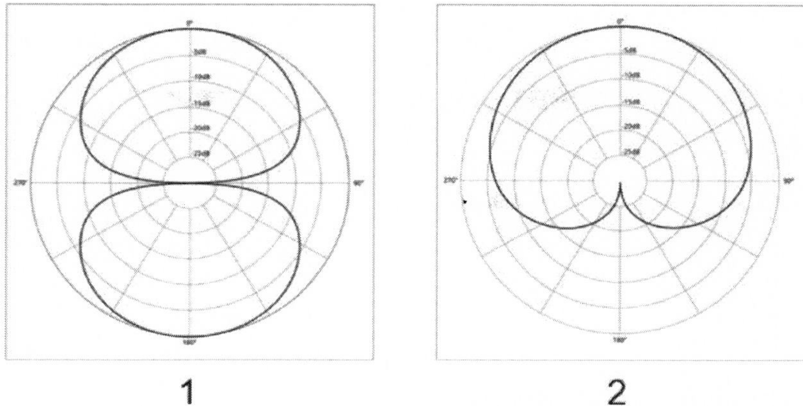

Figure 9.8. Diagram 1 represents a bidirectional pattern; diagram 2 represents a cardioid pattern. ***Creative Commons***

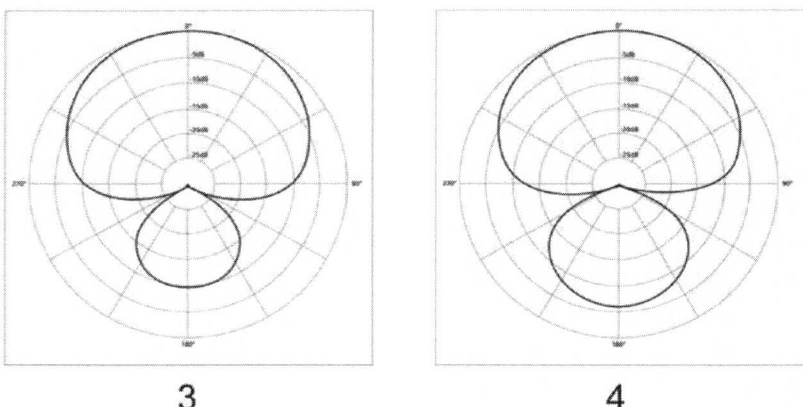

Figure 9.9. Diagram 3 represents a supercardioid pattern; diagram 4 represents a hypercardioid pattern. ***Creative Commons***

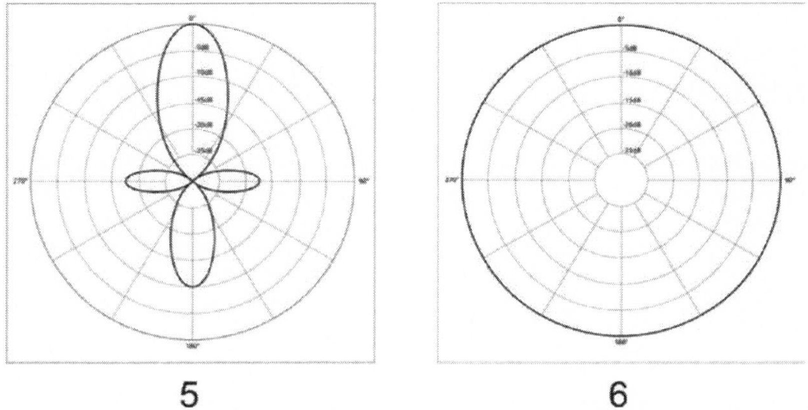

Figure 9.10. Diagram 5 represents a shotgun pattern; diagram 6 represents an omnidirectional pattern. ***Creative Commons***

Equalization (EQ)

Equalizers enable the audio engineer to alter the audio spectrum of the sound source and make tone adjustments with a simple electronic interface. Equalizers come in three main types: shelf, parametric, and graphic.

Shelf Shelf equalizers cut or boost the uppermost and lowermost frequencies of an audio signal in a straight line (see figure 9.11). While this style of equalization is not very useful for fine-tuning a singer's tone quality, it can be very effective in removing room noise. For example, if an air conditioner creates a 60-Hz hum in the recording studio, the shelf can be set at 65 Hz, with a steep slope. This setting eliminates frequencies below 65 Hz and effectively removes the hum from the microphone signal.

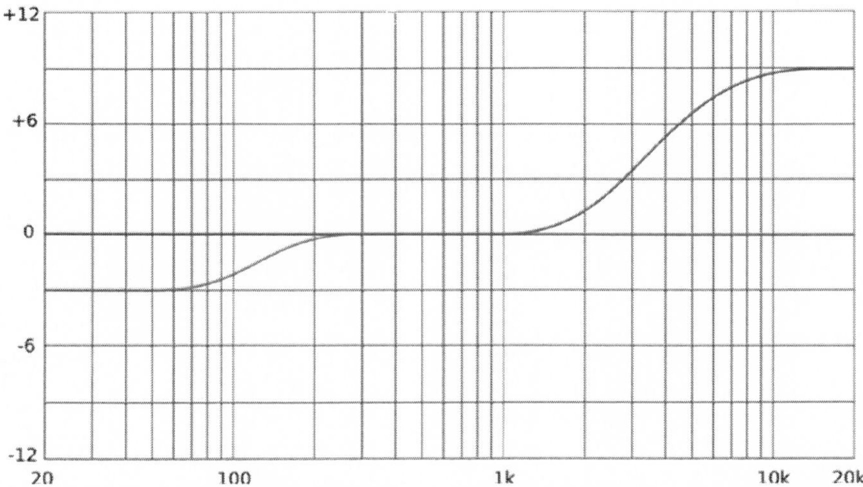

Figure 9.11. The frequency amplitude curves above show the effect of applying a shelf EQ to an audio signal. *Wikimedia Commons*

Parametric Parametric units simultaneously adjust multiple frequencies of the audio spectrum that fall within a defined parameter. The engineer selects a center frequency and adjusts the width of the bell curve surrounding that frequency by adjusting the "Q" (see figure 9.12). He or she then boosts or cuts the frequencies within the bell curve to alter the audio spectrum. Parametric controls take up minimal space on a soundboard and offer sufficient control for most situations. Therefore, most live performance soundboards have parametric EQs on each individual channel. With the advent of digital workstations, engineers can now use computer software to fine-tune the audio quality of each individual channel using a more complex graphic equalizer in

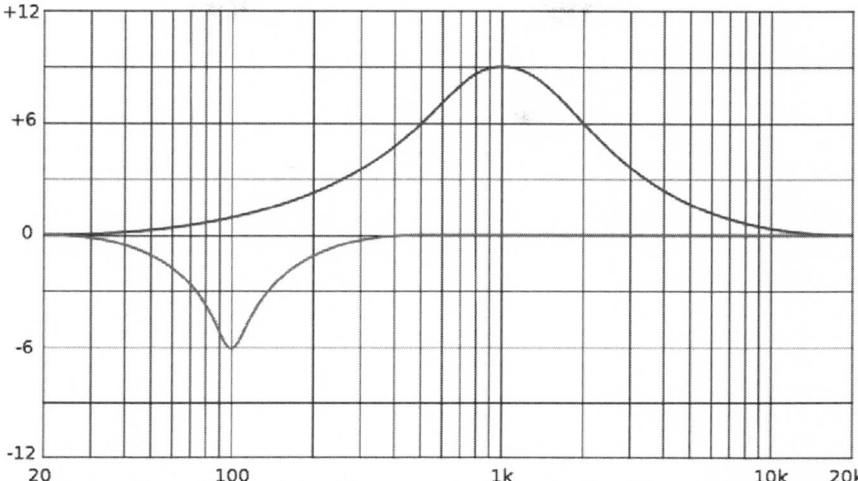

Figure 9.12. The frequency amplitude curves above display two parametric EQ settings. The top curve represents a boost of +8 dB set at 1 kHz with a relatively large bell curve—a low Q. The lower curve represents a high Q set at 100 Hz with a cut of −6 dB. *Wikimedia Commons*

both live and recording studio settings without taking up any additional physical space on the board. However, many engineers still prefer to use parametric controls during a live performance since they are usually sufficient and are easier to adjust mid-performance.

Parametric adjustments on a soundboard are made with rotary knobs similar to those in figure 9.13. In some cases, you will find a button

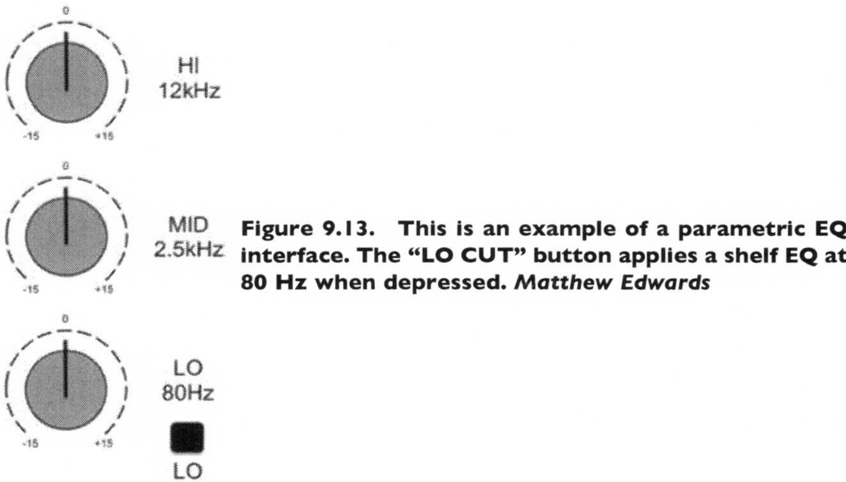

Figure 9.13. This is an example of a parametric EQ interface. The "LO CUT" button applies a shelf EQ at 80 Hz when depressed. *Matthew Edwards*

labeled "low cut" or "high pass" that will automatically apply a shelf filter to the bottom of the audio spectrum at a specified frequency. On higher-end boards, you may also find a knob that enables you to select the high pass frequency.

Graphic Graphic equalizers enable engineers to identify a specific frequency for boost or cut with a fixed frequency bandwidth. For example, a ten-band equalizer enables the audio engineer to adjust ten specific frequencies (in Hz): 31, 63, 125, 250, 500, 1K, 2K, 4K, 8K, and 16K. Graphic equalizers are often one of the final elements of the signal chain, preceding only the amplifier and speakers. In this position, they can be used to adjust the overall tonal quality of the entire mix.

Utilizing Equalization Opinions on the usage of equalization vary among engineers. Some prefer to only use equalization to remove or reduce frequencies that were not a part of the original sound signal. Others will use EQ if adjusting microphone placement fails to yield acceptable results. Some engineers prefer a more processed sound and may use equalization liberally to intentionally change the vocal quality of the singer. For instance, if the singer's voice sounds dull, the engineer could add "ring" or "presence" to the voice by boosting the equalizer in the 2–10 kHz range.

Compression

Many singers are capable of producing vocal extremes in both frequency and amplitude levels that can prove problematic for the sound team. To help solve this problem, engineers often use compression.

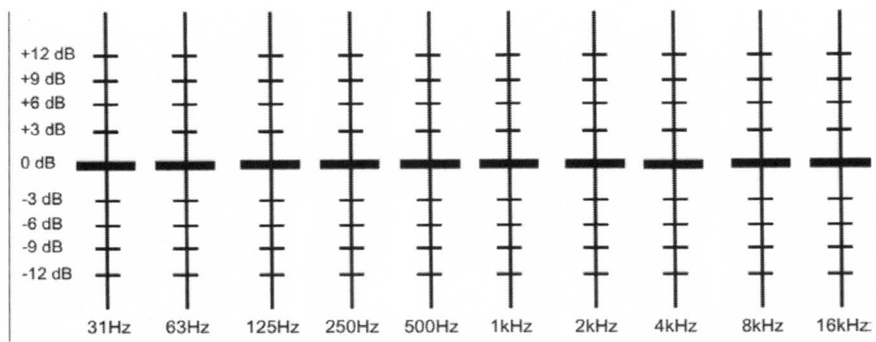

Figure 9.14. This is an example of a graphic equalizer interface.
Matthew Edwards

Compressors limit the output of a sound source by a specified ratio. The user sets the maximum acceptable amplitude level for the output, called the "threshold," and then sets a ratio to reduce the output once it surpasses the threshold. The typical ratio for a singer is usually between 3:1 and 5:1. A 4:1 ratio indicates that for every 4 dB beyond the threshold level, the output will only increase by 1 dB. For example, if the singer went 24 dB beyond the threshold with a 4:1 ratio, the output would only be 6 dB beyond the threshold level (see figure 9.15).

Adjusting the sound via microphone technique can provide some of the same results as compression and is preferable for the experienced artist. However, compression tends to be more consistent and also gives the singer freedom to focus on performing and telling a story. The additional artistic freedom provided by compression is especially beneficial

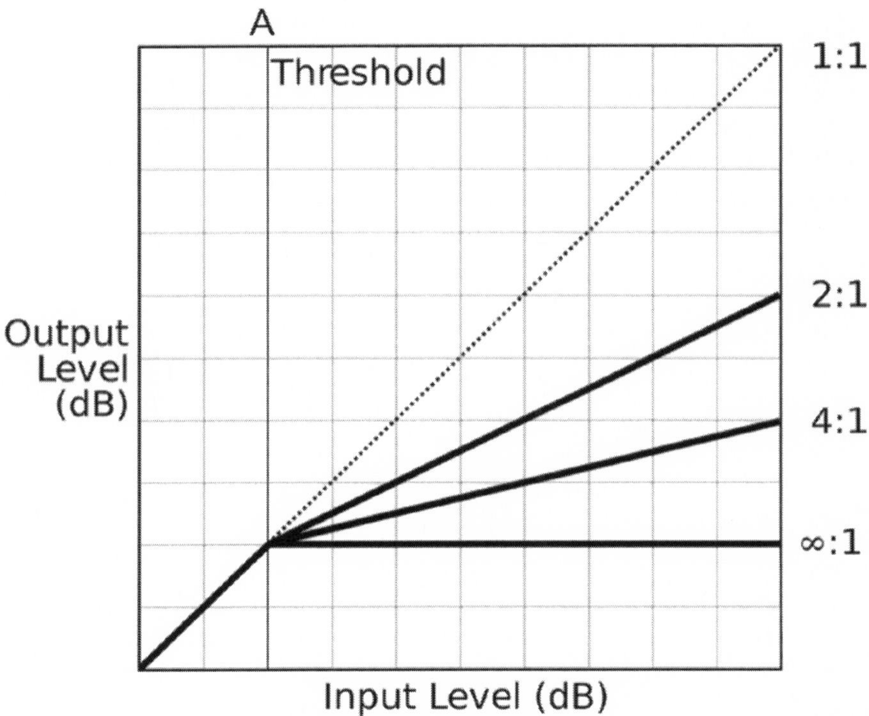

Figure 9.15. This graph represents the effects of various compression ratios applied to a signal. The 1:1 angle represents no compression. The other ratios represent the effect of compression on an input signal with the threshold set at line A. *Wikimedia Commons*

to singers who use head-mounted microphones, performers who switch between vocal extremes such as falsetto and chest voice, and those who are new to performing with a microphone. Compression can also be helpful for classical singers whose dynamic abilities, while impressive live, are often difficult to record in a manner that allows for consistent listening levels through a stereo system.

If a standard compressor causes unacceptable alterations to the tone quality, engineers can turn to a multiband compressor. Rather than affecting the entire spectrum of sound, multiband compressors allow the engineer to isolate a specific frequency range within the audio signal and then set an individual compression setting for that frequency range. For example, if a singer creates a dramatic boost in the 4-kHz range every time they sing above an A4, a multiband compressor can be used to limit the amplitude of the signal in only that part of the voice. By setting a 3:1 ratio in the 4-kHz range at a threshold that corresponds to the amplitude peaks that appear when the performer sings above A4, the engineer can eliminate vocal "ring" from the sound on only the offending notes while leaving the rest of the signal untouched. These units are available for both live and studio use and can be a great alternative to compressing the entire signal.

Reverb

Reverb is one of the easier effects for singers to identify; it is the effect you experience when singing in a cathedral. An audience experiences natural reverberation when they hear the direct signal from the singer and then, milliseconds later, they hear multiple reflections as the acoustical waves of the voice bounce off the side walls, floor, and ceiling of the performance hall.

Many performance venues and recording studios are designed to inhibit natural reverb. Without at least a little reverb added to the sound, even the best singer can sound harsh and even amateurish. Early reverb units transmitted the audio signal through a metal spring, which added supplementary vibrations to the signal. While some engineers still use spring reverb to obtain a specific effect, most now use digital units. Common settings on digital reverb units include wet/dry, bright/dark,

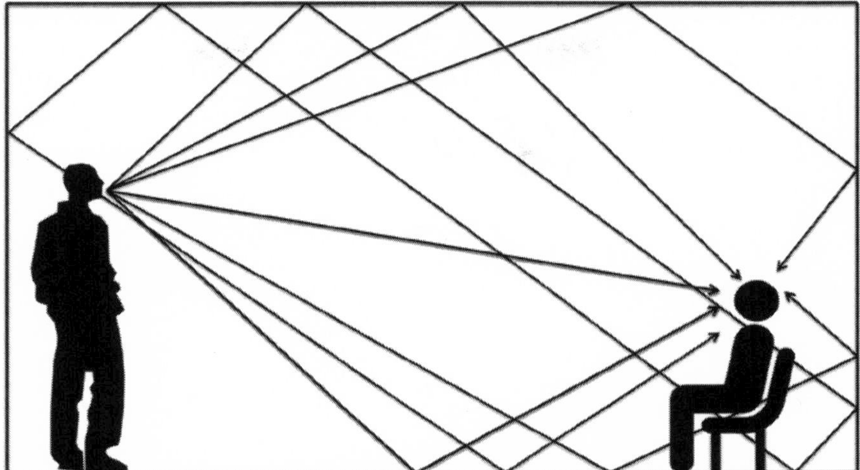

Figure 9.16. This diagram illustrates the multiple lines of reflection that create reverb. ***Matthew Edwards***

and options for delay time. The wet/dry control adjusts the amount of direct signal (dry) and the amount of reverberated signal (wet). The bright/dark control helps simulate the effects of various surfaces within a natural space. For instance, harder surfaces such as stone reflect high frequencies and create a brighter tone quality while softer surfaces such as wood reflect lower frequencies and create a darker tone quality. The delay time, which is usually adjustable from milliseconds to seconds, adjusts the amount of time between when the dry signal and wet signals reach the ear. Engineers can transform almost any room into a chamber music hall or concert stadium simply by adjusting these settings.

Delay

Whereas reverb blends multiple wet signals with the dry signal to replicate a natural space, delay purposefully separates a single wet signal from the dry signal to create repetitions of the voice. With delay, you will hear the original note first and then a digitally produced repeat of the note several milliseconds to seconds later. The delayed note may be heard one time or multiple times and the timing of those repeats can be adjusted to match the tempo of the song.

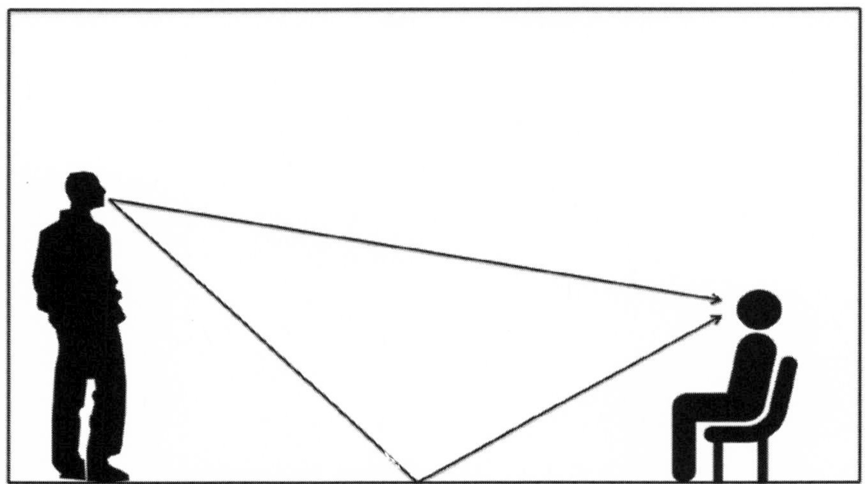

Figure 9.17. This diagram illustrates how a direct line of sound followed by a reflected line of sound creates delay. ***Matthew Edwards***

Auto-Tune

Auto-Tune was first used in studios as a useful way to clean up minor imperfections in otherwise perfect performances. Auto-Tune is now an industry standard that many artists use, even if they are not willing to admit it. Auto-Tune has gained a bad reputation in the past few years, and whether or not you agree with its use, it is a reality in today's market. If you do not understand how to use it properly, you could end up sounding like T-Pain.[2]

Both Antares and Melodyne have developed Auto-Tune technology in both "auto" and "graphical" formats. "Auto" Auto-Tune allows the engineer to set specific parameters for pitch correction that are then computer controlled. "Graphical" Auto-Tune tracks the pitch in the selected area of a recording and plots the fundamental frequency on a linear graph. The engineer can then select specific notes for pitch correction. They can also drag selected pitches to a different frequency, add or reduce vibrato, and change formant frequencies above the fundamental. To simplify, the "auto" function makes general corrections while the "graphic" function makes specific corrections. The "auto" setting is usually used to achieve a specific effect (for instance "I Believe" by Cher), while the "graphic" setting is used to correct small imperfections in a recorded performance.

Digital Voice Processors

Digital voice processors are still relatively new to the market and have yet to gain widespread usage among singers. While there are several brands of vocal effects processors available, the industry leader as of this printing is a company called TC-Helicon. TC-Helicon manufactures several different units that span from consumer to professional grade. TC-Helicon's premier performer-controlled unit is called the VoiceLive 3. The VoiceLive 3 incorporates more than twelve vocal effects, eleven guitar effects, and a multi-track looper with 250 factory presets and 250 memory slots for user presets. The VoiceLive 3 puts the effects at the singer's feet in a programmable stomp box that also includes phantom power, MIDI in/out, a USB connection, guitar input, and monitor out. Onboard vocal effects include equalization, compression, reverb, and "auto" Auto-Tune. The unit also offers µMod (an adjustable voice modulator), a doubler (for thickening the lead vocal), echo, delay, reverb, and several other specialized effects.[3] ♪

One of the most impressive features of digital voice processors is the ability to add computer-generated harmonies to the lead vocal. After the user sets the musical key, the processor identifies the fundamental frequency of each sung note. The computer then adds digitized voices at designated intervals above and below the lead singer. The unit also offers the option to program each individual song, with multiple settings for every verse, chorus, and bridge.

THE BASICS OF LIVE SOUND SYSTEMS

Live sound systems come in a variety of sizes from small practice units to state-of-the-art stadium rigs. Most singers only need a basic knowledge of the components commonly found in systems that have one to eight inputs. Units beyond that size usually require an independent sound engineer and are beyond the scope of this chapter.

Following the microphone, the first element in the live signal chain is usually the mixer. Basic portable mixers provide controls for equalization, volume level, auxiliary (usually used for effects such as reverb and compression), and, on some units, controls for built-in digital effects processors. Powered mixers combine an amplifier with a basic mixer, providing a compact solution for those who do not need a complex system. Since unpowered mixers do not provide amplification, you will need to add a separate amplifier to power this system.

The powered mixer or amplifier connects to speaker cabinets, which contain a "woofer" and a "tweeter." The woofer is a large round speaker that handles the bass frequencies while the tweeter is a horn-shaped speaker that handles the treble frequencies. The crossover, a component built into the speaker cabinet, separates high and low frequencies and sends them to the appropriate speaker (woofer or tweeter). Speaker cabinets can be either active or passive. Passive cabinets require a powered mixer or an amplifier in order to operate. Active cabinets have an amplifier built-in and do not require an external amplifier.

If you do not already own a microphone and amplification system, you can purchase a simple setup at relatively low cost through online vendors such as Sweetwater.com and MusiciansFriend.com. A dynamic microphone and a powered monitor are enough to get started. If you would like to add a digital voice processor, Digitech and TC-Helicon both sell entry-level models that will significantly improve the tonal quality of a sound system.

Monitors are arguably the most important element in a live sound system. The monitor is a speaker that faces the performers and allows them to hear themselves and/or the other instruments on stage. On-stage volume levels can vary considerably, with drummers often producing sound levels as high as 120 dB. Those volume levels make it nearly impossible for singers to receive natural acoustic feedback while performing. Monitors can improve aural feedback and help reduce the temptation to oversing. Powered monitors offer the same advantages as powered speaker cabinets and can be a great option for amplification when practicing. They are also good to have around as a backup plan in case you arrive at a venue and discover they do not supply monitors. In-ear monitors offer another option for performers and are especially useful for those who frequently move around the stage.

MICROPHONE TECHNIQUE

The microphone is an inseparable part of the contemporary commercial music singer's instrument. Just as there are techniques that improve singing, there are also techniques that will improve microphone use.

Understanding what a microphone does is only the first step to using it successfully. Once you understand how a microphone works, you need hands-on experience.

The best way to learn microphone technique is to experiment. Try the following exercises to gain a better understanding of how to use a microphone when singing:

- Hold a dynamic microphone with a cardioid pattern directly in front of your mouth, no farther than one centimeter away. Sustain a comfortable pitch and slowly move the microphone away from your lips. Listen to how the vocal quality changes. When the microphone is close to the lips, you should notice that the sound is louder and has more bass response. As you move the microphone away from your mouth, there will be a noticeable loss in volume and the tone will become brighter.
- Next, sustain a pitch while rotating the handle down. The sound quality will change in a similar fashion as when you moved the microphone away from your lips.
- Now try singing breathy with the microphone close to your lips. How little effort can you get away with while producing a marketable sound?
- Try singing bright vowels and dark vowels and notice how the microphone affects the tone quality.
- Also experiment with adapting your diction to the microphone. Because the microphone amplifies everything, you may need to underpronounce certain consonants when singing. You will especially want to reduce the power of the consonants [t], [s], [p], and [b].

FINAL THOUGHTS

Since this is primarily an overview, you can greatly improve your comprehension of the material by seeking other resources to deepen your knowledge. There are many great resources available that may help clarify some of these difficult concepts. Most important, you must experiment. The more you play around with sound equipment on your own, the better you will understand it and the more comfortable you will feel when performing or recording with audio technology.

NOTES

1. Paula Lockheart, "A History of Early Microphone Singing, 1925–1939: American Mainstream Popular Singing at the Advent of Electronic Amplification," *Popular Music and Society* 26, no. 3 (2003): 367–385.

2. For example, listen to T-Pain's track "Buy You a Drank (Shawty Snappin')."

3. "VoiceLive 3," TC-Helicon, www.tc-helicon.com/products/voicelive-3/ (accessed May 2, 2016).

APPENDIX

I Know Moonlight

From Slave Songs of the United States

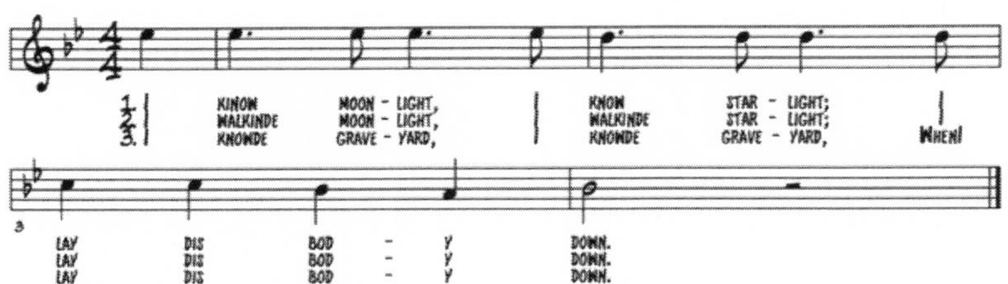

Appendix 1. "I Know Moonlight." ***Slave Songs of the United States***

Dere's No Rain

From Slave Songs of the United States

2. Dere's no sun to burn you.---O yes, etc.
3. Dere's no hard trials.
4. Dere's no whips a-crackin'.
5. Dere's no stormy weather.
6. Dere's no tribulation.
7. No more slavery in de kingdom.
8. No evil-doers in de kingdom.
9. All is gladness in de kingdom.

Appendix 2. "Dere's No Rain." ***Slave Songs of the United States***

No More Auction Block For Me

From Slave Songs of the United States

Appendix 3. "No Auction Block for Me." ***Slave Songs of the United States***

Appendix 4. Vocal warm-up. ***Eli Yamin and Darrell Lauer***

Appendix 5. 8-bar blues. ***Eli Yamin***

Appendix 6. 12-bar blues. ***Eli Yamin***

GLOSSARY

African retentions: The retention of African traits.

Angular: Every posture at an angle. One of the characteristics of Negro expression named by Zora Neale Hurston.

Areas of vocal production: Three areas of vocal production are *energy* source (breath, or *sound* source), larynx (sometimes called the voice box), and *resonators* (face, mouth, neck, and throat).

Asymmetry: In music, the use of syncopation and unpredictable phrasing. Asymmetry is one of the characteristics of Negro expression named by Zora Neale Hurston.

Blues: Mainly a solo art form created by African Americans defined by story, steady rhythm, and sound of the voice. The blues is designed to engage and uplift communities by transforming sadness and/or hardship into resilience, strength, and, sometimes, good humor. Embodying a system of immediate emotional communication with ancient roots yet infinitely modern, the blues traces its lineage to distinct sources in Africa that were uniquely combined during the crucible of slavery in the United States and gradually codified into the blues sometime between the end of the Civil War and the dawn of the recording age.

Blues form: The most common blues form is 12 measures long, using I, IV, and V chords like this: I/I/I/I/IV/IV/I/I/V/IV/I/I. The lyric structure for this form often begins with a statement that is repeated and then answered with a line commenting on the first and ending with a rhyme. Other blues forms include those of 8 bars and 16 bars (see appendix page 204).

Blues inflection: The way blues artists articulate melody to communicate blues feeling. Blues inflection includes a wide variety of devices uniquely adapted by each performer. These devices include scoops, slides, nasality, syncopation, hollers, moans, and cries.

Blues scale: A theoretical scale with flat third, fifth, and seventh that does not accurately render blues tonality. This author prefers Kubik's notion of *elastic scales* for describing blues melodicism.

Call-and-response: A give-and-take musical device with African roots commonly used in blues music. Blues uses call-and-response in a variety of ways, including between solo singer and an instrument or singer and the audience. The call-and-response nature of the blues contributes to its ability to deliver communal catharsis and is one of the enduring characteristics that makes it widely loved and practiced around the world.

Chest voice: The voice commonly used to speak (mode 2). The chest voice uses primarily the thyroarytenoid (TA) muscles in the larynx to create mostly lower sounds.

Commercial contemporary music (CCM): American-born styles of music including blues, pop, music theater, gospel, jazz, rhythm and blues, soul, U.S. folk, country, hip-hop, metal, rock, and electronic. The term was announced in 2000 at the *Science and the Singing Teacher in the New Millennium* conference, sponsored by the New York Singing Teachers Association and Mount Sinai Medical Center in New York City. The term is meant to collect all the styles previously called "nonclassical" under one umbrella and stop the practice of defining these styles by what they were not.[1]

Constriction: When a muscle is stuck in the contracted position and is not easily pliable; when this occurs, limitation in stamina also occurs, eventually resulting in fatigue and possibly causing damage.[2]

Constrictor muscles: The three sets of muscles that can contract and close the throat (like when swallowing or gargling).[3]

Cricothyroid (CT) muscles: These support vocal register mode 3. Mode 3 is the vocal register known as *falsetto* in men or *head register* in both women and men and is one of the primary vocal registers.

Elastic scales: A flexible scale named by Kubik that features flexible pitch areas around the third and the seventh in particular. These pitches can be raised and lowered as well as other scale degrees in a variety of ways depending on the particular moment, emotion, soundscape of the song, and blues tradition being employed.

Fry or pulse: The lowest vocal register, mode 1. Commercial contemporary music singers, including blues singers, use the fry effectively for a rough, gravelly effect.

Gospel: African American singing tradition praising God that draws together a range of African American musical and sacred traditions. Thomas Dorsey, widely considered the father of gospel music, was a blues pianist, singer, arranger, and composer before devoting himself full-time to composing and performing in the gospel tradition. His early composition "Take My Hand, Precious Lord," made famous by Mahalia Jackson, is one of gospel music's most treasured and widely known classics.

Growl: A vocal effect commonly used in African American singing styles with a raspy, gravelly tone. It can easily be found in blues singers such as Bobby Blue Bland, Koko Taylor, and Howlin' Wolf.

Head voice: The part of the voice used to sing higher pitches in a lighter tone color. The head voice, sometimes known as *falsetto*, uses primarily the cricothyroid (CT) muscles in the larynx.

Holler: A vocal effect commonly used in African American singing styles with an open throat projecting a loud and free sound on open vowels. Hollers were a common musical form during slavery and could be used to communicate messages over long distances as well as accompanying work. Many blues artists, ranging from Muddy Waters to Shemekia Copeland, use the holler technique to powerful effect when singing the blues.

Improvisation: In the blues, this is embellishing a melody and or story depending on the performer's mood, energy of the room, and interaction between performers and the audience.

Intercostal muscles: Several groups of muscles that help move the chest wall and are involved in the mechanical aspect of breathing.[4]

Jook: The word for a Negro pleasure house where the blues was born. "Singing and playing in the true Negro style is called 'jooking.'"[5]

Larynx: The hollow muscular organ forming a passage of air to the lungs and holding the vocal cords.[6]

Mix register: Where the singer combines mode 2 and 3 registers. For anyone struggling to sing high notes without strain, learning to sing consistently in *mix* is a lifesaver.

Mode 1: The pulse or vocal fry—the lowest register. Commercial contemporary music singers, including blues singers, use the fry effectively for a rough, gravelly effect. It is best used sparingly and should never be the default register because doing so for prolonged periods can cause vocal strain.

Mode 2: The thyroarytenoid (TA)—the register most people use to speak—is often referred to as the *chest register*. It is one of the primary registers.

Mode 3: The cricothyroid (CT) is the other primary register and is known as *falsetto* in men or *head register* in both women and men.

Mode 4: Flute or whistle register—the extremely high register that some high-voiced women can use effectively.

Onset: The beginning of the sound you make, especially at the top of phrases. Trineice Robinson-Martin identifies four types of onset:

Hard onset is when sound is initiated abruptly without a smooth flow of air. This draws the vocal folds together quickly and creates a pressed, rough sound.

Breathy onset is where you hear an excessive amount of air before the vocal folds are drawn together to make the sound. The sound tends to be weaker and can be interpreted as more emotionally vulnerable.

Balanced onset is where there is a smooth initiation of the sound and an optimal amount of airflow draws the vocal folds together. There is no noticeable popping or pressed quality in the initiation of tone.

Gravel onset is also important in blues and this is accomplished by beginning the sound in a vocal fry and then sliding into a pitched tone.[7]

Polyp: Vocal polyp. A mass that forms on the vocal folds due to excessive vocal use and abuse. It is almost always larger than a vocal nodule and is usually a softer and more movable lesion. It is usually on one vocal fold in contrast to vocal nodules, which are almost always in pairs.

Polyrhythm: Two or more rhythms occurring simultaneously.

Ring shout: An African American worship tradition involving particular movement and vocal practices that create a trance effect.

Shuffle rhythm: A fundamental blues rhythm resembling the heartbeat.

Slide: Vocal slides—descending and ascending pitches used by blues singers of all eras.

Soulful: In music, often used to describe performances exhibiting African American style characteristics.

Spiritual: Traditional African American songs with sacred text that often convey multiple meanings.

Stomp/clap: A fundamental four-beat rhythm of American music derived from African American church music with foot stomps on beats 1 and 3 and hand claps on beats 2 and 4.

Swing rhythm: A fundamental American rhythm that contains uneven eighth notes suggesting a polyrhythmic framework featuring simultaneous duple and triple time.

Thyroarytenoid (TA) muscle: This supports vocal register mode 2—often referred to as the *chest register*—and is one of the primary registers. Chest register is what most people use to speak.

Underground Railroad: Not an actual railroad but a network of safe houses and well-intentioned people working together to help enslaved African Americans escape northward to freedom from slavery.

Vocal registers: Parts of the voice that make up the entire range of a singer. Each register uses a different combination of muscles in the throat with modes 2 and 3 being the most actively used.

Wavy intonation: Varying pitches up and down. Can be used to evoke feeling and a particular language of vocal expression, such as in the blues or the Muslim call to prayer.

Will to adorn: Embellishing a melody through spontaneous improvisation as the spirit of the song moves you. Will to adorn is one of the characteristics of Negro expression named by Zora Neale Hurston.

Work song: A song tradition from the times of American slavery when workers would sing songs that would match the rhythm of the work they were doing.

NOTES

1. Jeannette LoVetri, "Classical and Contemporary Commercial Music: A Comparison," 2014, http://www.thevoiceworkshop.com/pdfs/LoVetri%20Chapter%20Mordern%20Singer.pdf.

2. Trineice Robinson-Martin, *So You Want to Sing Gospel* (Lanham, MD: Rowman & Littlefield, 2017), 230.

3. Robinson-Martin, *So You Want to Sing Gospel*, 230.

4. Robinson-Martin, *So You Want to Sing Gospel*, 231.

5. Zora Neale Hurston, "Characteristics of Negro Expression," 1933; Robert O'Meally, *The Jazz Cadence of American Culture* (New York: Columbia University Press, 1998), 298.

6. Robinson-Martin, *So You Want to Sing Gospel*, 231.

7. Robinson-Martin, *So You Want to Sing Gospel*, 87.

BIBLIOGRAPHY

Albertson, Chris, and Gunther Schuller. *Bessie Smith: Empress of the Blues*. New York: Schirmer, 1975.

Allen, William Francis, Charles Pickard Ware, and Lucy McKim Garrison, eds. *Slave Songs of the United States: The Classic 1867 Anthology*. New York: Dover, 1995.

Baraka, Amiri. *Blues People*. New York: Harper Perennial, 1963.

Blackmon, Douglas A. *Slavery by Another Name: The Re-Enslavement of Black Americans from the Civil War to World War II*. New York: Doubleday, 2008.

Boyer, Horace. *How Sweet the Sound: The Golden Age of Gospel*. Montgomery, AL: Elliott and Clark Publishing, 1995.

———. *Lift Every Voice and Sing II: An African American Hymnal*. New York: Church Publishing, 1993.

Bradford, Sarah. *Harriet, the Moses of Her People*. New York: Geo R. Lockwood and Son, 1886.

Broonzy, Big Bill. *Big Bill Blues: William Broonzy's Story as Told to Yannick Bruynoghe*. New York: Oak Publications, 1955.

Brown, Oren. *Discover Your Voice: How to Develop Healthy Voice Habits*. Norwich: Singular Publishing, 1996.

Brown, William Wells. *The Anti-Slavery Harp: A Collection of Songs for Anti-Slavery Meetings*. Boston: Bela Marsh, 1848.

———. *My Southern Home*. Boston: A. G. Brown, 1880.

Carawan, Guy, and Candi Carawan. *Sing for Freedom: The Story of the Civil Rights Movement through Its Songs*. Montgomery, AL: NewSouth Books, 2007.

Charters, Samuel B. *The Country Blues*. New York: Da Capo, 1975.

———. *The Poetry of the Blues*. New York: Oak Publications, 1963.

———. *The Roots of the Blues*. London: Marion Boyars Publishers, 1981.

———. *Walking a Blues Road: A Blues Reader 1956–2004*. New York: Marion Boyars Publishers, 2004.

Cohn, Lawrence. *Nothing but the Blues*. New York: Abbeville Press, 1993.

Cohodas, Nadine. *Queen: The Life and Music of Dinah Washington*. New York: Pantheon, 2004.

Davis, Angela. *Blues Legacies and Black Feminism*. New York: Random House, 1998.

DeSalvo, Debra. *The Language of the Blues from Alcorub to Zuzu*. New York: Billboard Press, 2000.

Dixon, Willie, with Don Snowden. *The Willie Dixon Story: I Am the Blues*, New York: Da Capo, 1990.

Douglass, Frederick. *My Bondage and My Freedom*. New York: Penguin, 1855; reprint, 2004.

Duval Harrison, Daphne. *Black Pearls: Blues Queens of the 1920s*. New Brunswick, NJ: Rutgers University Press, 1988.

Edwards, Honeyboy. *The World Don't Owe Me Nothin': The Life and Times of Bluesman Honeyboy Edwards*. Chicago: Chicago Review Press, 1997.

Edwards, Matthew. *So You Want to Sing Rock 'n' Roll*. Lanham, MD: Rowman & Littlefield, 2014.

Ellington, Duke. *Piano Method for Blues*. New York: Robbins Music Corporation, 1943.

Evans, David. *Big Road Blues: Tradition and Creativity in the Folk Blues*. Berkeley, CA: Da Capo, 1982.

Ferris, William. *Blues from the Delta*. New York: Da Capo, 1978.

———. *W. C. Handy's Blues—An Anthology*. Jackson: University of Mississippi Press, 1990.

Friedwald, Will. *Jazz Singing: America's Great Voices from Bessie Smith to Bebop and Beyond*. New York: Da Capo, 1996.

Garner, Kelly K. *So You Want to Sing Country*. Lanham, MD: Rowman & Littlefield, 2017.

Gordon, Robert. *Can't Be Satisfied: The Life and Times of Muddy Waters*. Boston: Back Bay Books, 2003.

Graves, Tom. *Crossroads: The Life and Afterlife of Blues Legend Robert Johnson*. Spokane, WA: Demers Books, 2008.

Handy, W. C. *Blues: An Anthology*. New York: Dover, 1949.

———. *Father of the Blues: An Autobiography*. New York: Da Capo, 1941.

James, Etta, and David Ritz. *Rage to Survive: The Etta James Story*. New York: Villard, 1995.

Kay, Jackie. *Bessie Smith*. Somerset: Absolute Press, 1997.

Keil, Charles. *Urban Blues*. Chicago: University of Chicago Press, 1966.

Kemble, Frances Anne. *Journal of a Residence on a Georgia Plantation in 1838–1839*. New York: 1864. University of Georgia Press, Reprint edition (March 1, 1984).

King, B.B., with David Ritz. *Blues All Around Me: The Autobiography of B.B. King*. New York: HarperCollins, 1996.

Kubik, Gerhard. *Africa and the Blues*. Jackson: University Press of Mississippi, 1999.

Mance, Junior. *Blues Piano Course*. Miami Beach, FL: Hansen House, 1967.

Mississippi Department of Archives and History. *All Shook Up: Mississippi Roots of American Popular Music*. Jackson: Mississippi Department of Archives, 1995.

Morgenstern, Dan. *Living with Jazz*. New York: Pantheon, 2004.

Murray, Albert. *The Blue Devils of Nada: A Contemporary American Approach to Aesthetic Statement*. New York: Random House, 1996.

———. *Stompin' the Blues*. New York: Da Capo, 1976.

Niemack, Judy. *Exploring the Blues*. New York: Second Floor Music, 2012.

Northup, Solomon. *Twelve Years a Slave*. Los Angeles: Graymalkin Media, 1853.

Oliver, Paul. *Barrelhouse Blues*. New York: Basic Civitas Books, 2009.

———. *Blues Fell This Morning: Meaning of the Blues*. New York: Cambridge University Press, 1960.

———. *The Meaning of the Blues*. New York: Collier Books, 1960.

Olmsted, Frederick Law. *Journey in the Seaboard Slave States: With Remarks on Their Economy*. New York: Dix and Edwards; London: Sampson Low, Son & Co., 1856.

O'Meally, Robert. *The Jazz Cadence of American Culture*. New York: Columbia University Press, 1998.

Palmer, Robert. *Deep Blues*. London: Penguin, 1981.

Pearson, Barry Lee, and Bill McCulloch. *Robert Johnson Lost and Found*. Champaign: University of Illinois Press, 2003.

Pleasants, Henry. *The Great American Popular Singers*. New York: Simon and Schuster, 1974.

Porter, Bob. *Soul Jazz: Jazz in the Black Community, 1945–1975*. Bloomington, IN: Xlibris, 2016.

Reagon, Bernice Johnson. *If You Don't Go, Don't Hinder Me: The African American Sacred Song Tradition*. Lincoln: University of Nebraska Press, 2001.

———, ed. *We'll Understand It Better By and By: Pioneering African American Gospel Composers*. Washington, DC: Smithsonian Institution Scholarly Press, 1992.

Robinson-Martin, Trineice. *So You Want to Sing Gospel*. Lanham, MD: Rowman & Littlefield, 2017.

Schuller, Gunther. *Early Jazz, Its Roots and Musical Development*. New York: Oxford University Press, 1968.

Segrest, James, and Mark Hoffman. *Moanin' at Midnight: The Life and Times of Howlin' Wolf*. New York: Pantheon, 2004.

Shapiro, Jan. *So You Want to Sing Jazz*. Lanham, MD: Rowman & Littlefield, 2016.

Shapiro, Nat, and Nat Hentoff. *Hear Me Talkin' to Ya*. New York: Dover, 1955.

Shirley, Kay. *The Book of the Blues*. New York: MCA Music, 1963.

Southern, Eileen. *The Music of Black Americans: A History*. New York: Norton, 1997.

Stewart-Baxter, Derrick. *Ma Rainey and the Classic Blues*. London: Studio Vista, 1970.

Tate, Greg. *Everything but the Burden: What White People are Taking from Black Culture*. New York: Harlem Books, 2003.

The Rolling Stone Encyclopedia of Rock & Roll. 3rd ed. New York: Simon and Schuster, 2001.

Wald, Elijah. *The Blues: A Very Short Introduction*. Oxford University Press, 2010.

———. *Escaping the Delta*. New York: HarperCollins, 2004.

Ward, Greg. *Blues 100 Essential CDs: The Rough Guide*. London: Penguin, 2000.

White, Newman I. *American Negro Folk Songs*. Cambridge, MA: Harvard University Press, 1928.

Wilkerson, Isabel. *The Warmth of Other Suns*. New York: Vintage, 2010.

ARTICLES

Baldwin, James. "The Creative Process." Creative America, Ridge Press, 1962.

Barretta, Scott. "Central Mississippi/Jackson." *Living Blues Magazine: The Mississippi Blues Trail* 45, no. 5 (issue 233, 2014): 82.

———. "The North Delta." *Living Blues Magazine: The Mississippi Blues Trail* 45, no. 5 (issue 233, 2014): 18.

———. "North and East Mississippi." *Living Blues Magazine: The Mississippi Blues Trail* 45, no. 5 (issue 233, 2014): 66.

———. "The South Delta." *Living Blues Magazine: The Mississippi Blues Trail* 45, no. 5 (issue 233, 2014): 46.

———. "South Mississippi." *Living Blues Magazine: The Mississippi Blues Trail* 45, no. 5 (issue 233, 2014): 94.

Boyer, Horace. "Take My Hand, Precious Lord, Lead Me On." In *We'll Understand It Better By and By: Pioneering African American Gospel Composers*, edited by Bernice Johnson Reagon. Washington, DC: Smithsonian Institution Scholarly Press, 1992.

"Chicago Blues." Thelonious Monk Institute of Jazz. http://www.jazzinamerica.org.

Edwards, David. "Honeyboy." Interview with Elijah Wald, 1997.

Encyclopedia of Chicago. "Blues." http://www.encyclopedia.chicagohistory.org/pages/151.html.

Hughes, Langston. "Music at Year's End." *Chicago Defender*, January 9, 1943.

Hurston, Zora Neale. "Characteristics of Negro Expression." 1933.

Joplin, Scott. "School of Ragtime." In *44 Original Ragtime Hits*. Naples, FL: Ashley Publications, 1987.

Keepnews, Peter. "Etta James." Obituary. *New York Times*, January 20, 2012.

Kelly, Robin D. G. "Reds, Whites, and Blues People." In *Everything but the Burden*, edited by Greg Tate. New York: Harlem Books, 2003.

King, Martin Luther, Jr. "On the Importance of Jazz." Letter to 1963 Berlin Jazz Festival.

LoVetri, Jeannette. "Classical and Contemporary Commercial Music: A Comparison." 2014. http://www.thevoiceworkshop.com/pdfs/LoVetri%20Chapter%20Mordern%20Singer.pdf.

———. "Voice Students: What Is Healthy Belting?" 2013. https://majoringinmusic.com/voice-students-what-is-healthy-belting.

Pullum, Geoffrey K. "African American Vernacular English Is Not Standard English with Mistakes." In *The Workings of Language*, edited by Rebecca S. Wheeler. Westport, CT: Praeger, 1999.

Robeson, Paul. "The Culture of the Negro." *The Spectator* (London) (1934), 86–87.

Staig, Laurence. "Obituary: Thomas Dorsey." *Independent*, January 26, 1993.

Wald, Elijah. "Leroy Carr—The Bluesman Who Behaved Too Well." *New York Times*, July 17, 2004.

Welding, Pete. "Ramblin' Johnny Shines." *Living Blues*, no. 22, July–August 1975, 29.

Wight, Phil, and Fred Rothwell, comps. "The Complete Muddy Waters Discography." http://www.bluesandrhythm.co.uk/documents/200.pdf.

FILMS

Chicago Blues. Documentary. Produced and directed by Harley Cokeliss. 1970.

Too Close to Heaven: The History of Gospel Music. 1997. Produced by Leo St. Clair. Directed by Alan Lewens for the BBC. Distributed by Films Media Group, Princeton, NJ. VHS, color, 3 parts, 51 minutes each.

RADIO

Manzarek, Ray. "The Blues of Howlin' Wolf." *Morning Edition*. National Public Radio, 2004, https://www.npr.org/templates/story/story.php?storyId=3249069.

INDEX

ABOUT THE AUTHOR

Eli Yamin is an internationally presented pianist, composer, educator, and singer. He is the cofounder and managing artistic director of the Jazz Power Initiative, a nonprofit organization whose mission is to ignite the power of jazz arts education to transform lives by fostering self-expression, leadership, collaboration, and diversity. He is also the founding director of Jazz at Lincoln Center's Middle School Jazz Academy, leading its first decade. His three youth-centered musicals—*Nora's Ark*, *Holding the Torch for Liberty*, and *Message from Saturn*—have been performed internationally in four languages and across the United States, bringing diverse communities together through jazz and blues to tell socially uplifting stories. He has trained more than 1,000 teachers in Jazz Power Pedagogy, and his instructional videos for Jazz at Lincoln Center's Jazz Academy have received more than 1 million views. As a jazz and blues ambassador for the United States, he has performed in more than 25 countries and in the United States at Lincoln Center, Carnegie Hall, the Kennedy Center, and the White House. His recordings include *You Can't Buy Swing* with his jazz quartet; *I Feel So Glad* with his blues band; *Louie's Dream*, dedicated to "our jazz heroes," with New Orleans–based clarinetist Evan Christopher; and *Live In Burghausen* with jazz icon Illinois Jacquet. He teaches jazz and blues history, piano, and voice at Lehman College of the City University of New York and at Marymount Manhattan College and lives with his wife, Lorraine, and daughter, Mani, in New York City.